# THE NEW
## *Pennsylvania Dutch*
## Cook Book

# THE NEW
# Pennsylvania Dutch
# Cook Book

### By RUTH HUTCHISON

ILLUSTRATED BY TIM PALMER

HARPER & ROW · PUBLISHERS
*New York, Evanston, and London*

FOR
*Nell Woodroofe*
*with love*

# Contents

|     | INTRODUCTION TO 1958 EDITION | ix |
|-----|------------------------------|-----|
|     | INTRODUCTION | xi |
| I | SOUPS | 1 |
| II | BREAD AND BREADSTUFFS | 17 |
| III | MEATS | 55 |
| IV | POULTRY | 78 |
| V | EGGS | 89 |
| VI | CHEESE | 95 |
| VII | FISH AND SEAFOOD | 100 |
| VIII | OF HEXEL AND MUMMIX | 106 |
| IX | VEGETABLES | 114 |
| X | SWEETS AND SOURS | 132 |
| XI | PIES AND PASTRIES | 150 |
| XII | CAKE | 168 |
| XIII | COOKIES | 187 |
| XIV | OTHER DESSERTS | 206 |
| XV | CANDIES | 219 |
|     | INDEX | 229 |

# Introduction to 1958 Edition

Two centuries ago the word went out, probably from Bethlehem in the colony of Pennsylvania. Twenty years later the word had spread throughout the colonies, for soldiers have a way of finding out where there is good food, congressional delegates like to eat, and travelers make a specialty of eating.

The word went out that the people of southeastern Pennsylvania were the best cooks in the colonies!

In 1758 the Moravian citizens of Bethlehem had built an inn. A year or so later it was licensed by King George II. From the very beginning the Sun Inn was successful; before long it was famous. Travelers said there was no better food this side of London and perhaps not there. Considering that it offered dinners for a shilling, combined a night's lodging, shave, and breakfast for sixpence, and served excellent brandy and Madeira, it would seem that it deserved its popularity. What more could a traveler want?

A lot more! Guests at the Sun Inn wanted asparagus, strawberries, shad, oysters, and good roast beef, if they could get them. They could at the Sun Inn. And the guests were demanding almost at once the delectable dishes with the strange names that they discovered there—sauerkraut, *Schnitz un Knepp*, coleslaw, *Rosina Boi*, *Ebbelkuche*. . . . There was something called shoofly pie, sweet with molasses and an inch deep in crumbs, there was a not-to-be forgotten cheese cake, and there were even some salted curlicues that accompanied the local beer—Pennsylvanians called them pretzels. It is no wonder that the traveling public, accustomed to little more than a weary joint and lukewarm potatoes in the inns of the day, marked Bethlehem's inn as not to be missed. They had a way with cookery at the Sun Inn.

Swinging overhead, the inn sign radiated comfort and cheer—a round, golden sun, with rays shooting in all directions. Inside, the inn kept the sign's promise. Set down at the intersection of Cow Lane and the main street, the Sun Inn was fortunate, for before long, with the advent of the Revolution, this corner became the crossroads of the colonies. Up and down the inn steps went the great men of the colonies—General Washington (his lady too), Benjamin Franklin, John Hancock, John Adams, congressmen by the score— and Lafayette, DeKalb, Pulaski and Von Steuben, among our military allies. Benedict Arnold slept there and so did the hapless Major André, shortly after his capture. Everyone slept at the Sun Inn, but, more importantly, he ate there.

There was coach service to Bethlehem and the inn's entrance faced the mountain. On a Thursday afternoon, when the Philadelphia coach topped the rise, the driver signaled the inn. That set off a scurry of preparation in the inn kitchen, and I like to think that the passengers leaned forward eagerly, anticipating the inn's pleasures and that, as they got out of the coach and hastened inside, their greatest concern was to sniff the tantalizing odors wafted from the kitchen—perhaps there would be chicken and corn pie, or some of that delicious coffee cake, golden with butter and thickly flecked with brown sugar.

Yes, the word had gone out. After the war there was an inevitable borrowing of recipes—and even cooks! This, I like also to think, was the start of basic American cookery. And the word has been going out ever since. For of Pennsylvania cookery there is no end. That I know. Ten years ago, when the first edition of this book was published, I thought, in my ignorance, that I had told all I could of Pennsylvania cookery. I had—then—but there was more to learn and I kept on learning. You see, once a recipe collector, always a hoarder of bits and scraps of paper with "cups of" this and "teaspoons of" that scrawled all over them. Before I knew it my file was bulging again. There were recipes that hadn't been in the first book and some that seemed even better than those I'd had. I had a hankering to do it all over again. This new book is the result.

The addition of so many new recipes calls for renewed thanks, to the former tried-and-true contributors and to the generous new ones. The list is so long by this time that it can't be printed here, but just the same I am grateful. And, for that matter, no list of contributors is needed—you will find the names of all these kind people and wonderful cooks attached to their own recipes. If you like this cookery, they are the people who have made this collection possible. And to them I say, thank you so much!

# Introduction

FROM their earliest days the Pennsylvania Dutch, in their villages and farm-steads, have been building bulwarks of food against their atavistic dread of wars and invasions. For centuries their homes overseas had been demolished by barbarians, devastated by feudalism, and desolated by religious controversy. Somewhere along the weary course of their history the Rhinelanders had become Christians and had evolved in to a variety of sects, many with a mystical quality. For these Pietists believed in deed rather than creed and were determined to live according to their religious convictions. Accordingly, when in the seventeenth century Louis XIV invaded the Low Countries and when William Penn sought colonists for the New World, they made their decision—they would go to America.

The first of the Plain Sects to sail for Philadelphia in 1683 were the Mennonites. These were followed by the Amish, Seventh-Day Baptists, Dunkards, Schwenkfelders, and Moravians. Later came the Lutherans and Reformed, so that by the time of the Revolutionary War there were so many Germanic people in Pennsylvania it was feared they outnumbered the English. Strictly speaking, there was no Germany in that day, but emigrants from the Low Countries were loosely called Germans, most of them spoke Low German, and the first of their American settlements was called Germantown.

The newcomers spread out over the southeastern part of the colony of Pennsylvania. The English had taken up most of the easily cleared land, but the Germans preferred woodland. They knew that black walnut trees indicated the presence of limestone and they knew that limestone in the land meant that farming there would be good. So they searched for the black walnut trees and where they found them they cleared the forest and established their farms.

The Rhinelanders understood planting routines, crop rotation, and soil con-
servation. They were such excellent farmers that they considered that *was Man
gert ist keine Arbeite*—doing what you like to do is easy work. They were
willing to toil ceaselessly in the wilderness, to sacrifice what they must, if they
could be at last free men. And they were determined to so secure their families
in the New World that their children and grandchildren, generation after
generation, might still be free.

Since their farms were sequestered, families functioned as units and large
families were cause for rejoicing. The farmer and his sons tilled the soil, the
farm women cooked and baked, spun and wove together. When industry and
intelligence produced bountiful crops and full larders, frugality motivated the
sale of surplus food to less fortunate—or less provident—neighbors. For themselves, the Pennsylvania Germans needed to buy little except salt and spices.

As the children grew up and made their own homes in the vicinity, family
gatherings became frequent. "The Folk," as they called themselves, came together to feast, to worship, and sometimes to mourn. Well aware of the changing seasons, they marked springtime and harvest with festivals. They were
grateful for God's good gift of life in the new land and, Pietists though many
of them were, they were humanists in the sense that they loved and savored
this life on earth.

The cloistered at Ephrata, it is true, led monastic lives along communistic
lines. The Brethren there were said at one time to have been so poor that they
built narrow doorways "to restrain the flesh" and low doorways to teach
humility! But music and the other arts flourished among them and their book-
making was the finest in the colonies. The Plain People of what is now Lancaster County forswore buttons and other frivolities of dress, adopted a uniform garb with invisible fastenings, and, in a gesture of pious humility, washed
one another's feet at communion services. But between the Sunday "preachings" they indulged in hearty dinners, met their friends and neighbors to talk
and catch up on the news, were gregarious and content.

The Germans were craftsmen and could make for themselves just about
whatever they needed. Their great, stone-sided "Swiss" barns were built
soundly and ornamented with what have been called "hex signs." It is doubt-
ful that these designs were ever intended to keep off witches, or even lightning,
but they were satisfactorily ornamental and unconsciously mystical. They built
their houses of native stone, as solidly and truly as those of their Quaker neighbors. They made their own furniture, painting chairs and chests in bright
colors, adorning them with pomegranates and lilies, angels and birds. Their

ancestors across the seas had loved these motifs—here in Pennsylvania the lilies bloomed again. They wove their coverlets in patterns of tulips and stars, houses and rosetrees. They pieced their bright quilts in similar designs. Their blacksmiths made iron-lace trivets, their tinkers shaped cookie cutters to delight the children. Even the butter molds were carved in designs and the *Boi Schissel* (pie dish) bore quaint painted figures under its glaze. Their *Schmutz Amschels* (literally, grease robins) were little iron lamps with suspended wicks that burned fat—and they *did* resemble birds. By their flickering light the pioneer labored at keeping his family records, carefully lettering names and dates in German script and ornamenting the completed *Fraktur* with swelling heart, swirling vines, stars, and angels—and, if it was seemly, a pair of birds "conjugally facing." Nowadays the *Fraktur*, the pottery, and the cooking utensils of the Pennsylvania Germans have been collected and treasured in museums. There you can see the birth certificates, house blessings, pie dishes, butter molds, cups, flagons, trivets, and spice boxes in profusion. So many of them are concerned with food—"Here is Meat and Sauerkraut" reads the legends on one old plate, "Our maid she is a bride in the year 1810." The plate, a pretty one, with light slip ground, touches of green, and lilies in sgraffito, commemorates a wedding. But the food is mentioned before the bride! The Rhinelanders, you see, even in times of plenty, cast backward looks at their years of privation.

The harmony between Palatine farmers and Pennsylvania soil produced, in colonial days, an abundance that was duly noted by some of the less successful neighbors. Envy consumed them, the language barrier disturbed them—so they implemented their lack of understanding with ridicule. And indeed some of the Germans, by their customs and costumes, lent themselves to easy caricature. Thus they who called themselves simply "Deutsch" or "the Folk" became in frontier parlance first "Deitsch," then "Dutch," and occasionally "Dumb Dutch." Just who was "dumb" was open to debate, but the misnomer persisted and was bitterly resented. With the passing of time, the term "Pennsylvania Dutch" came to serve well enough to distinguish between these descendants of Swiss and Low Country (German) pioneers and the nineteenth-century German immigrants. But in earlier days the name separated these people from their neighbors, set them apart cruelly, and sealed them into a double isolation of distance and language. For solace, the "Dutch" turned to their music and handicrafts, "Pennsylvania folk art" developed, and Bethlehem music-making evolved into the famous Bach Festival. But all this, of course, took generations. In the beginning the Folk were too busy to worry about what their neighbors thought of them. "Think what you please," ran one of their adages, "but not too loud." Another was, "Better die eating than fighting." However, when the Revolution began, when the cause of Liberty overshadowed every other, many of these people fought and fought well. Although they remained steadfastly peace-loving, they knew that freedom must be won and held. Those sects among them whose beliefs would not permit the bearing of arms helped in many other ways, maintaining hospitals or collecting supplies. The Revolutionary cause made large use of their skills, and Pennsylvania Dutch voices were heard in its councils. Pennsylvania-made rifles turned the tide in more than one battle and Pennsylvania's cannon and cannon balls, cast in Pennsylvania furnaces, were indispensable to victory. There came dark days when the fate of the nation seemed to depend upon Pennsylvania's Conestoga wagons—creaking into Valley Forge, heavy-laden with Pennsylvania's stone-ground flour, or even loaves of freshly baked bread.

We are told that General Washington's cook that long, terrible winter was a Pennsylvania Dutchman. And that when at last the general went home to Mount Vernon he took with him a fondness for Pennsylvania cookery that lasted his lifetime. But he was not the only one, for soldiers from other colonies had learned the goodness of Dutch cooking too and went home to talk about it. Meantime, the Quaker and Scotch-Irish neighbors of the Dutch housewives had been learning to bake, preserve, and pickle from them—gradually Pennsylvania Dutch cookery came to be considered the best in the land.

This cookery had come a long way from the valley of the Rhine, from the villages of Switzerland, from the towns of Alsace. It had suffered a sea change, of course, and for a time it had fared badly under the rigors of pioneer life. It had waited, of necessity, upon the herds and the harvests—for milk, butter, and flour were at first luxuries in the new land. It had been neglected while the farm wives eked out meals, living perforce upon fish and game, fruit and berries, and whatever could be had. They cooked their "poor man's dishes" as well as they could, but the memory of good food dies hard and as soon as better times arrived Pennsylvania housewives returned to their grandmothers' techniques. They got out their old handwritten cook books and began to study and practice the old methods of cookery. As soon as Pennsylvania's bounty rewarded the farmers with bumper crops, their wives experimented with the fruits of the New World and were emboldened to add some of their own recipes to their grandmothers'—in the same German script. Thus Pennsylvania Dutch cookery developed.

Pennsylvania Dutch cooks still use their handwritten cook books. Except that nowadays they are usually written in English, they are very like the old ones. One is still likely to find a table of measurements in the front and a few household remedies in the back. The everyday recipes are skipped over without a qualm, but there is a spate of rules for cakes and pies, sweets and sours. The details of these are considered important, but, since anyone is supposed to be able to make the stews and pot roasts, they are gone over lightly. Mrs. Ganseleiter won the blue ribbon at the county fair for her marble cake, so Mrs. Ganseleiter's technique is carefully noted. The fact that the cook book already contains several recipes for marble cake makes no difference. It is the nuances of baking, the tricks of famous cooks, that are all-important. Aunt Katie uses "eating molasses" in her cake, Mrs. Weaver bases her success upon a certain kind of sugar—so various recipes for the same cake must be included. So the Pennsylvania Dutch housewife may patiently copy twenty recipes for the same cake; if a dish offers little scope for her culinary imagination, she may skip it entirely and trust to her memory for that one. This, of course, is why so many cherished Pennsylvania Dutch cook books appear to be a bit lopsided as to content. Gold cake, silver cake, sunshine cake, feather cake, sponge cake, angel food cake, devil's food cake, pound cake—so runs the list. Sweet dough, dumplings, noodles, soup balls—these you will find. But for a recipe for brown stew or pot roast you must search long and hard. Unless it is somehow unusual. For, certainly, there is no need to put down what everyone knows!

So it is that the making of a Pennsylvania Dutch cook book can become arduous. The best-liked dishes seem to be the most difficult to hunt down; the housewife is astonished to be asked about them. When she does agree to tell what she does, the problem of measurements arises immediately. She gives little thought to proportion and measures by feeling. Cooking is instinctive as she practices it, and "butter the size of a walnut," "one and a half eggshells of water," "flour to stiffen," "as large as an apple" are measurements that do little to hearten the timidly accurate amateur. Standardization has been known, moreover, to take the life right out of a good Pennsylvania recipe. The cupful: it may be the uniform measuring cup, but it is more likely to be a teacup that has lost its handle or a coffeecup—a large, cracked one that still has its uses. You can't be sure, with Pennsylvania measurements, but you strive for accuracy and hope for luck. For Pennsylvania Dutch cookery is a combination of expediency, imagination, and artistry, in that order!

This book does not pretend to cover the whole body of cookery because the

Pennsylvania Dutch traditionally make small use of certain foods. The recipes offered here are either indigenous to Pennsylvania or have through the years become incorporated into its cuisine. To fill the gaps would make small contribution to Pennsylvania Dutch cookery, and I have no intention of doing so. The Pennsylvania Dutch make simple salads, about three kinds of cheese, their cheese dishes are usually cheese cake or cheese pie, and their manner of cooking fish is not unusual. So you will not find much of salad, cheese, or fish.

As a matter of fact, the typical Pennsylvania Dutch menu is so generous and satisfying that it has little need for some of the time-killers that are used to clutter menus elsewhere. A full-rounded Pennsylvania dinner is not to be taken lightly. This cookery was brought from overseas with certain continental embellishments that were soon lost to the exigencies of pioneer life and it was adapted to become farm food for hearty trenchermen. In spite of the addition of many ingredients now available but unthought of in the early days, it is much the same today as in the beginning—Pennsylvania dinners are still man size. So, unless possessed of a redoubtable appetite, you will do well to try these recipes one at a meal!

The sturdy folk who developed Pennsylvania Dutch cookery have long since been added to their fathers. But they bequeathed to their sons their fondness for hearty fare, and their daughters have inherited their skill in preparing it. Certainly, each substantial, satisfying dish bears witness to a folk's love of food, and to a people's historic need of food for sustenance and security.

# Soups

*Montgomery County log house*

‖‖‖‖‖‖‖‖‖‖‖‖‖‖‖‖‖‖‖‖‖‖‖‖‖‖‖‖‖‖‖‖‖‖‖‖‖‖‖‖‖‖‖‖‖‖‖‖‖‖‖‖‖‖‖‖‖‖‖‖‖‖‖‖‖‖‖‖‖‖‖‖‖‖‖‖‖‖‖‖‖‖‖‖‖‖‖‖‖‖

"THE poor must eat what they have," said the early Pennsylvania settlers, and "You don't have to have teeth to eat soup." They had a lot of adages concerning soup and it is no wonder—often it was all there was to eat. But the soup of the pioneers was a far cry from the polite consommés and bland purées regarded nowadays as mere preludes to eating. Soup in those days was the all-purpose food. It had to be hearty enough to build young bones, stick to the farmer's ribs, and sustain the breath of life in the old folks who sat in the chimney corner.

It took time to clear the land, raise the first crops, collect cattle and poultry —but people had to eat. They could not wait for the harvest and the butchering. Soup was frugal, soup was filling. Whatever food was available could be dropped into the soup kettle, and soup would keep body and soul together for a while. Even if there was nothing but milk and flour to be had, they would make two kinds of soup: brown flour soup and *Rivvel* soup. Milk, potatoes, and onions would make two more kinds of soup: potato soup and onion soup. Thus the "milk soups" came into being; sometimes the Pennsylvania Dutch called them "poor man's soups." But to the end of their lives they remembered how good they had tasted—and smelled. "You can tell onion soup by the smell," ran an old saying, adding ruefully, "You can smell scorched soup from afar." In later days, the descendants of the pioneers went right on making milk soups. It happened that they liked them.

As their flocks and herds increased, as field and garden yielded grains, vegetables, and herbs, the Pennsylvania Dutch began making more substantial soups. There was a piece of meat for them nowadays, and the soups were rich; they could be "stretched." When the unexpected visitor arrived, his

1

name could go into the pot along with a little water; it did no harm. But the old settlers had a word about that, too, and when they held a poor opinion of something they would say, "It is not worth the water in a plate of soup."

The story of Stone Soup has long been a part of Pennsylvania folklore. No doubt it crossed the sea with the first immigrants, for they went right on telling it to their children in the New World—in Pennsylvania Dutch! Once there was a farmer's wife and she had a visitor. He was a devious sort of fellow who, instead of saying that he was hungry, told her that he could make Stone Soup. The farm wife had made soup from just about everything in her day, but she had never tried to make soup from a stone. "First," directed her visitor, "find me a fine, round stone in the fields. Wash and polish it carefully, then drop it into a kettle of boiling water. On second thought, I'll get the stone. You boil the water. But not too much water. . . ." When he returned with the stone the soup-making began. He dropped the stone into the kettle with a flourish. "Now," he said, "we need some potatoes, some cabbage, and some onions. Oh, yes, some corn and some string beans. And, let's see . . . some tomatoes. Better add a little parsley and seasoning, too. While you're at it, just toss in a good-sized piece of meat. There now, I think that is all. This is Stone Soup." And so in due time they ate it.

## POOR MAN'S SOUPS

### RIVVEL SUPP

| | |
|---|---|
| 4 cups milk | 2 heaping tablespoons flour |
| 2 eggs | ½ teaspoon salt |
| | ⅛ teaspoon pepper |

Heat the milk. Beat the eggs and cut into the flour with a knife until the mixture flakes. *Rivvel* in Pennsylvania Dutch means flakes or lumps, so sometimes this is called Lump Soup. *Rivvels* are made by rubbing the mixture through the hands, letting it fall into the soup in flakes. Turn down the heat and let simmer for a few minutes, until the flour is perfectly blended with the milk. Season and serve, adding minced parsley if desired. Serves 4.

*Mrs. F. C. Wunder*

### BROWN FLOUR POTATO SOUP

| | |
|---|---|
| 4 cups water | 4 tablespoons flour |
| 8 medium-sized potatoes | 2 tablespoons butter |
| 4 cups milk | Salt and pepper to taste |

Cube the peeled potatoes and boil in salted water until tender. Add milk and simmer together. Brown the flour in melted butter at low heat and add to the soup. Blend carefully, bring to the boiling point. Season and serve at once, with minced parsley or grated hard-boiled eggs to garnish. Serves 6.

*Mrs. Herman Oswald*

## GRUMBERA SUPP

4 large potatoes
1 large onion
4 cups boiling water
4 cups milk

½ teaspoon salt
⅛ teaspoon pepper
1 large lump butter
2 teaspoons chopped parsley

(*Grumbera*, literally, ground pear, means potato in Pennsylvania Dutch.) Peel and dice the potatoes, peel the onion and slice very thin. Boil together in the water until they are tender. Add milk, stirring constantly until soup reaches the boiling point. Turn down heat and let simmer for a few minutes. Season, add butter, sprinkle with parsley, and serve. Makes 8 servings.

*Mrs. Thomas B. Keck*

## TZVIVVELLE SUPP
### (Onion Soup)

2 cups chopped onions
3 cups boiling water
3 cups milk
1 large lump butter

½ cup grated cheese
½ teaspoon salt
⅛ teaspoon pepper
6 slices toast

Peel onions and put through a food chopper, measuring 2 cups. Cook in boiling water until tender, add milk, simmer together 10 minutes. Add butter and seasoning. Place a slice of toast in each large soup dish, heap grated cheese on the toast, pour soup over it and serve immediately. Serves 6.

*Mrs. Edward S. Shepherd*

## TZVIVVELLE SUPP II

3 tablespoons butter
2 tablespoons flour
1 cup milk

Salt and pepper
2 cups chopped onions
4 cups boiling water
3 cups milk

Melt butter in saucepan and blend with flour until thick and smooth. Slowly add 1 cup milk, stirring and blending constantly. Season and set aside. Boil onions in the boiling water for 10 minutes, or until tender. Pour off water. Add the white sauce and 3 cups milk. Simmer until blended. Serves 4.

*Mrs. C. C. Helffrich*

## TZVIVVELLE SUPP III

3 tablespoons flour
1 egg, beaten
2 cups chopped onions

3 tablespoons butter
6 cups beef bouillon
Salt and pepper

Blend the egg into the flour with a spatula until small lumps, or *Rivvels,* are formed. Put onions through food chopper, melt the butter, and cook the onions in it until lightly browned. Heat the broth, add onions, bring to a boil, then simmer. Rub the *Rivvels* through the hands and let fall in flakes into the soup. Simmer until *Rivvels* are cooked—about 10 minutes. Serves 6.

## TZVIVVELLE SUPP IV

3 tablespoons butter
2 cups chopped onions
5 cups beef broth or bouillon

Salt and pepper
6 slices toast
½ cup grated cheese

Melt butter, add chopped onions, cook until onions are lightly browned. Add bouillon and simmer 15 minutes. Season with salt and pepper if broth is used, go easy if commercial bouillon is used—it's usually salty. Place toast in soup bowls, pour soup over it, and sprinkle thickly on top with cheese. The cheese may be placed on the toast before the soup is poured or can be sprinkled on top afterward. Serves 6.

*Elizabeth Treible*

## TOMATO SOUP

3 tablespoons flour
¼ cup butter
4 cups milk
2 cups home-canned tomatoes

1 teaspoon sugar
1 teaspoon salt
⅛ teaspoon pepper
1 teaspoon chopped parsley

Blend flour and melted butter to smooth paste. Scald the milk and add carefully, stirring together. Simmer tomatoes about 10 minutes, add sugar and strain into the milk in a double boiler. Turn heat low and keep warm for about 10 minutes. Season, sprinkle with parsley, and serve. Serves 4.

*Mrs. Edward S. Shepherd*

## PRETZEL SOUP

2 tablespoons flour
2 tablespoons butter
6 cups milk

12 pretzels
Dash of cayenne pepper
1 tablespoon chopped parsley

Sift flour, blend with butter over low flame. Add milk gradually, stirring constantly. Bring just to a boil, then simmer 10 minutes. No salt should be needed; pretzels are salty. Add pepper and parsley. Break pretzels into 4 large bowls, pour in soup, and serve at once. Men like this for a snack after late parties. They say that sometimes it's the thing for Sunday breakfast (same reason).

*Robert Butz Keck*

## POPCORN SOUP

1 egg
1 cup flour
5 cups milk
1 large lump butter

2 teaspoons chopped parsley
2 hard-boiled eggyolks
2½ cups popcorn
Dash of cayenne pepper

Beat the egg, sift the flour, and blend together, chopping lightly with a spatula until batter flakes into *Rivvels,* or lumps. Bring milk to a boil, add butter, and simmer. Drop *Rivvels* into the soup a few at a time, stirring until they are cooked —about 10 minutes. Add parsley and grated egg yolks. Divide the popcorn into four large bowls, pour soup on top, sprinkle with pepper (and salt if needed), serve at once. Same comment for this as for pretzel soup! Serves 4.

*William W. Meixell*

## BUTTERMILK POP

1 quart buttermilk          3 tablespoons cornmeal
Brown sugar or maple syrup

Place buttermilk on stove in a wide pan. Heat gently, stirring constantly, to prevent separation into curds and whey. Just as it begins to boil, sift in the cornmeal gradually, stirring until it thickens the buttermilk. Add salt if needed, pour into bowls, and serve. Sweeten it at the table with brown sugar or maple syrup to taste.

This is a very old recipe, supposed to have been intended for the children's supper. But the story goes in my family that my father arrived weary and hungry after journeying to the bride's house for his wedding and found himself relegated to a corner where the children were being fed buttermilk pop. Everyone was too busy to bother with him, so he was given a bowl of the concoction. Always afterward he said that if he lived long enough he might learn to like the stuff but he doubted it. Then he would add that no doubt the buttermilk pop was the reason why he tried to black his shoes with stove polish! Stove polish and buttermilk pop were synonymous terms in my family when we were growing up. I never tasted it because Mother never dared to make it.

## CORN SOUP

| | |
|---|---|
| 6 ears corn | Large lump butter |
| 2 cups water | ½ teaspoon salt |
| 2 cups milk | ⅛ teaspoon pepper |

Cut the corn from the cob, cook it in the water until tender and the water has boiled down a bit. Add milk, bring to the boiling point, then simmer for 10 minutes. Add butter and seasoning. Make *Rivvels* (flaky lumps) by blending:

1 beaten egg
2 tablespoons flour

Blend and cut through with a spatula until the mixture can be flaked gradually into the soup. Let the soup simmer about 7 minutes longer, or until the *Rivvels* seem well cooked. Serves 4.

*Mrs. Floyd Siegfried*

## DRIED BEAN SOUP

| | |
|---|---|
| 2 cups dried soup beans | 1½ tablespoons butter |
| 2 quarts water | ½ teaspoon salt |
| ¼ teaspoon soda | ¼ teaspoon pepper |

Wash the beans, cover with cold water, and soak overnight. Next morning, drain, put in kettle with 2 quarts fresh water. Boil, drain again, cover the beans with boiling water this time, add soda, simmer gently until beans are soft. Press through a colander, return to the kettle with water in which they were cooked, simmer a few minutes longer. Add butter and seasoning and serve at once. Makes 6 large servings.

*Elizabeth Sanders*

## OYSTER STEW

| | |
|---|---|
| 5 cups milk | ½ cup water |
| 1 cup cream | ¼ cup butter |
| 25 oysters and liquor | Salt and pepper |

Use double boiler with water boiling briskly. In upper part, put milk and cream. Bring milk to a boil, then turn down heat to simmer. Place oysters, with their liquor in saucepan, adding ½ cup water. Simmer until oysters become plump and edges begin to curl. Skim the oysters from the pan and add to the heated milk and cream. Melt the butter in small iron pan, add salt and pepper, and strain into it the remaining oyster liquor. Stir together and add to the stew. Pour into heated tureen and serve at once with oyster or Exton crackers that have been warmed. Serves 6.

*Mrs. Edward S. Shepherd*

## SMALL OYSTER STEW

¼ cup butter
1 pint oysters
2 cups milk

½ teaspoon salt
⅛ teaspoon pepper
1 cup cream

2 teaspoons chopped parsley

Melt the butter, heat the oysters in their own liquor, and add to the butter. Heat the milk separately, add to oysters and butter. Season and simmer until oysters rise to the surface—about 10 minutes. Heat the cream and add last. Sprinkle with parsley, season, and serve. Serves 2 or 3.

*Mrs. Donald L. Helfferich*

## CLAM SOUP

25 clams and liquor
Enough water to make 3 cups
3 cups milk

1 tablespoon butter
½ teaspoon salt
⅛ teaspoon pepper

Heat clams in their own liquor, adding enough water to make 3 cups. Simmer for 10 minutes. Heat the milk separately, adding butter, salt, and pepper. Add this slowly to the heated clam broth. Simmer together for 10 minutes. Serves 4.

*Mrs. Thomas B. Keck*

# RICH SOUPS

## PHILADELPHIA PEPPERPOT

2 pounds tripe
2 pounds honeycomb tripe
1 veal knuckle
2 small onions
1 bay leaf
4 potatoes

1 bunch pot herbs
½ teaspoon salt
⅛ teaspoon cayenne pepper
1 red pepper
½ pound beef suet
2 cups flour

2 teaspoons parsley, minced

Wash tripe 3 times in ice water. Cover and boil slowly for a long time. The old recipes said 6-8 hours, but about 4 will do. Cool, remove from water, and cut into small pieces. Wash the veal, put in kettle, and cover with water, simmer slowly for 3 hours, skimming frequently. Remove from water, cut veal away from the bones and into small pieces. Set aside. Strain the broth and return to the kettle. Add chopped onion and bay leaf, simmer for another hour. Add the diced potatoes. Use whatever pot herbs you prefer or, if you use dried herbs, tie them in a bag and remove later. Add veal, tripe, and seasoning. Make dumplings by blending suet (or same amount of butter) with the flour and adding a little salt. Add just enough ice water to make a paste that can be rolled with floured fingers into balls the size of walnuts. Handle the dumplings lightly, sprinkle with a little flour, and drop into the bubbling soup. Simmer for 5 minutes, the kettle covered. Don't peek. Sprinkle with parsley and serve. Serves 6. (This was my grandmother's recipe.)

## DUTCH PEPPERPOT

| | |
|---|---|
| 1½ pounds cubed beef | 2 potatoes |
| 1 green pepper | Noodles |
| 1 onion | Salt and pepper |

Cube the beef and cook in water until nearly tender. Add chopped pepper, diced onion, and diced raw potatoes. Season. Mix paste for noodles:

3 eggs
Flour to make soft paste
¼ teaspoon salt

Beat the eggs, mix with the sifted flour and salt, blend together. Roll out lightly on a floured board, until very thin. Cut in squares and let dry on a cloth for about an hour.

Add noodles to the soup. Simmer for 15 minutes, or until noodles are thoroughly cooked. Serves 4.

*Mrs. Herman Oswald*

## BEAN SOUP
### (Amish Preaching Soup)

| | |
|---|---|
| 1 pound dried soup beans | ½ cup chopped onions |
| 1½ pounds ham | ¼ teaspoon pepper |
| 2 cups diced celery | 2 teaspoons chopped parsley |

Soak beans in water to cover overnight. Cover the ham with water and boil until tender. Skim the fat from the broth, add beans, drained, and then the celery, onions, and pepper. Simmer all together until ham is well cooked, the beans soft, and the whole well blended. Garnish with parsley and serve. Serves 6.

Bean soup is sometimes called "Amish Preaching Soup" because it was served traditionally by the House Amish between Sunday preachings. The House Amish are so-called because this distinguishes them from the Church Amish. Their Sunday services are held turn about in the houses of the congregation; the serving and eating of "Preaching Soup" is common practice. Usually the soup is accompanied by homemade bread and butter, an array of "sweets and sours," and Schnitz Pies.

## SPLIT PEA SOUP

2 cups dried split peas
2 large onions
1 stalk celery
2 tablespoons butter

2 quarts water
4 tablespoons breadcrumbs
1 cup mashed potatoes
1 teaspoon salt

¼ teaspoon pepper

Wash the peas and soak overnight. Peel and slice the onions, dice the celery, and brown both in the butter. Drop this mixture into the kettle with the water. Add the bread crumbs. Drain the peas, add them to the soup, and cook all together for about an hour. Put through a sieve, return to the kettle, add the mashed potatoes, bring the soup to a boil, season, and serve. Makes 6 large servings.

*Elizabeth Sanders*

## LENTIL SOUP

2 cups lentils
2 quarts cold water
1 minced onion

½ pound smoked sausage
Salt and pepper
2 teaspoons chopped parsley

Wash the lentils and put in kettle, cover with the cold water, bring to a boil. Add onion and simmer for 1½ hours. Add the smoked sausage, cut into small pieces, simmer ½ hour longer, or until lentils are soft. Season, add parsley, and serve. Makes 6-8 servings. "This is Mother Bachman's recipe. She always served it to her family on New Year's Day, to bring good luck, health, and prosperity for the year."

*Frances C. Bachman*

## CHESTNUT SOUP I

2 cups chestnuts
Cooking oil
¼ cup melted butter
4 cups veal stock

1 cup cream
½ teaspoon sugar
Few grains cayenne pepper
Salt to taste

Score the chestnuts crosswise, place in pan with cooking oil, and heat in oven, shaking now and then, until shells can be removed easily. Melt the butter, add the chestnuts, cook slowly but do not permit to brown. Add chestnuts in butter to the veal stock and cook gently until chestnuts are tender. Remove them and put through a sieve. Return to stock, bring it to a boil, add cream, sugar, and seasoning. Serves 4.

*From* The Pennsylvania German, *1908*

## CHESTNUT SOUP II

1 cup chestnuts, peeled      8 cups chicken stock
Cooking oil      ½ teaspoon salt
⅛ teaspoon pepper

Score the chestnuts crosswise, place in pan with a little cooking oil, and heat in oven until shells can be removed easily. Cool and peel. Place 2 cups of the chicken stock in a kettle and cook the chestnuts in it about 20 minutes, or until they are tender. Remove chestnuts, drain, and season lightly. Set aside. Add the stock in which they were cooked to the remainder of the stock and bring to a slow boil. Put the chestnuts in a tureen, pour the stock over them, and serve at once. Serves 6.

*Mrs. Thomas B. Keck*

## VEGETABLE SOUP I

1 cup dried soup beans      ¼ cup barley
1 soup bone      ½ cup diced carrots
2 stalks celery, chopped      1 cup canned tomatoes
4 potatoes, diced      ¾ teaspoon salt
2 cups corn      ¼ teaspoon pepper
½ head cabbage      2 tablespoons chopped parsley

Soak the beans overnight and drain. Choose a soup bone with some meat on it, cover it with water in a kettle, and cook until meat is tender. Remove the bone, cut off the meat, and cook the beans in the broth until they are soft. Add the soup meat, celery, potatoes, corn, cabbage, barley, and carrots. Simmer. Add the canned tomatoes (or use 3 fresh tomatoes—in which case cook until they are soft), season sharply, add parsley, and serve. Serves 6-8.

*Elizabeth Sanders*

## VEGETABLE SOUP II
### (with noodles)

3 pounds stewing beef      2 onions
2 quarts water      ½ teaspoon salt
3 potatoes      ⅛ teaspoon pepper

Cook the beef 1½ hours, or until tender. Add diced potatoes, onions, and seasoning. Simmer until they are soft, then drop in the noodles:

| | |
|---|---|
| 2 eggs | ¼ teaspoon salt |
| Flour to stiffen | ½ eggshell cold water |

Beat the eggs, mix with the sifted flour and salt, add the water and stir the mixture to a paste that can be rolled on a floured board. Roll very thin, shape into a long, narrow roll, and slice across the roll, very thin, with a sharp knife. Unroll and drop the noodles in the boiling soup. Cook 15 minutes longer. Serves 6.

*Mrs. Victor Boyer*

## VEGETABLE SOUP III
### (with butter balls)

| | |
|---|---|
| 1 soup bone, with meat | 2 cups diced carrots |
| ½ head cabbage | 1 cup string beans |
| 4 potatoes | ¼ cup barley |
| ½ cup diced turnips | 1 cup tomatoes |
| 2 cups corn | ½ teaspoon salt |

⅛ teaspoon pepper

Cover the soup bone with water and cook until the meat is tender, 2-2½ hours. Add chopped cabbage, diced potatoes, and turnips. Cook 10 minutes, add corn, carrots, and string beans, cut fine. Add barley, and lastly the tomatoes. When all are well cooked, turn down the heat, season, and simmer a minute or two. To make the butter balls:

| | |
|---|---|
| 1 teaspoon butter | ½ teaspoon salt |
| 3 tablespoons flour | 1 tablespoon water, to blend |

Form mixture into balls with floured fingers—about the size of walnuts. Drop into the bubbling soup, cover tightly, and boil for 5 minutes. Serves 8.

*Elizabeth Sanders*

## CHICKEN NOODLE SOUP

| | |
|---|---|
| 1 4-pound chicken | 1 bay leaf |
| 3 quarts cold water | 1 tablespoon minced parsley |
| 1 small onion | ½ teaspoon salt |

¼ teaspoon pepper

Put chicken in kettle, cover with water, and simmer until tender, with the onion and bay leaf. Remove the chicken, cut the meat from the bones, and return it to the kettle. Add parsley, seasoning, and noodles. To make the noodles:

2 eggs                                  ¼ teaspoon salt
Flour to stiffen                        ½ eggshell cold water

Beat the eggs, sift in the flour and salt, add the water to make paste. Roll out paper-thin on a floured board and dry for about an hour, spread on a cloth. Shape into a long, narrow roll, slicing across with a sharp knife to make noodles as thin as possible. Unroll as noodles are dropped into the soup. Simmer until they are thoroughly cooked (probably about 15 minutes). Serves 6.

*Carrie Meixell*

## CHICKEN CORN SOUP

1 5-pound chicken                       2 raw (or chopped, hard-boiled) eggs
½ cup noodles                           1 teaspoon chopped parsley
1 cup fresh young corn                  Salt and pepper to taste

Cut up the chicken and stew in water to cover until tender. Take the chicken from the kettle and set aside the legs and breast for future potpie. Cut up the rest of the meat and return to the kettle. There should be a quart or more of the stock. To make the noodles:

2 eggs                                  ¼ teaspoon salt
Flour to stiffen                        1 tablespoon cold water

Mix the beaten eggs with sifted flour and salt, adding water to make paste. Roll out very thin on floured board, roll up like jelly roll and slice across, very thin, with sharp knife. Measure about ½ cup of noodles and unroll them as they are dropped into the soup. Boil together for 5 minutes. Add corn, boil 3 minutes longer. Stir in the eggs (raw eggs add more flavor but use chopped hard-boiled eggs if you prefer), add parsley and seasoning. Serve with slices of home-baked bread.

"A pinch of saffron adds delicate flavor and golden coloring. Every well-run house once had its saffron bed. The star-shaped blossoms are a beautiful lavender and resemble clematis. Only the pistils are dried and used for coloring. Nowadays saffron must come from the drugstore. . . . This soup is a favorite summer soup in Lancaster County. It has been used for generations for Sunday School picnic suppers."

*Mrs. Ira F. Zartman*

## CHICKEN CORN SOUP WITH BUTTER BALLS

1 3-pound chicken                       Pinch of saffron
1 cup diced celery                      Fresh, grated corn, 6-8 ears
1 tablespoon chopped parsley            Salt and pepper to taste

Boil chicken in water to cover until tender. Remove from broth and cut into small pieces. Return to kettle. Add celery, parsley, saffron, and salt and pepper. Grate the corn and add to the stock. Cook 3 minutes longer, add butter balls, cover and cook 5 minutes longer. Serve at once. To make butter balls:

| | |
|---|---|
| 2 tablespoons butter | ½ teaspoon salt |
| Scant cup sifted flour | Milk to blend |

Mix together to make paste, with floured fingers. Add more butter if needed but too much will cause balls to crumble in the broth. They should be size of small walnuts. Chill in refrigerator.

## CHICKEN SOUP WITH ALMOND BALLS

| | |
|---|---|
| ½ cup almonds | 2 tablespoons oil or lard |
| ⅓ cup bread crumbs | 2 quarts chicken stock |
| ¼ teaspoon salt | 1 tablespoon minced parsley |
| 2 egg whites | Salt and pepper |

Blanch and chop the almonds, rather fine. Mix with bread crumbs, salt, and beaten egg whites. (Reserve a little of the egg white.) With lightly floured fingers form the mixture into marble-sized balls, roll in the remaining egg white, drop into the hot fat and brown quickly, shaking the pan gently to prevent burning. Drain on brown paper. Heat the chicken stock, put the almond balls in tureen, and pour soup over them. Sprinkle with parsley and salt and pepper. Serves 6-8.

*Elizabeth Sanders*

## TURKEY BONE SOUP

| | |
|---|---|
| Turkey bones | 1 carrot, chopped |
| Water to cover | 1 onion, minced |
| (stuffing) | (beef bouillon) |
| (herbs for seasoning) | 2 tablespoons rice or barley |
| 2 stalks celery, chopped | Salt and pepper |

Put leftover turkey bones in deep kettle, cover with cold water, bring to a boil. Add stuffing if there is any left. If not, remember to add some herbs for seasoning, whatever you prefer. Add celery, carrot, and onion. Cover and simmer for about an hour. (If broth lacks flavor, add 2 cups beef bouillon.) Remove turkey bones, pull off the meat, cut it into small pieces. Strain the soup, return to kettle with turkey meat. Add rice or barley and simmer about ½ hour, or until cereal is cooked. Serves 4-6.

## MARROW BALL SOUP

2 quarts soup stock
1 large soup bone, cracked, to yield:
¼ cup marrow
½ cup bread crumbs

1 teaspoon grated onion
1 egg
½ teaspoon salt
¼ teaspoon pepper

Use broth of beef or veal, or combination of both. Have the butcher crack the soup bone. Remove the marrow, measuring ¼ cup. Mix marrow with bread crumbs, season, and add onion and the beaten egg yolk. With floured fingers form into tiny balls the size of marbles, roll quickly in the beaten egg white, and drop into the bubbling soup stock. When the marrow balls rise to the top of the soup they are cooked and the soup is done. Simmer a minute or two longer and serve. Serves 6-8.

*Mrs. Arthur J. McShane*

## LEVVERKNEPP SUPP I
### (Liver Dumpling Soup)

1 soup bone, with meat
Dumplings
1 tablespoon chopped parsley

2 stalks celery, chopped
½ teaspoon salt
¼ teaspoon pepper

Place soup bone in kettle, cover with cold water. Simmer until the meat on the bone is tender—about 2 hours. Remove bone, cut off the meat, strain the broth, return broth and meat to the kettle. Reheat and simmer. Add parsley, celery, and seasoning. To make the dumplings:

1 pound calf's liver
1 cup bread pieces, soaked in milk
  or water
¼ cup butter

2 teaspoons minced onion
2 eggs
2 tablespoons flour
Salt and pepper

Chop liver. Soak the bread, drain off the excess milk or water, and add to the liver. Brown the onions in the butter and add to the mixture. Beat egg yolks and add. Sprinkle part of the flour over the paste with salt and pepper and blend. Add beaten egg whites last. Use balance of the flour to mold the balls with the fingers—to the size of walnuts. Drop into the bubbling stew and boil *uncovered* for 20 minutes. Serves 6-8.

*Mrs. Arthur J. McShane*

## LEVVERKNEPP SUPP II

1 soup bone
1 pound boiling beef
1 teaspoon salt

¼ teaspoon pepper
1 onion
2 stalks celery

Put soup bone in kettle and cover with water, adding beef cut in bite-sized pieces. Add salt and pepper. Cook with the whole onion and celery stalks until meat is tender—about 2½ hours. Turn down heat and simmer ½ hour longer, while making *Knepp* or dumplings:

| | |
|---|---|
| 1 pound beef liver | ¼ cup shortening |
| ½ cup chopped onions | 1 cup bread crumbs |
| ½ cup chopped celery | 1 egg |
| ¼ cup butter | Salt and pepper |

Skin the liver and remove fiber. Put onion and celery through food chopper, measuring 1 cup. Put liver through the food chopper. Melt butter and shortening and sauté the onions and celery in it until golden yellow. Do not brown. Add chopped liver, bread crumbs, beaten egg, and salt and pepper. Blend. Remove soup bone, onion, and celery from the broth and, when it is bubbling, drop the dumplings by spoonfuls into the stew. Cook 8-10 minutes, when the dumplings will start to rise to the surface. Serve at once. Serves 6.

*Pauline Annas*

## POOR MAN'S DINNER I

| | |
|---|---|
| 2 quarts thin soup | 2 cups mashed potatoes |
| 3 eggs | 2 slices bread, soaked in |
| ½ teaspoon salt | milk |
| Flour to make paste | |

Use whatever soup is on hand, just so it is not thick. Add beaten eggs and salt to the mashed potatoes. Press the milk from the bread lightly, and add to the mixture with a little flour to make a soft paste. Blend. Drop the dumplings from a spoon into the soup, season, cover tightly, and cook for 10-15 minutes. Serves 4.

*Mrs. Rose Preschman*

## SOUP WITH EGG BALLS

| | |
|---|---|
| 1 tablespoon soft butter | 2 hard-boiled egg yolks |
| 2 tablespoons sifted flour | Salt and pepper |
| 1 egg white | 2 quarts soup stock |

Blend butter with flour, add beaten egg white and egg yolks that have been pressed through a sieve. Season and mold into small balls with lightly floured fingers. If too soft, add a very little more flour, but mixture must not be too stiff. Drop into bubbling soup and cook for 5 minutes. Serves 6-8.

*Elizabeth Sanders*

## SOUP WITH DUMPLINGS

2 quarts soup stock
1 egg
½ cup flour, scant

1 heaping tablespoon butter
½ teaspoon salt
Milk to form paste

Salt and pepper

Use any preferred soup stock—or chicken broth. Season to your liking. Make dumplings by blending beaten egg with sifted flour and melted butter. Add salt and just enough scalded milk so that the mixture may be dropped from a teaspoon into the gently boiling soup. Cover tightly and continue to boil for 10 minutes. Serves 6-8.

*Mrs. Victor Boyer*

*Bake oven, Ephrata Cloisters*

# Bread and Breadstuffs

FROM the beginning baking has been an art in Pennsylvania. Pioneer women made their own yeast, used whatever kind of flour was available—and baked perfect bread in primitive ovens! Bread and soup were so often the whole meal that the bread *had* to be good. Loaves were expected to be crisp and golden on the outside and soft and moist inside. If there were any holes under the crust, "the baker was in it," they said, and it was not acceptable.

And because bread was so literally the staff of life, folklore attended it— Friday was considered a lucky day, so it became baking day. But there were many tasks that the housewife must *not* do on Friday—sweep the floor, cultivate her plants, or sow peas or beans. Goodness knows, what with a week's baking to do for a large and hungry family, there really wasn't time for anything but baking. Local folklore, however, had a full set of rules for the task:

Loaves must never be placed upside down on the table; the family would quarrel. They must not be placed on their sides either; the angels would weep. A loaf with a broom must be sent ahead to a new house when the family moved; this would ward off homesickness. The dough trough must be carried into the house before anything else; this would assure the family of food. As for yeast, the names of three capable women must go into the pot when it was "started." This was to make sure of perfect bread. Of course, to begin, the yeast had to be borrowed. No doubt that is where the three capable women came in.

The homemade yeast was kept in the "sotz crock" on the kitchen shelf and stirred into the flour at night. Then the dough was set to rise. For this purpose the early settlers wove baskets with small holes in the center, so that when the

17

basket was overturned the dough could be loosened with the finger. Later the dough trough came into use; it could be pulled up to the hearth for the proper temperature. Early in the morning the dough was kneaded, the loaves shaped, and carried outside to the bake oven.

Pioneer bakehouses were of plastered masonry, with a tile-roofed shed across the front to protect baker and loaves from bad weather. Shelves ranging down the sides of the shed were for the loaves as they came from the oven. The oven, elevated for convenience, was floored and arched with brick and had an iron door. Early in the morning a cordwood fire was built inside and allowed to burn furiously until it was reduced to ashes. Then the ashes were shoveled out with the *Kitch,* the oven floor was swabbed out with the *Huddel Lumpa,* and all was ready for the baking. The loaves were transferred from the paddle-shaped, long-handled *Schiesel* to the bottom of the oven and the baking began. Usually some wood ash stuck to the bottom crusts, but this was considered to improve the flavor of the bread.

As the bread baked the housewife busily made her pies and cakes, and when the bread came out and the loaves were lined up on the shelves the pies went in. But that was not all: as the heat of the oven slowly dwindled, trays of fruit were placed inside to dry. By the time the bake oven had cooled the shelves were filled with row after row of golden brown loaves, an array of cakes and pies that smelled too good to last a whole week, and perhaps some sticky buns or a crumb-covered coffee cake. At this point, if the weary baker gave a thought to her neglected peas and beans, tomorrow was another day.

The tantalizing aroma, of course, drew the children to the bake oven like little homing pigeons—and they were not disappointed. For them were little pie shells filled with left-overs: a little milk or molasses and a touch of spices produced *Flitche*. These they devoured with a bite or two and then it was their duty to carry the loaves, pies, and cakes into the farmhouse. They would have to wait until mealtime for further delights.

Many of these old bakehouses still stand in farmhouse environs but there are modern stoves in the kitchen nowadays and baking tasks have been lightened. The amount and variety of baking done is still impressive, however, for there is and always has been more to bread dough than just bread in Pennsylvania. With a twist here and a sprinkle of sugar and cinnamon there, the housewife produces the most delectable poppy-seed rolls, cinnamon buns, "Dutch" cakes, and the like that can be imagined. Fruit-filled, crumb-topped, hot and buttery, these confections cross the border line between bread and cake so wantonly that they are hard to classify. Sometimes "cakes" are enclosed in pie crust and sometimes they are rolled or twisted. The word "cake" means many things in Pennsylvania Dutch.

## BREAD I

| | |
|---|---|
| 1 yeast cake, dissolved in | 1½ teaspoons sugar |
| ½ cup lukewarm potato water | 1 teaspoon salt |
| 2½ cups water | 6 cups flour (plus) |

1 tablespoon butter

Dissolve the yeast cake in the ½ cup lukewarm water in which potatoes have been boiled, add 2½ cups water, turn into a large mixing bowl, add sugar and salt. Sift the flour 3 times, adding gradually to the mixture until about 4 cups of flour have been added. Stir vigorously with a wooden spoon while adding the flour. When the dough forms a ball that does not stick to the sides of the bowl, place upon a floured board and knead with floured hands, adding more flour as needed. Knead for 15 minutes, or until smooth and elastic in the hands. Return to bowl, cover tightly, and set in warm place until doubled in size. Then knead again, adding more flour if necessary. Chop in the butter and set aside in the bowl in a warm place for an hour to rise. Shape into loaves, place loaves in pans 3½ x 7½ inches that have been greased. Half fill the pans with dough, grease the tops of the loaves with melted butter or lard, let rise another hour. When the loaves have doubled in size, bake in a 450° oven for 5 to 10 minutes, when the loaves will have begun to brown. Reduce heat to 350° and finish baking. This will take 45 minutes to 1 hour. Makes 2 good-sized loaves.

*Mrs. Arthur J. McShane*

## BREAD II

| | |
|---|---|
| 2 yeast cakes, dissolved in | 2 teaspoons salt |
| ½ cup lukewarm water (or | 1 cup scalded milk |
| potato water) | 1 cup cold water |
| 2 tablespoons sugar | 6 or 7 cups bread flour |

1 heaping tablespoon butter

Dissolve the yeast cakes in the lukewarm water, turn into a large mixing bowl, add sugar and salt, milk and water. Add sifted flour gradually, stirring until about 4 cups flour have been added. Place dough upon a floured board and let it stand there for about 10 minutes. Knead vigorously for about 10 minutes, cover, and let rise in a warm place until doubled in size. Then knead the rest of the flour into the dough to make a stiff sponge. Chop in the butter, set the dough aside to rise again. When well risen, knead once more, shape into loaves, dust lightly with flour, brush with melted butter, place in 3½ x 7½ inch breadpans, the loaves half-filling the pans. Let rise in the pans for another hour, or until the loaves rise above the tops of the pans. Bake in 450° over for 10 minutes, or until loaves begin to brown. Reduce heat to 350°, bake about 45 minutes longer. Makes 2 large loaves.

*Mrs. Edward S. Shepherd*

## BREAD III

| | |
|---|---|
| 1 yeast cake, dissolved in | 2 teaspoons salt |
| 2 cups scalded milk | 1 tablespoon sugar |
| 1 cup mashed potatoes | 6 cups flour (plus) |

1 heaping tablespoon butter

Dissolve the yeast cake in the lukewarm milk, turn into large bowl with the potatoes, add sugar and salt. Sift the flour 3 times, adding gradually to the mixture until about 4 cups have been added. Stir vigorously with a wooden spoon while adding the flour. When dough forms a ball that leaves the sides of the bowl turn out upon a floured board. Knead with floured hands, adding more flour as needed. Knead for about 15 minutes, or until dough is smooth and elastic in the hands. Return to bowl, cover tightly, and set in a warm place to rise. When doubled in size, knead again, adding more flour if necessary. Chop in the butter (avoiding gas bubbles) and set bowl aside in a warm place to rise for an hour. Shape into loaves, place in 3½ x 7½ inch pans, half filling them with the loaves. (The pans, of course, have been greased.) Grease the tops of the loaves with melted butter, let rise another hour in warm place. When loaves have doubled in size, bake in 450° over for 5 to 10 minutes or until loaves begin to brown, then reduce heat to 350° and bake 45 minutes to 1 hour. Makes 2 good-sized loaves.

*Mabel E. Mulock*

## FEDERAL BREAD

| | |
|---|---|
| 4 tablespoons butter | 3 cups flour |
| ½ yeast cake dissolved in | 3 eggs |
| 2 cups scalded milk | 1 tablespoon sugar |

½ teaspoon salt

Drop the butter into the milk while it is scalding. Sift flour into a large bowl, make a hole in the middle, pour in the milk, butter, and yeast mixture, also the eggs, sugar, and salt. Mix. Pour into a well-greased pan, set aside to rise in a warm place —for an hour, or until the loaf has doubled in size. Bake in 350°-375° oven for 50 minutes to 1 hour. Bread should not be sliced but torn from the loaf, buttered, and eaten hot. Makes 1 loaf.

*Mabel E. Mulock*

## POPPY SEED TWISTS

½ cup mashed potatoes
1 tablespoon lard
2 tablespoons butter
1 teaspoon salt

1½ tablespoons sugar
1½ yeast cakes, dissolved in
½ cup lukewarm potato water
5 cups bread flour, approximately

2 cups water

Place the mashed potatoes, melted lard and butter, salt and sugar in a large bowl and stir in the yeast and potato water. Add sifted flour and the 2 cups of water alternately, mixing well until the sponge is rather stiff. Add more flour if necessary. Turn out on a floured board and knead vigorously, 25 minutes by the clock. Shape the sponge into a ball, rub with soft lard or butter, place in bowl, cover tightly, and let stand in a warm place. When double in size, (a sponge that stands too long will sour) knead well again, roll out on floured board. Divide dough into 6 long strips. Pinch the ends of 3 strips together and braid, to make a loaf. Place loaves in greased 3½ x 7½ inch bread pans. Let stand for 1 hour, or until doubled in size. Brush tops of loaves with a little milk, sprinkle with poppy seeds, and let stand to rise for a few more minutes. Bake in 450° oven from 5-10 minutes, or until loaves have just begun to brown. Reduce heat to 350° and bake 40-45 minutes longer. Makes 2 large loaves.

*Mrs. Arthur J. McShane*

## GRUMBERA TWISTS
(Potato Twists)

1 cup hot mashed potatoes
1 tablespoon lard
2 tablespoons butter
1 teaspoon salt
1½ tablespoons sugar

1 cup scalded milk
1 egg
1½ yeast cakes, dissolved in
½ cup potato water
6 cups flour (approximately)

Early in the morning, place the mashed potatoes, melted lard and butter, salt and sugar in a large mixing bowl. Stir in the cooled, lukewarm scalded milk. Let stand 5 minutes. Beat the egg lightly and add. Add the yeast in potato water. Stir in the sifted flour gradually, stirring until the paste leaves the side of the bowl. Cover tightly, set aside in a warm place to rise—about 1 hour. Turn out on a floured board and knead vigorously, adding more flour to stiffen if needed. Return dough to greased bowl. Let rise again. Turn out and knead some more, chopping through the dough with a knife, for fine texture. Return ⅓ of the dough to the bowl. Divide remaining dough into 2 parts. Roll one of these parts into 3 long, narrow strips. Pinch together at the ends and braid to form a loaf. Repeat with the remaining part. Place these large braids in 3½ x 7½ inch breadpans. Moisten tops with a little milk. Repeat the process with the dough in the bowl, separating it to make 2 smaller braids. Place small braids on top of large braids in pans. Brush with melted butter. Let rise until loaves have doubled in size. Bake in 450° oven for a few minutes—until loaves have begun to brown. Reduce heat and finish baking—about 45-50 minutes. Makes 2 large loaves.

*Mrs. Thomas B. Keck*

## RICH BREAD

1 yeast cake
1 cup lukewarm water
1 cup scalded milk

2 tablespoons shortening
2 tablespoons sugar
2 teaspoons salt

### 5 cups flour

Dissolve the yeast in the lukewarm water, add scalded milk cooled to lukewarm, shortening, sugar, and salt. Let mixture stand until it foams a little on top. Mix, add sifted flour. Knead the paste on a floured board until it is smooth and elastic—about 7 or 8 minutes. Roll into a ball and put in a greased bowl, rub melted butter over top and sides of dough, cover, and let rise at temperature of about 80° until doubled in size (from 1½-2 hours). Turn out on floured board, punch down, cut through several times with a knife to improve texture, shape into 2 loaves. Let rise another ½ hour. Reshape and place in greased loaf pans. Cover with a cloth and let stand again in warm place until loaves have doubled in size. Bake in moderate oven (350°-400°) for about 45 minutes. Brush loaves with melted butter. Makes 2 loaves.

*Mrs. Floyd Siegfried*

## RAISED CORNMEAL BREAD

1 yeast cake, dissolved in
1 cup lukewarm milk
2 tablespoons butter

2 scant tablespoons sugar
2 teaspoons salt
2 cups flour (plus)

### ½ cup stone-ground cornmeal

Scald the milk, dissolve the yeast in it, add butter, and when the butter has melted pour the mxiture into a large bowl. Add sugar and salt. Sift in the flour. Mix well and place bowl in a warm place (80°-85°), to rise until doubled in size (about 1 hour). Add cornmeal and blend. Knead the paste on a well-floured board, adding as much more flour as is needed to form a stiff dough. Place in a greased bowl, rub melted butter on sides and top of the ball of dough, cover tightly, and let rise again in a warm place—for about 1½-2 hours. Shape into a loaf, place in a 3½ x 7½ inch breadpan, cover, let rise until doubled in size. Bake in 350° oven for about 45 minutes. Makes 1 large loaf.

*Tim Palmer*

While you are bread-making, here are two variants that you can make with some of the dough:

## MUSH BREAD

| | |
|---|---|
| 4 cups boiling water | 1 cup cold water |
| 1 cup cornmeal | 1 teaspoon salt |

Place the boiling water in the top of a double boiler. Mix the cornmeal, cold water, and salt. Stir this mixture into the boiling water. Cook together gradually, stirring for 3 minutes, steaming, covered, for 15 minutes. When the mush is smooth, cool and add:

| | |
|---|---|
| 4 cups bread dough | 1 scant cup molasses |
| | ½ teaspoon salt |

There should be 4 cups of the mush. Mix the batter well together; it should be thin. Pour into 4 small, greased breadpans, let rise, covered, in a warm place until doubled in size. Bake about 1¼ hours in 350°-375° oven. Makes 4 small loaves.

*Mary Faas*

## CINNAMON BREAD

| | |
|---|---|
| ½ cup soft butter | 4 cups bread dough |
| 1 cup sugar | ⅓ cup raisins |
| 2 eggs | Melted butter, sugar, and cinnamon |

Cream the butter and sugar, add egg yolks, well beaten, cream again. Mix with the bread dough, add raisins, fold in egg whites (beaten). Let rise, covered, in a warm place until doubled in size. Shape into loaves, place in greased breadpans, brush with melted butter, sprinkle thickly with sugar and lightly with cinnamon, let rise again for ½ hour. Bake in 350° oven for 50-60 minutes. Makes 3 loaves.

*Mary Faas*

## RYE BREAD

| | |
|---|---|
| 1 yeast cake, dissolved in water to cover | 2 teaspoons salt |
| | 1½ tablespoons sugar |
| 1½ cups lukewarm water | 6 cups rye flour |
| 3 tablespoons melted butter | ½ cup dry milk (scant) |
| | 1 egg white |

Soften the yeast in a little water and set aside. Combine the lukewarm water, melted butter, salt, and sugar in a large bowl. Mix thoroughly. Add 4 cups of the sifted rye flour and the dry milk. Mix. Add balance of the flour and mix together with a wooden spoon until dough is stiff. Place on a floured board and knead for 5 minutes. Turn into a greased bowl, cover, and let rise in a warm place for 1½ hours. Punch down and cut through the bubbles with a knife, turn the dough, and repeat. Cover, let rise again—½ hour. Place dough on a floured board, divide into 2 balls. Put loaves in 2 greased, round pans. Prick the loaves several times with a fork. Cover, let rise for 1 hour. Bake in 350° oven for 50 minutes. Cool, brush tops of loaves with beaten egg white. Makes 2 loaves.

## WHOLE WHEAT BREAD

| | |
|---|---|
| 1 yeast cake | 2 tablespoons sugar |
| ¼ cup lukewarm water | ½ teaspoon salt |
| 1 cup scalded milk | 1 cup white flour |
| 1 tablespoon butter | 2 cups (plus) whole wheat flour |

Dissolve yeast in the lukewarm water; add butter, sugar, and salt to the milk, cool mixture to lukewarm. Add the yeast and water and mix. Sift in the flour. When dough leaves the sides of the bowl it is ready to be turned out on a floured board and kneaded until it blisters. Roll into a ball, place in greased bowl, cover, and let stand in warm place (80°-85°) until doubled in bulk. Shape into loaves, let stand until loaves have risen, then bake 1 hour in 400° oven. Makes 1 large or 2 small loaves.

*Mabel E. Mulock*

## COFFEE BREAD

| | |
|---|---|
| 1 yeast cake, dissolved in | ½ teaspoon salt |
| ½ cup lukewarm water | 2 tablespoons flour |
| 2 tablespoons butter | 2 eggs |
| 2 tablespoons sugar | 4 cups flour, approximately |
| | 2 cups milk |

Cover the yeast with the lukewarm water and set aside. Mix the butter, sugar, salt, and the 2 tablespoons flour in a large bowl. Add yeast and water. Mix together and set aside in a warm place to rise, about 1 hour. Add beaten eggs and two-thirds of the sifted flour. Let rise, covered, another hour, then add milk and balance of the flour. Turn out on floured board and knead vigorously for about 10 minutes. Roll out dough into 4 1-inch cakes, place in pie tins, and brush with melted butter. Let rise until doubled in size. Bake in 350° oven for about 20 minutes. Makes 4 "cakes."

*Mrs. Victor Boyer*

## KAFFEEKUCHE
### (Coffee Cake)

3 tablespoons sugar
½ cup lard and butter, mixed
½ teaspoon salt
1 yeast cake, dissolved in
½ cup lukewarm potato water

2 tablespoons flour
4 egg yolks
½ cup cream
4 cups flour
1 cup scalded milk
2 egg whites

Mix sugar with lard and butter and salt in a large bowl. Add the yeast cake in warm water (that potatoes have been boiled in) and 2 tablespoons flour. Set aside, covered, in a warm place (80°-85°) to rise—about an hour. Beat in the egg yolks and cream. Sift flour 3 times and add, alternating with the lukewarm milk. Fold in beaten egg whites last and set bowl aside for another hour. Slightly warm deep pie tins, grease them, flour lightly, and fill two-thirds with the paste. Set pans aside to rise until the dough has risen to the tops of the pans. Brush cakes with a little melted butter. For crumbs, mix:

1 cup sifted flour
½ cup granulated sugar

½ cup brown sugar
1½ teaspoons cinnamon
⅓ cup lard

Spread this mixture thickly over the cakes and bake in 350° oven for about 25 minutes—or until golden brown on top. Makes 6 7-inch cakes. A common term for this confection is "Dutch Cake," especially in Pennsylvania regions not "Dutch."

*Eleanor-Rose Roth*

## SCHWENKFELDER CAKE

1 tablespoon sugar
1 tablespoon flour
1 teaspoon salt

½ cup mashed potatoes
1 cup lukewarm potato water
1 yeast cake

Dissolve the yeast cake in the lukewarm water and add to the other ingredients, mixed in a large bowl. A little saffron may be added if wished for color and flavor. Set the bowl in a warm place for about 2 hours, or until foamy on top. Mix, in another bowl:

1 cup granulated sugar
½ cup mashed potatoes

½ cup melted butter or lard
1 cup warm milk
1 egg

When thoroughly mixed, add the first mixture to this with enough flour to make a thick batter:

### About 4 cups (flour)

Let rise in warm place, covered, until doubled in size. Add more flour:

### 1 or 2 cups (flour)

Knead dough until spongy and until it leaves the sides of the bowl. Cover and let rise again about an hour. Form into cakes and roll cut on floured board (lightly) to ½-inch thickness. Place in well-greased pie tins. Let rise, spread with lard or butter and crumbs:

| | |
|---|---|
| 1 cup flour | 1 teaspoon cinnamon |
| 1 cup brown sugar | ⅓ cup lard |

Blend the mixture lightly to make crumbs, spread on the cakes, and bake in 350° oven for 20-25 minutes until nicely browned. Makes 6 7-inch "Dutch Cakes."

*Irma Schultz*

(The Schwenkfelders emigrated to America from Silesia in the early days. They are among the most learned of the sects and have always interested themselves particularly in education. They have a fascinating museum at Pennsburg, Pennsylvania, and it contains some of the finest *Fraktur* to be found.)

## LIGHT CAKE WITH DOLLARS

| | |
|---|---|
| 1 cup hot mashed potatoes | 1 yeast cake, dissolved in |
| 1 cup soft sugar | ½ cup lukewarm potato water |

Mix these ingredients and let stand in warm place, covered, to rise—for several hours. Then add:

| | |
|---|---|
| 1 cup sugar | ¾ cup melted butter |
| 1 cup milk | 3 eggs, well beaten |

### 3 cups flour, approximately

Stir together until well mixed, cover, and let stand in a warm place until doubled in size. Turn out on floured board, knead lightly, let rise again, shape into loaves. Brush the tops of the loaves with a little milk, place in 3½ x 7½ inch pans, let stand until loaves have nearly filled the pans. To make the "dollars":

| | | |
|---|---|---|
| 1 cup sugar | ½ cup flour | ½ cup butter, or enough to bind |

Mix flour and sugar, cream with the butter, form into a roll, and place in the refrigerator until the roll hardens. Slice into "dollars," dot these over the top of the cake, and bake in 375° oven for about ½ hour. Makes 2 loaves.

*Mrs. David A. Miller*

## EBBELKUCHE
### (Apple Cake)

| | |
|---|---|
| 1½ yeast cakes | ¼ cup butter |
| 1 tablespoon sugar | ½ cup sugar |
| 1 cup milk, scalded and cooled | 2 eggs |
| 3½ cups sifted flour | ¼ teaspoon salt |

Peeled apples, cut in eighths

Dissolve the yeast and the tablespoon of sugar in the lukewarm milk. Add half of the sifted flour to make a sponge. Beat until smooth. Cover and set bowl aside in a warm place until light—about ½ hour. Cream ½ cup sugar with the butter, add to the sponge, then add the well-beaten eggs. Add the balance of the sifted flour (or enough to make a soft dough) and the salt. Knead lightly, roll into a ball, and return to greased bowl. Turn over in the bowl to grease whole surface of the sponge. Let rise for about 2 hours, Roll out on a floured board to ½-inch thickness, place in well-greased, shallow pans, brush with butter, sprinkle with sugar. Cut the apples in eighths and press into the dough with sharp edges downward. Sprinkle with cinnamon and let rise for ½ hour. Bake 20 minutes in 350° oven, keeping covered with pans on top of cakes for the first 10 minutes of baking. This makes sure that the apples are cooked. Uncover and finish baking.

*Mrs. Henry Lang*

## RAISIN BREAD

| | |
|---|---|
| 1 cup mashed potatoes | ½ cup sugar |
| 1 yeast cake, dissolved in | 3½-4 cups sifted flour |
| ½ cup potato water | 2 eggs, beaten |
| ½ cup scalded, lukewarm milk | 1 cup raisins |
| ½ cup potato water | ¼ teaspoon cloves |
| ¼ cup melted butter | ½ teaspoon cinnamon |

Mix the mashed potatoes, the yeast cake dissolved in potato water (which should be lukewarm), and let rise, covered, in a warm place. After ½ hour add lukewarm milk and balance of potato water, creamed butter and sugar, sifted flour, and well-beaten eggs. Mix well, set aside to rise for about 2 hours. Add raisins, cinnamon, and cloves, roll out and knead on floured board, return to greased bowl, and let rise until doubled in size. Return to floured board, chop through with knife, knead lightly, and divide into 2 parts. Shape into loaves, bake in 2 small, greased breadpans in 450° oven for 5 minutes, or until loaves have begun to brown. Reduce heat to 350° and finish baking—40-45 minutes. Makes 2 small loaves.

*Helen B. Bailey*

## RAISED NUT BREAD

| | |
|---|---|
| 1 cup white flour | 1 cup scalded milk |
| 1 yeast cake, dissolved in | 2 tablespoons brown sugar |
| ¼ cup lukewarm water | 1 teaspoon salt (scant) |
| 1 tablespoon butter | ½ cup nutmeats |

1 cup whole wheat flour

The early settlers used hickory nuts for this bread. Sift the white flour, dissolve the yeast cake in the lukewarm water, set a sponge of the sifted white flour, yeast in water, butter, and milk, cooled to lukewarm. Cover in bowl and set aside in a warm place for about 2 hours until it has risen and is light. Add sugar, salt, nutmeats (in small pieces), and sifted whole wheat flour, making paste as stiff as can be stirred with a spoon. Let rise again, rolled into a ball in the greased bowl, for ½-1 hour. Shape into a loaf on floured board, put in greased breadpan, and allow to rise until doubled in size. Bake about 50 minutes in 375° oven. Makes 1 good-sized loaf.

*Mabel E. Mulock*

## RAISED CAKES

| | |
|---|---|
| 1 cup mashed potatoes | ½ cup butter |
| 1 cup lukewarm water | ½ teaspoon salt |
| 1 yeast cake | 5 cups flour (approximately) |
| 2 cups sugar | 2 eggs |

Mix the mashed potatoes, the yeast cake dissolved in the potato water, the sugar, butter, salt, and a little of the sifted flour—in a large bowl. Let rise in a warm place for an hour. Add the beaten eggs and the balance of the sifted flour. Mix. Let rise again for an hour. Knead the dough on a floured board, shape into 4 flat 1-inch cakes, place in greased pie pans, and let rise until doubled in size. Brush with butter, sprinkle with crumbs:

| | |
|---|---|
| 1 cup sugar | ½ cup molasses, thinned with water |
| ¼ cup butter | ½ cup flour |

1½ teaspoons  cinnamon

Mix ingredients together lightly to form crumbs. Spread on the cakes and bake in 350° oven until golden brown on top—about 25 minutes. Makes 4 7-inch cakes.

*Mrs. Victor Boyer*

## MORAVIAN SUGAR CAKES

1 cup hot mashed potatoes
1 cup sugar
1 cup melted butter
1 teaspoon salt

2 yeast cakes, dissolved in
1 cup lukewarm water
4-5 cups sifted flour
2 eggs

For topping: melted butter, brown sugar, cinnamon.

Mix the mashed potatoes, sugar, butter, and salt in a large bowl, adding a little of the flour. Add yeast in lukewarm water. Sift in the flour, using 4 cups and as much more as seems needed. Add the beaten eggs. Let rise in a covered bowl, in a warm place. When doubled in size, roll out on a floured board, knead lightly, roll out to ¾-inch thickness, and place in greased pans. Let rise for about 2 hours. Brush surface with melted butter, press holes about 2 inches apart across the top (with the thumb), fill the holes with melted butter and brown sugar. Sprinkle with a little cinnamon. Bake in 375° oven for about ½ hour, or until golden brown.

The dough can be shaped into 2-inch balls and flattened a little, to make buns. They should be brushed with butter and sprinkled with sugar. These buns are traditional at Moravian love feasts.

*Marilyn Buckner*

## SCHNECKE
### (Snails)

1 cup milk, scalded
1 yeast cake
¼ cup sugar (white)
1 teaspoon salt
3 cups flour

1 egg and 1 egg yolk
¼ cup melted butter
½ cup yellow sugar
2 teaspoons cinnamon
½ cup raisins

½ cup blanched shredded almonds

Scald the milk and cool to lukewarm. Dissolve the yeast in it, add salt and sugar. Cover and let stand ½ hour. Add half of the sifted flour. Mix, cover, and set aside in a warm place to rise (about 1 hour). Add the beaten eggs, melted butter, and the balance of the flour. Knead lightly and set aside to rise. Roll out on a floured board to about ¼-inch thickness, brush liberally with melted butter, sprinkle with mixed yellow sugar and cinnamon, dot thickly with raisins and almonds. Roll up like a jelly roll and slice to 1½-inch thickness with a very sharp knife. Place in greased pans, brush tops with butter, sprinkle with more cinnamon and sugar. (Yellow sugar will not burn.) If you want the *Schnecke* to be sticky, use brown sugar instead of yellow and sprinkle some on the bottom of the pan before the *Schnecke* are put in. Bake 25 minutes in a 375° oven.

*Mrs. John N. Mealey*

## STRICKLE SHEETS

4 cups milk
4 eggs
4 tablespoons butter

1 yeast cake, dissolved in a little
lukewarm water
1 teaspoon salt
2 cups sugar

5 cups flour (approximately)

Scald the milk, let it cool, add beaten eggs and melted butter. Add yeast and water it was dissolved in, salt, sugar, and enough of the sifted flour to form a thin batter. Beat vigorously for about 10 minutes. Cover bowl tightly and place in a warm place. When doubled in size, add the balance of the sifted flour to make a stiff dough. Knead on a floured board for 10 minutes, cutting the dough with a knife to make it fine-textured. Set aside in bowl to rise again. When the sponge is light, roll out on a floured board to ¾-inch thickness and cut in small rounds. Place rounds in greased pans and let rise again until doubled in size. Mix the following:

2 cups light brown sugar
2 heaping tablespoons butter

4 scant tablespoons sifted flour
4 tablespoons boiling water

Blend ingredients into a syrup and spread over the rounds. Bake 20 minutes in 350° oven. The biscuit shapes will have run together, with the syrup binding them into a sheet.

*Mrs. Arthur J. McShane*

## BUTTERSEMMELN

½ cup mashed potatoes
½ cup sugar

½ yeast cake, dissolved in
¼ cup lukewarm water

Mix these ingredients into a batter and set aside to rise. Several hours later add:

2 cups milk
2 eggs (beaten)
½ cup sugar

½ cup mixed butter and lard
¼ teaspoon salt
5-6 cups sifted flour

Mix well together. Set aside in warm place, tightly covered, to rise. When doubled in size, knead lightly on a floured board, roll out to ¼-inch thickness. Brush with melted butter, cut in 2-inch squares. Bring up the corners of each square to the center, rather like an old-fashioned valentine. Place in greased pans, well apart, and let rise for ½ hour. Bake 15-20 minutes in 375° oven. As soon as taken from the oven brush with butter and sprinkle with powdered sugar. Makes about 4 dozen.

*Mrs. Philip B. Woodroofe*

## DUTCH ROLL-UPS

1 yeast cake, dissolved in
   a little lukewarm water
1 cup scalded milk
6 tablespoons sugar

1 teaspoon salt
2 egg yolks
1 cup butter
4 cups flour

Dissolve yeast in lukewarm water. Cool milk to lukewarm and mix with sugar and salt. Combine lightly beaten egg yolks and softened butter with yeast and water, add to the milk mixture. Stir in 1/4 of the sifted flour, mix well. Add balance of flour. Turn out on floured board, knead dough until smooth and elastic. Place in greased bowl, cover, set in warm place, and let rise for 1 hour. Divide into halves on floured board and roll out to thickness of 1/8 inch. Spread with this mixture:

1 cup walnut meats, finely chopped   1/2 cup light brown sugar
   1/2 teaspoon cinnamon

Roll as for jelly roll, slice into pieces 1 1/2 inch thick with sharp knife, place on greased sheet, brush tops with butter, sprinkle with a little more of the sugar and cinnamon, and bake about 35 minutes in 350° oven.

*Mabel E. Mulock*

## CINNAMON BUNS I

2 medium-sized potatoes, boiled
   and mashed
1 tablespoon sugar

1 tablespoon flour
1/2 teaspoon salt
1 cup lukewarm potato water

Mix together. Add:

1 yeast cake, dissolved in   1/2 cup lukewarm potato water

Stir together. Let rise for 1 hour in a covered bowl in a warm place. Now measure the paste. There should be 5 cups. Add:

2 cups sugar
1/2 cup melted butter

1/2 teaspoon salt
5 cups flour, approximately

Use enough flour to make a not too stiff paste. Let rise again until the bowl is filled. Take up a portion of the dough, toss on a floured board, roll out to 1/2-inch thickness. Spread with melted butter, light-brown sugar (brown sugar will stick), cinnamon, and raisins that have been soaked in water. Roll up as for jelly roll, cut in 1-inch sections with a very sharp knife, place rolls on buttered tins, crowding about 7 in a 9-inch pan. Sprinkle the tops with sugar and pecans. Let rise until doubled in size. Bake in 375° oven for 25-30 minutes, or until golden brown. Makes about 35.

*Mrs. C. A. Haas*

We had been lucky enough to eat Mrs. Haas's cinnamon buns for years, and when the first edition of this book was written my mother decided to get her recipe for the wonderful buns—the best we had ever eaten or hoped to eat. They had a lot of difficulty. Mrs. Haas was perfectly willing to tell how she made the buns, but the trouble was she made them so automatically that she could not tell, for the life of her, just how. Finally, after a whole afternoon of give-and-take, they evolved the foregoing recipe.

## CINNAMON BUNS II

2 yeast cakes, dissolved in     1 tablespoon sugar
½ cup scalded, lukewarm milk     1 tablespoon flour
          ¾ teaspoon salt

Place the yeast, scalded milk, sugar, flour, and salt in a large bowl. Mix together and set aside to rise in a warm place for about 1 hour. Add:

2 scant cups sugar     ¾ teaspoon salt
1 cup melted butter     5-6 cups flour

This should make a rather stiff sponge. Add more flour if not stiff enough. Add:

### 5 whole eggs

Beat the mixture well and set aside to rise again. Roll out on a floured board lightly to ½-inch thickness, spread with butter, sprinkle with sugar and cinnamon, adding raisins if desired. Roll up, slice into 1-inch sections, place on greased pans. Sprinkle tops with sugar, cinnamon, and press pecans down into the dough. Let stand until well risen. Bake about 20 minutes in 375° oven. Makes 6 9-inch panfuls.

*Elizabeth Schramek*

## CINNAMON BUNS III

1 yeast cake     ¼ cup shortening
1 cup scalded milk     ½ cup butter
¼ cup white sugar     1 cup brown sugar
4 cups flour     ¾ teaspoon cinnamon

Dissolve the yeast cake in a little lukewarm water. Add sugar and scalded milk, cooled to lukewarm. Mix. Add 2 cups of the sifted flour, melted shortening. Stir, adding the balance of the flour. Cover bowl, let paste rise in a warm place for about 1 hour, or until doubled in size. Turn out on floured board, roll to ¼-inch thickness, spread with half the soft butter and brown sugar and cinnamon, mixed. Roll up like jelly roll, slice with sharp knife into 1½-inch sections. Place the rest of the butter and brown sugar, mixed, in bottom of pans and put the rolls in the pans. Let rise until doubled in size. Sprinkle nuts over tops if desired, sprinkle with cinnamon, and bake at 375° for 25-30 minutes, or until golden brown on top.

*Mrs. Floyd Siegfried*

## STICKY BUNS I

| | |
|---|---|
| 1 yeast cake, dissolved in | 6 cups sifted flour |
| ½ cup lukewarm water | ½ cup butter |
| 2 cups scalded, lukewarm milk | 1 cup brown sugar |
| 2 cups sugar | 2½ teaspoons cinnamon |
| 1 teaspoon salt | ½ cup raisins |

½ cup currants

Dissolve the yeast in the lukewarm water, add to the lukewarm scalded milk. Add sugar, salt, and flour and stir well together. Place in a greased bowl, shaping the sponge into a large, round ball. Butter the sides and the top. Cover and set aside to rise in a warm place. About 2 hours later, or when the paste is more than doubled in size, roll out on a floured board to 1½-inch thickness. Spread with melted butter, brown sugar, and cinnamon. Soak raisins and currants in warm water, to soften, dot over the surface, roll up like jelly roll and cut into 1-inch slices with sharp knife. Place rolls in buttered tins which have been well greased and sprinkled thickly with brown sugar. Seven will fit a 9-inch pan. Sprinkle tops with brown sugar, a little cinnamon. Let stand to rise until doubled in size. Bake in 400° oven for 5 minutes, turn down heat, and bake at 350° for 15 minutes longer. Makes 6 pans.

*Mrs. John M. Mealey*

## STICKY BUNS II

| | |
|---|---|
| ¼ cup butter | 1 cup scalded, lukewarm milk |
| ¼ cup lard | 2 eggs |
| Sugar | Grated rind of 1 orange |
| 1 teaspoon salt | 4 tablespoons orange juice |
| 1 yeast cake, dissolved in | 5 cups flour, approximately |
| ¼ cup lukewarm water | |

Place softened butter, lard, sugar, and salt in large bowl and mix together. Add yeast in lukewarm water and lukewarm milk. Stir. Add well-beaten eggs, grated orange rind, orange juice, and half the sifted flour. Beat vigorously, add remaining flour, to make a stiff paste. (Add ½ cup more sifted flour if dough seems too soft.) Beat. Let rise, covered, in a warm place for 1 hour. Turn out on floured board, knead until smooth and elastic. Roll dough into a ball, place in a greased bowl, buttering the top and sides of the dough. Let rise until doubled in bulk. Turn out on floured board, punch down and cut through with a knife to improve texture, roll to 1/4-inch thickness. Brush with:

### 3 tablespoons melted butter

Sprinkle with:

1/2 cup brown sugar                              2 teaspoons cinnamon

Roll, as for jelly roll, and cut into 1 1/2-inch slices with sharp knife. Combine:

2 tablespoons butter                             1 cup brown sugar
                    2 tablespoons water

Bring to a boil, simmer 1/2 minute, pour this mixture into greased pans, sprinkle nuts on top (optional), place the rolls in the pans, let rise until doubled in size. Bake 25 minutes in 375° oven. Makes 25.

*Helen B. Bailey*


## POCKETBOOK ROLLS

1 yeast cake, dissolved in            1/4 teaspoon salt
1/4 cup lukewarm water                1/4 cup sugar
1 cup scalded milk                    4 cups sifted flour
                    1/4 cup butter

Dissolve the yeast in the lukewarm water, using water in which potatoes have been boiled, if you like; scald the milk, cool to lukewarm. Mix together the salt, sugar, sifted flour, and melted butter. Add yeast-and-water and milk. Stir together. Cover bowl, set aside in a warm place to rise for an hour or 2—until paste has risen to top of bowl. Punch down, cut through with a knife several times, let rise again—about 1/2 hour. Turn out on floured board, knead until smooth and elastic, form dough into a ball, return to greased bowl, and let rise, covered, in a warm place. (If you turn the dough over when you have put it into the bowl, you will not have to butter the top and sides.) When doubled in size, knead again, roll out on floured board to 1/4-inch thickness, cut in rounds with cookie cutter, dot rounds with butter, fold double, and place on greased cookie sheet. Let stand until doubled in size. Bake in 375° oven until rolls are golden brown—about 25 minutes. Makes about 25.

*Mabel E. Mulock*


## RAISED BISCUIT

1 yeast cake, dissolved in            3 tablespoons butter
1/4 cup lukewarm water                3 tablespoons sugar
1 cup scalded milk                    2 eggs, well beaten
3 1/2 cups sifted flour               1/2 teaspoon salt

Dissolve yeast in lukewarm water, place in bowl with scalded milk, which has been cooled to lukewarm. Add half the sifted flour to make a sponge. Beat until smooth. Cover and set aside in a warm place to rise—about 1 hour. Cream the butter and sugar, add to the sponge, then add the balance of the flour. Add well-beaten eggs and salt. Knead lightly, place in greased bowl. Cover, set aside to rise for about 2 hours. Roll out on floured board to ½-inch thickness, cut in rounds with biscuit cutter, place in greased pans, brush tops with butter, let stand ½ hour longer, to rise again. Bake 20-25 minutes in 375° oven. Makes about 2 dozen, depending upon size of biscuits.

*Mrs. Karl L. Lubrecht*

## FASTNACHTKUCHE I
### (Raised Doughnuts)

| | |
|---|---|
| 1 cup hot, unsalted mashed potatoes | 1 yeast cake, dissolved in |
| 1 cup sugar | 1 cup lukewarm water |

1 cup sifted flour

Mix together, using, if you prefer, potato water for the cup of lukewarm water required. Several hours later, add:

| | |
|---|---|
| 1 cup sugar | 3 eggs |
| 1 cup lukewarm water | 1 teaspoon salt |
| ¾ cup melted butter or lard | 6 cups sifted flour |

Mix well together, cover, let rise until doubled in size. Then knead lightly, adding additional flour to make stiff paste if needed. Let rise from 1 to 2 hours or until well risen. Take up ⅓ of the paste and toss on floured board. Roll out to ¼-inch thickness, shape with floured cutter, and fry quickly in deep, hot fat. Repeat with balance of the paste—or, if you prefer, use the rest of the dough to make rolls or buns, since this is a basic recipe. The original *Fastnacht* was, of course, cut in diamond shape and slit across with a knife. Makes about 6 dozen doughnuts.

*Mrs. W. H. Anewalt*

## FASTNACHTKUCHE II
### (Raised Doughnuts)

| | |
|---|---|
| 3 potatoes, boiled and mashed | ½ teaspoon salt |
| 1 yeast cake, dissolved in | 1 cup sifted flour |
| ¼ cup lukewarm potato water | |

Mix together, then cover the bowl and let the paste rise for several hours in a warm place. Then add:

| 5 cups sifted flour | 2 cups scalded, lukewarm milk |

Mix well together, let rise, covered, until doubled in size. Then add:

| 4 beaten eggs | 1 cup sugar |
| ½ cup melted butter | ½ teaspoon mace |

Knead vigorously on a floured board until stiff enough to roll out. Add more flour if necessary to stiffen. Return to bowl, brush top and sides of dough with melted butter. Let rise until doubled in size. Roll out on floured board to ¼-inch thickness. Cut in shapes with doughnut cutter and let stand a little longer to rise again. Fry quickly in deep, hot fat, turning until both sides have browned. Cut out one lot while the other is frying in order to give doughnuts one more chance to rise a little before they go into the fat. Makes about 5 dozen.

*Mrs. C. C. Helffrich*

## RAISED DOUGHNUTS I

| 1 yeast cake | 3 tablespoons butter |
| 1 tablespoon sugar | ½ cup sugar |
| 1½ cups scalded milk, cooled to lukewarm | ½ teaspoon salt |
| | ⅓ teaspoon mace |
| 4½ cups sifted flour | 2 eggs |

Dissolve the yeast and 1 tablespoon sugar in the lukewarm milk. Add half the flour and beat well. Cover paste in a large bowl and set aside in a warm place for about 1 hour, or until bubbles burst on top. Add the creamed soft butter, sugar, salt, mace, the well-beaten eggs, and the balance of the flour to make a soft dough. Knead lightly on a floured board, roll into a ball, place in a well-greased bowl, turn over the dough so that it is greased, cover, and let rise again in warm place for 1½ hours. When the dough is light, turn out on the floured board, roll to ¼-inch thickness, cut with floured doughnut cutter. Cover the doughnuts on floured board, place in warm place, and let rise again until light (about 45 minutes). Drop doughnuts into deep, hot fat with the side uppermost that has rested on the board. (When a film begins to rise from the hot fat, the temperature is correct for frying.) Doughnuts made in this way do not absorb the fat, for they rise *before* and not *after* they are dropped into the fat. Makes about 4 dozen doughnuts.

*Mrs. Henry Lang*

## RAISED DOUGHNUTS II

| 2 cups mashed potatoes | 2 yeast cakes, dissolved in 1 cup lukewarm potato water |

Mix together in a large bowl and let rise, covered, in a warm place. After an hour or two add:

| | |
|---|---|
| 1 cup scalded milk, cooled to lukewarm | 2 eggs |
| | 1 cup butter |
| 1 cup lukewarm potato water | 6 cups flour (approximately) |
| ½ cup sugar | |

Mix and set aside, covered, to rise. When light and doubled in size, turn out on a floured board, roll thin, shape with floured doughnut cutter, spread out on a floured board, again covered, to rise for another ½ hour. Fry quickly in deep, hot fat. May be rolled in powdered sugar when cool. Makes about 6 dozen doughnuts.

*Mrs. Victor Boyer*

As you can see from the last four recipes, *Fastnachtkuche* and raised doughnuts are the same thing. The difference is mainly in the shape, for the pioneers made diamond-shaped "fried cakes" and slit them across. When and why and how they came to be round, with holes in the middle, I cannot tell. However, the ingredients are much the same, so long as they are made with yeast instead of baking powder, with or without the addition of mashed potatoes or potato water. But every year, without fail, when Shrove Tuesday arrives, the Pennsylvania Dutch bake their *Fastnachtkuche*. Indeed, Shrove Tuesday is called Fastnacht Day! The doughnuts are baked in the morning, and by dinner time plates of the confection are ready to be enjoyed. It would be a sad Pennsylvania Dutch household that had to go without *Fastnachts* on Shrove Tuesday. Usually the housewife has been at her doughnut frying since early morning and Dutchmen have started the day with *Fastnachts* for breakfast. Traditionally, the last of the dough, probably a cluster of "holes," is dropped together into the hot fat and the resultant fried cake is reserved for the last one down to breakfast. He finds it on his plate when he arrives and is called a "lazy *Fastnacht*" throughout Shrove Tuesday.

Everyone knows that this custom of using up the fats derives from long-ago days when they had to be used before the advent of Ash Wednesday. So England has its "Pancake Day" and the Pennsylvania Dutch eat *Fastnachtkuche*—just in time for Lent to begin. But there are those who believe that the custom is even earlier than that of Lent, and that these doughnuts are a survival of the burnt offerings that primitive ancestors living along the Rhine made to their goddess of spring, Oestara. Certainly her name is significant! When the Germanic tribes became Christian, they celebrated Easter rites for the spring festival and ate the little cakes themselves—on Shrove

Tuesday! When the Rhinelanders reached America they ate doughnuts on the day simply to make sure, they said, of living until the next Shrove Tuesday.

## QUICK BREADS, COFFEE CAKES

Here we cross the line between bread and cake, calling it pretty much whichever we like. We have been doing that with the recipes in the preceding chapter, talking about coffee cake and coffee bread, raised cakes and light cakes—yet all were made with yeast and based on bread dough. In this section we are exploring the breads and cakes made with baking powder. Whereas the setting and rising of bread dough is a long, careful process, and in the early days necessitated the setting aside of one whole day for baking, the quick breads can be turned out in a jiffy with the help of soda, baking powder, or cream of tartar. And they are pretty much foolproof.

The Pennsylvania Dutch love coffee—at any hour of the day or night. Dutch housewives had their "coffee breaks" in midmorning long before coffee and doughnuts became a national custom. They had been busy for hours anyhow by the time they paused to put the coffeepot on the stove and offer the neighbor who had stopped in for a minute a steaming cup and a generous slice of nut bread at the kitchen table. More than likely the neighbor had brought a covered dish containing a still warm coffee cake, topped with crumbs. The hostess lifted the fringed napkin, admired the golden brown goodness beneath, and then set it aside for the next meal, bringing out her own confection for her friend. If their menfolk had gone to the village or even "to town," it was a safe bet that at the same time they were dunking doughnuts or crullers into their coffee, lined up at a restaurant counter. Later in the day there might be *Kaffeeklatches*, which have been defined as "gossiping coffee parties." Whatever the social occasion, there was bound to be coffee and all sorts of "cakes" to accompany it.

### FRIED CAKES
#### (Crullers)

| | |
|---|---|
| 1 teaspoon soda, dissolved in | 4 cups flour (approximately) |
| 1 cup sour milk or cream | ½ teaspoon salt |
| 1 cup sugar | 2 eggs |

Place soda and sour milk in a large bowl, add sugar, sift in the flour, using just enough to stiffen the batter, add salt and beaten eggs. Mix into a stiff paste, roll out on a floured board, cut into shapes, and fry quickly in deep, hot fat. When cool roll in powdered sugar. Makes 2 dozen.

*Mrs. Susan Laudenslager*

## CRULLERS II

1 tablespoon soda
2 cups sour milk
6 cups sifted flour (approximately)

3 eggs
1 tablespoon butter
1½ cups sugar

Dissolve the soda in the sour milk, add flour gradually, using enough to make a stiff paste, and well-beaten eggs. Cream the sugar and butter and add. Beat well together, roll out on a floured board, cut into shapes, fry in deep, hot fat. Makes about 3 dozen.

*Mrs. Victor Boyer*

## CRULLERS III

1 egg and 1 egg yolk
1 cup sugar
1½ teaspoons soda, dissolved in
1 cup sour milk or cream

4 cups flour, approximately
1½ teaspoons salt
1½ teaspoons cream of tartar
¼ teaspoon nutmeg or cinnamon

Beat the eggs and the egg yolk, adding sugar gradually. Then add the sour milk in which the soda has been dissolved. Sift in the rest of the ingredients and mix well together. Add a little more sifted flour if needed. Roll out on a floured board to ¼-inch thickness, cut in shapes. Fry in deep, hot fat. Makes about 3 dozen.

*Mrs. Victor Boyer*

## BREAKFAST CAKES

2 cups flour
2 cups sugar
4 teaspoons baking powder

2 teaspoons butter
2 cups milk
1 tablespoon melted butter

Brown sugar and cinnamon

Sift the flour, sugar, and baking powder together, work the butter into the mixture, add milk, and beat well together. Grease 4 7-inch piepans and fill with mixture. Brush the tops with melted butter and sprinkle thickly with brown sugar and cinnamon. Bits of butter may be dotted across the tops. Makes 4 cakes.

*Eleanor-Rose Roth*

## MRS. GOTTSHALL'S STREUSEL-FILLED COFFEE CAKE

*Cake*

| | |
|---|---|
| 1½ cups sifted flour | ¼ cup shortening |
| 3 teaspoons baking powder | 1 egg |
| ½ teaspoon salt | ½ cup milk |
| ¾ cup sugar | 1 teaspoon vanilla |

*Streusel*

| | |
|---|---|
| ½ cup brown sugar, firmly packed | 2 teaspoons cinnamon |
| 2 tablespoons sifted flour | 2 tablespoons melted butter |

½ cup finely chopped nutmeats

Sift together the flour, baking powder, salt, and sugar. Cut in the shortening as when making pie. Add the well-beaten egg, milk, and vanilla. Divide the batter and put half of it into an 11-inch pan, spreading well over the bottom of the (greased and floured) pan. Mix the Streusel until it is stiff and breaks into crumbs. Sprinkle thickly over the cake, add another layer of the batter, top with balance of the streusel. Bake in 375° oven for about ½ hour. Makes 1 large cake.

*Mrs. Donald L. Helfferich*


## DER BENNER BREAKFAST CAKE

| | |
|---|---|
| 1 cup granulated sugar | 2 cups flour, sifted with |
| 2 tablespoons lard or shortening | 1 teaspoon soda |
| ½ teaspoon salt | Brown sugar |
| 1 cup milk | Cinnamon |

Mix together all ingredients except last two. Spread batter in a greased, floured pan, mix brown sugar and cinnamon, and sprinkle over the top. Bake in 350° oven for 35-40 minutes. Makes 1 cake.

*Jeanette Heimbach*


## "DUTCH" CAKE

| | |
|---|---|
| 1 cup granulated sugar | 1 cup butter and lard, mixed |
| 2 teaspoons baking powder | 1 cup milk |
| 4 cups flour | 1 egg |

*Topping:*   2 tablespoons melted butter
¼ cup brown sugar
1 tablespoon cinnamon

Mix together the dry ingredients and sift. Mix with the shortening, add milk and beaten egg, blend. Spread into 2 greased, floured pans, indent the surface at intervals with the finger, drop melted butter, brown sugar, and cinnamon into the holes. Bake in 350° oven until browned. To be served with coffee on New Year's Eve, at intermission in Watch Night Services, and at "Putzings."

*From* The Pennsylvania German, *1907*

## BROWN SUGAR CRUMB CAKE

2 cups flour
2 teaspoons baking powder
½ teaspoon salt
2 cups brown sugar, loosely packed

6 tablespoons shortening
1 egg, beaten
½ cup milk
¾ teaspoon vanilla

Sift flour, baking powder, salt. Add brown sugar, work in shortening. Reserve 1 cup of mixture for crumbs. To the rest, add egg, milk and vanilla. Place in loaf pan, sprinkle with crumbs, bake in 350° oven for 45 minutes.

*Mrs. R. M. Thomas*

## LANCASTER COUNTY CRUMB CAKE

1½ cups sugar
3½ cups flour
2 teaspoons baking powder

½ cup shortening
2 eggs
Milk

Cinnamon

Mix sifted sugar, flour, and baking powder with shortening. Break eggs into a cup and beat. Fill up cup with milk. Remove half the dry mixture and set aside for crumbs. Stir the cup of egg and milk into the other half of the mixture. Grease and flour an 8-inch cake tin and spread with batter. Sprinkle with reserved half of crumbs, then with cinnamon. Bake in 350° oven for about ½ hour. Makes 1 cake.

*Mrs. Henry A. Reninger*

## BLITZKUCHEN
### (Lightning Cake)

4 tablespoons butter
1 cup powdered sugar
2 eggs
1¼ cups flour
1½ teaspoons baking powder

¼ teaspoon salt
½ cup milk
1 teaspoon vanilla
Cinnamon and sugar
Chopped walnuts

Cream butter and sugar, add well-beaten egg yolks. Sift flour, resift with baking powder and salt, gradually beat into the batter, alternating with milk. Add vanilla. Whip egg whites and fold in. Place in greased and floured 9 x 12 inch pan and sprinkle top thickly with sugar, cinnamon, and nuts. Bake slowly in 325° oven for about 40 minutes. Cut in squares.

*Mrs. Victor Boyer*

## JOURNEY CAKE
### (Johnny Cake)

| | |
|---|---|
| 2 cups Indian meal | 1 cup wheat flour |
| ¼ cup boiling water | 2 teaspoons baking powder |
| 2 cups scalded milk | 1 teaspoon salt |

3 eggs

Sift meal into bowl, scald with a little boiling water, cool. Cool milk to lukewarm and add. Sift flour, baking powder, and salt into bowl, mix, add well-beaten eggs and a little sugar, if you prefer. Mix and bake on hot griddle.

*From* The Pennsylvania German, *1907*

## CORN BREAD

| | |
|---|---|
| 1 cup sifted flour | 1 scant teaspoon salt |
| ½ teaspoon soda | ⅔ cup cornmeal |
| 2 scant teaspoons baking powder | 3 eggs |
| 1 tablespoon sugar | 1 cup sour milk or buttermilk |

3 tablespoons bacon fat

Sift the flour twice, then sift again with soda, baking powder, sugar, and salt. Sift in the cornmeal. Beat the eggs, combine with sour milk and melted bacon fat. Stir the mixture into the dry ingredients quickly, pour into greased breadpan. Bake at 425° for 30 minutes. Makes 1 loaf.

*Mary Faas*

## BROWN BREAD

| | |
|---|---|
| 1 teaspoon soda | 1 cup graham flour |
| 1 cup buttermilk | 1 cup cornmeal |
| ½ cup molasses | ½ teaspoon salt |

½ cup raisins

Mix soda with buttermilk, add molasses. Sift the flour, cornmeal, and salt. Add liquid ingredients to the dry mixture in the bowl. Mix well together, then add raisins. Grease a tin can that has a cover, fill it two-thirds with the batter, cover, steam in hot water for 2 hours. Remove, bake in 400° oven for 10 or 15 minutes. Makes 1 loaf.

*Mary Faas*

## MOLASSES BREAKFAST CAKE

1 cup sour milk
1 teaspoon soda
½ cup molasses

1 cup light brown sugar
2 cups flour
1 heaping tablespoon shortening

Place sour milk in bowl, add soda. Stir and add molasses and brown sugar. Sift in the flour, add melted shortening. Mix well. Bake in a greased pan at 325° for 25-30 minutes.

*Mrs. Allen Wenner*

## SHOOFLY PIE

Shoofly Pie is a molasses breakfast cake enclosed in a pie shell. It is intended to accompany the morning coffee. There are all sorts of explanations for its name; all more or less plausible—that it derives from descriptive French or German words, or that it is so temptingly sweet that it will draw ... well, flies! But no matter, because there's another discussion about Shoofly Pies to settle: whether to make them with "wet" or "dry" bottoms. That's entirely a matter of personal preference. Offered below are recipes, one of each kind.

## SHOOFLY PIE I (LANCASTER COUNTY)

*Filling*

1½ cups boiling water
1 teaspoon baking soda
1 cup molasses

*Crumbs*

4 cups sifted flour
2 cups brown sugar
1 cup shortening
¼ teaspoon salt

Use any pastry recipe you prefer and roll out 2 crusts, placing one in each of 2 pie tins. Pour boiling water over soda in a bowl and stir in molasses. Pour filling into pie shells, half filling. Mix ingredients for crumbs and sprinkle thickly on top of the pies. Bake in 350° oven for 30-40 minutes until nicely browned. Makes 2 8-inch pies.

*Mrs. D. L. Helfferich*

## SHOOFLY PIE II (LEHIGH COUNTY)

*Filling*
1 cup molasses
1 heaping teaspoon soda
1 cup boiling water
⅔ of crumb mixture

*Crumbs*
3 heaping cups sifted flour
1 cup sugar
½ cup butter
Pinch of salt

Line 2 pie plates with rich pastry. Dissolve soda in molasses, stir until it foams, add boiling water. Mix crumbs. Add ⅔ of crumb mixture to filling mixture, blend, and spread on bottom of pies. Scatter balance of crumbs on top. Bake in 375° oven for about ½ hour, until crumbs and crust are golden. Makes 2 8-inch pies.

*Mrs. W. H. Anewalt*

## SOFT GINGERBREAD

½ cup soft butter
1 cup white or brown sugar
2 eggs
2 cups sifted flour
1 teaspoon soda

½ teaspoon salt
1 teaspoon cinnamon
1 teaspoon cloves
1 teaspoon ginger
½ cup molasses

½ cup boiling water

Cream shortening and sugar and beat in eggs separately. Sift the flour twice, then resift with soda, salt, cinnamon, cloves, and ginger. Combine the boiling water and molasses and add to the mixture alternately with the sifted dry ingredients. Beat well all the time. Pour batter into greased loaf pan, bake in 350° oven for 40 minutes. Makes 1 loaf.

*From* The Pennsylvania German, *1907*

## NUT BREAD I

3 cups graham flour
1 cup wheat flour
4 teaspoons baking powder
¼ teaspoon salt

1 cup sugar
1 egg
1 tablespoon table syrup
1½ cups milk

1 cup chopped walnuts

Sift the flour several times, add baking powder and salt, sift again. Mix sugar and beaten egg with the dry ingredients. Stir in syrup and milk. Mix well together. Dredge the walnuts in a little flour, add last. Grease two 3½ x 7½ inch loaf pans, pour in mixture, let it stand a few minutes to rise. Bake in 350° oven for 45-50 minutes. Makes 2 loaves.

*Mrs. C. C. Helffrich*

## NUT BREAD II

4 cups sifted flour
4 teaspoons baking powder
½ teaspoon salt
1 cup soft butter

2 cups granulated sugar
2 eggs, well beaten
2 cups milk
1 cup chopped nutmeats

Sift together the flour, baking powder, and salt in a large bowl. Cream the butter and sugar, add the beaten eggs, stir together until mixture is light. Add mixture to the dry ingredients alternately with the milk. Fold in the nuts which have been lightly dredged in flour. Pour batter into 2 greased breadpans and bake in 350°-375° oven for 50 minutes to 1 hour. Makes 2 loaves.

*Helen B. Bailey*

## NUT BREAD III

4 cups flour
4 rounded teaspoons baking powder
1 egg
1 cup sugar

2 cups milk
¼ teaspoon salt
1 cup chopped walnuts
¾ cup raisins

Sift the flour with the baking powder several times. Beat the egg, add the sugar, milk, and salt. Add 2 cups of the sifted flour. Mix the rest of the flour with the nuts and raisins. Add to the first mixture. Pour batter into 2 well-greased loaf pans, 3½ x 7½ inches. Let rise for ½ hour, to make a lighter cake. Bake in 350° oven for 50-60 minutes. Makes 2.

*Mrs. Victor Boyer*

## DATE AND NUT BREAD

1 cup chopped dates
1 teaspoon soda
1 cup boiling water
2 cups sifted flour
½ teaspoon salt

1 cup chopped walnuts
1 cup brown sugar
1 tablespoon butter
1 beaten egg
1 teaspoon vanilla

Pit and chop the dates, dissolve the soda in the boiling water, and mix with the dates. Set aside to cool. Sift the flour with the salt. Mix ⅓ of the flour with the walnuts and reserve. Cream the sugar and butter, add the beaten egg. Add date mixture and flour alternately. Add floured nuts and vanilla. Bake in 350° oven for 1 hour. Makes 1 large loaf.

*Mary Huyett*

## BISCUIT I

2 cups sifted flour                     ½ teaspoon salt
3 teaspoons baking powder               2 tablespoons shortening
                     ¾ cups milk, scant

Sift together the flour, baking powder, and salt—3 or 4 times. Work in shortening
with the fingertips. Add milk gradually, mixing to a soft paste. Roll out with a light
touch on a floured board to ¾ inch thickness. Cut in small rounds (about the size
of a half dollar) with floured biscuit cutter. Place on greased pan rather close
together. Bake in 450° oven for about 12 minutes. Makes 25 small biscuits.

*Mrs. Edward S. Shepherd*

## BISCUIT II

3 cups sifted flour                     2 tablespoons soft butter
3 tablespoons baking powder             ½ teaspoon soda
½ teaspoon salt                         1 scant cup sour milk

Sift flour, baking powder, and salt together 3 or 4 times. Add butter by softening it
and cutting it through the flour. When batter is well mixed, dissolve the soda in the
sour milk, blend quickly with the flour, stirring with a fork, taking care not to use
too much milk. Roll out lightly to ¾ inch thickness on floured board. Cut in rounds
and bake in 450° oven for 12-13 minutes. Makes 2 dozen large biscuits.

*Mrs. Victor Boyer*

## BISCUIT III

5 cups sifted flour (approximately)     1½ cups sugar
¾ teaspoon soda                         ¾ cup melted butter
¾ teaspoon cream of tartar              3 eggs

Sift 4 cups of the flour with the soda and cream of tartar. Cream the butter and
sugar and add the well-beaten egg yolks. Sift in the flour, beating the mixture
together to make a very stiff dough. If needed, add the fifth cup of flour. Fold in
the egg whites. Set aside to rise for about an hour, then roll out on a floured board
to ¾-inch thickness, cut with floured cutter, and bake in 450° oven for 12-15
minutes, or until golden brown. Makes about 4 dozen.

*Helen B. Bailey*

## SHORTCAKE I

2 cups sifted flour                     ½ teaspoon salt
2½ teaspoons baking powder              2 tablespoons soft butter
                     1 scant cup milk

Sift the flour, baking powder, and salt 3 or 4 times. Rub in the butter, add milk gradually, to make a smooth paste. Turn out on a floured board, roll into a large cake, about ¾-inch thick. Bake 20 minutes in a greased pan in 450° oven.

When baked, split the cake and butter generously while still hot. Spread with mashed strawberries, or whatever fruits you prefer, that have been sweetened with sugar. Top with second half of the cake, butter this, spread with more crushed berries. Save some whole berries for the top. Serve with a pitcher of thick, sweet cream. Strawberry shortcake is a Sunday night supper all by itself.

*Mrs. Edward S. Shepherd*

### SHORTCAKE II

| | |
|---|---|
| 3 cups sifted flour | 1 tablespoon melted butter |
| 3 teaspoons baking powder | 1 cup sugar |
| ¼ teaspoon salt | 1½ scant cups milk |

Sift the baking powder with the flour. Add salt, work in the butter, add sugar. Add milk gradually, beating to blend. Turn out on a floured board, roll to ¾-inch thickness. Bake on greased pan in 450° oven for about 20 minutes. Split, spread with butter and crushed peaches (or whatever berries or fruit you prefer). Place second half on top, butter, spread with more fruit. Serve hot. Makes 4 to 6 portions.

*Mrs. Victor Boyer*

# MUFFINS, GRIDDLE CAKES, AND WAFFLES

There was no mistake about breaking one's fast in the early days in Pennsylvania. Breakfast was truly an eye-opener with sleep-sharpened appetites more than willing to be confronted with ham and eggs, buckwheat cakes and sausage, fried mush dripping with maple syrup, country-fried potatoes, gingerbread hot from the oven, the ubiquitous shoofly pie (and most likely two or three other kinds of pie), doughnuts or crullers, of course, and, just to round things off, some hot biscuit, sticky buns, or muffins or waffles, not to mention the fresh-churned butter and array of jams and jellies that accompanied them. It is a wonder that anyone ever got up from those old-time breakfast tables at all. But people got up early those mornings; indeed they couldn't be kept in bed when the tempting odors swirled upward from the kitchen. And no one could deny that people in those days got a good start for the day. Once they had managed to push themselves away from the table, they were fortified to endure any weather and accomplish any task. No Pennsylvania Dutchman would have dreamed of going without his breakfast—it was the best meal of the day.

Here are some recipes for muffins, griddle cakes, waffles, and the like, just to prove that Pennsylvania Dutch breakfasts are an incentive to early rising!

## GRAHAM MUFFINS

| | |
|---|---|
| 2 cups graham flour | ½ teaspoon salt |
| ½ cup sugar | 1 egg |
| 2 teaspoons baking powder | 1 cup milk |

Sift the dry ingredients, mix with the egg and the milk, beat the batter well until blended, and bake in greased muffin pans at 375° for 25 minutes. Makes 12.

## CORN MEAL MUFFINS

| | |
|---|---|
| ¾ cup cornmeal | ½ teaspoon salt |
| 1 cup sifted flour | 1 egg |
| 2½ teaspoons baking powder | ¾ cup milk |
| 1 tablespoon sugar | 1 tablespoon melted butter |

Sift the dry ingredients together. Mix egg, milk, and melted butter in a bowl, sift in the dry mixture. Bake in greased muffin pans in 350° oven for 20-25 minutes. Makes 10.

## BRAN MUFFINS

| | |
|---|---|
| 2 cups bran | 1½ cups flour |
| ½ cup brown sugar | 1 teaspoon salt |
| 1 scant teaspoon soda | 2 cups buttermilk |

Place the bran in a mixing bowl and sift the other dry ingredients together. Mix with the bran. Add buttermilk and stir. Bake in greased muffin pans at 350°-375° for about ½ hour. Makes 20.

## FEATHER MUFFINS

| | |
|---|---|
| ¼ cup sugar | 2 cups sifted flour |
| ¼ cup butter | 3 teaspoons baking powder |
| 1 egg | ½ teaspoon salt |
| ¾ cup milk | |

Cream the sugar and butter. Add the beaten egg and mix. Sift the flour several times, then sift into the bowl with the salt and baking powder, alternating with the milk. Mix quickly, then bake in greased muffin pans in 400° oven for 20 minutes. Makes 12.

## RAISED MUFFINS

1 cup milk, scalded
1 tablespoon butter
1 tablespoon shortening
1 tablespoon sugar

1½ teaspoons salt
1 yeast cake
2 eggs
3 cups flour

Pour scalded milk in mixing bowl, add butter, shortening, sugar, and salt. Cool. When lukewarm add yeast. Mix and add beaten eggs. Sift in flour gradually, blending well until soft paste is formed. Grease muffin pans, half fill with paste, let rise at 80°-85° for about an hour, or until doubled in size. Bake at 375° for 25 minutes. Makes 12.

## HUCKLEBERRY MUFFINS

⅓ cup sugar
¼ cup butter
1 egg
3 cups flour (scant)

4 teaspoons baking powder
½ teaspoon salt
1 cup milk
Huckleberries

Cream the sugar and butter, add the well-beaten egg. Sift the flour twice and reserve a little to dredge the huckleberries. Sift the rest with the baking powder and salt. Add to mixture, alternating with the milk. Fold in the floured berries. Bake in greased muffin pans in 375°-400° oven for 20 minutes. Makes 18.

## RUSKS

1 cup milk, scalded
¾ yeast cake, dissolved in
¼ cup warm water
½ cup shortening

3½ cups flour (approximately)
¾ teaspoon salt
2 tablespoons sugar
1 egg

Cool the milk to lukewarm, add the yeast and water and the shortening. Sift the flour, salt, and sugar together, add half to the mixture, stir in the egg, add balance of the flour. Mix well, turn out on a floured board, and knead lightly. Set in warm place until doubled in bulk—about an hour—then roll out and shape with floured biscuit cutter. Place on greased cookie sheet, let rise for ½ hour, bake in 400° oven for 15-20 minutes. Makes 12.

## GRIDDLE MUFFINS

2 cups sifted flour  
4 teaspoons baking powder  
2½ teaspoons sugar  

½ teaspoon salt  
¼ cup butter  
2 eggs  

½ cup milk

Sift the flour twice, then sift with the baking powder, sugar, and salt. Work in the butter, add well-beaten eggs and milk. Mix well. Turn out on a floured board, roll lightly to ¾-inch thickness. Cut in rounds, brush with milk, sprinkle with a little sugar. Bake in 450° oven for 15 minutes, or on top of stove on greased griddle, baking slowly to avoid burning, turning once. (Currants may be added to the batter if preferred.) Makes 12.

## SOUR CREAM PANCAKES

1 cup sour cream  
1¼ cups sifted flour  
¼ teaspoon salt  

¾ teaspoon soda (level measure)  
1 scant tablespoon sugar  
1 egg

Place sour cream in mixing bowl, sift in the dry ingredients. Add well-beaten egg. Mix lightly. Bake on hot griddle, turning once. Makes 15.

## HUCKLEBERRY PANCAKES

2 cups sifted flour, approximately  
½ teaspoon salt  
2 cups milk, scant  

4 eggs  
1 pint huckleberries  
Sugar

Sift the flour and salt into the mixing bowl, adding milk gradually. Beat the egg yolks and add. Whip the egg whites and fold in. Add the berries, lightly floured. Bake on hot griddle, using plenty of butter. Brown carefully and turn. Sprinkle with sugar and serve at once. Makes 2 dozen.

## CRUMB GRIDDLE CAKES

½ cup bread crumbs  
2 cups sour milk  
2 eggs  

1 teaspoon soda, dissolved in  
a little water  
2 teaspoons melted butter  

½ cup cornmeal, approximately

At night soak the bread crumbs in part of the sour milk. In the morning add the well-beaten egg yolks, soda and water, butter, and the balance of the sour milk. Add enough cornmeal to make a smooth batter. Last stir in the beaten egg whites. Makes about 30 cakes.

*Mrs. Herman Kirkpatrick*

## CORNMEAL HOT CAKES

| | |
|---|---|
| 1 teaspoon soda | 1 teaspoon salt |
| 1 cup sour milk | 2 cups cornmeal |
| 1 tablespoon flour | 1 egg, beaten |

Dissolve the soda in the sour milk, add the flour, salt, and cornmeal. Add the egg last. Fry on hot griddle. Makes about 25.

*Mrs. Herman Kirkpatrick*

## FLANNEL CAKES I

| | |
|---|---|
| 1 cup milk, scalded | 1 yeast cake, dissolved in |
| 1 heaping tablespoon butter | lukewarm water |
| 1 cup cold milk | ½ teaspoon salt |
| 2 egg yolks | 4 cups flour |
| 2 egg whites | |

Scald the milk, melt the butter in it, add cold milk. Beat the egg yolks and add. Add yeast in lukewarm water; sift salt with flour and add enough to make a stiff batter. Let rise, covered, in a warm place overnight. In the morning add the beaten egg whites. If additional flour has to be used, add and set bowl aside to rise a second time. Fry on a hot griddle. Makes 35-40.

*Mrs. Herman Kirkpatrick*

## FLANNEL CAKES II

| | |
|---|---|
| 2 cups flour | 3 eggs |
| 2 teaspoons baking powder | 2 cups milk |
| ¼ teaspoon salt | ½ cup butter |

Sift together the dry ingredients in a large bowl. Add the beaten egg yolks, milk, and melted butter, mixing well. Add beaten egg whites last. Fold in. Fry on a hot griddle. Makes about 30.

*Mrs. Victor Boyer*

## BUCKWHEAT CAKES I

| | |
|---|---|
| ½ yeast cake | 2 tablespoons molasses |
| 2 cups lukewarm water | 2 cups buckwheat flour |
| 1 teaspoon salt | (approximately) |
| 1 scant teaspoon soda | |

Dissolve the yeast cake in a little of the lukewarm water, place in a bowl with the salt and molasses, adding the balance of the water and the sifted flour alternately until the batter is thin and smooth. Let rise covered in a warm place overnight. Next morning beat down the batter and add the soda, dissolved in a little water. Beat well. Bake on a hot griddle, turning once. Cakes should be very thin and evenly browned. Makes about 2 dozen.

*Frances C. Bachman*

## BUCKWHEAT CAKES II

1 teaspoon soda
2 cups buttermilk
1 tablespoon molasses

1 teaspoon salt
2 cups buckwheat flour
1 egg

Mix the soda with the buttermilk in a large bowl. Add the molasses. Sift in the salt and flour, add the well-beaten egg. Set aside for a few minutes, then stir well, adding more flour if needed. The batter should be thin enough to be poured from a pitcher. Bake an even brown on a hot griddle, turning once.

*Mary Faas*

## BUCKWHEAT CAKES III

1 yeast cake, dissolved in
    warm water
3 cups buckwheat flour
1 cup milk or water

1 scant teaspoon salt
2 tablespoons molasses
1 cup water
1 cup milk

Mix the yeast, flour, and milk in a large bowl, to make a stiff batter. Let stand, covered, in a warm place overnight. In the morning add the salt, molasses, and water, thinning the batter with the milk. Use just as much of the cup of milk as is needed to make the batter thin enough to pour from a pitcher. Bake on a hot griddle. Makes about 40.

*From* The Pennsylvania German, *1907*

## RAISED BUCKWHEAT CAKES

½ yeast cake
2 cups lukewarm water
¾ teaspoon salt

1½ cups buckwheat flour
½ cup cornmeal
½ teaspoon soda

Dissolve the yeast in a little of the lukewarm water, put in a bowl with the water and salt, sift in the flour and cornmeal, cover and let rise in a warm place overnight. In the morning, beat down, add the soda in a little warm water, mix well, and bake on a hot griddle, browning both sides of the cakes. Makes about 30.

*Mary Faas*

## DRECHTERKUCHE
### (Funnel Cakes)

4 cups milk
4 eggs
½ teaspoon soda, dissolved in
    a little lukewarm water

2 tablespoons sugar
4 cups sifted flour, approximately
¼ teaspoon salt
Powdered sugar

The directions that came with this recipe read: "Flour enough to form a batter that will run slowly through a funnel into hot lard. Form the cakes any size or shape desired." The only thing to do is to start with, say, 3 cups of the flour and keep on adding until the batter seems satisfactory. After that the frying becomes quite an art, because all sorts of shapes can be achieved by quick twists and turns of the funnel and covering and uncovering the opening. Serve at once, sprinkled with powdered sugar.

*Kaye Schneitman*

## WAFFLES I

1 teaspoon soda
2 cups sour milk
½ cup cream

¼ cup melted butter
2½-3 cups flour
3 eggs

Dissolve the soda in the sour milk. Place in bowl with cream, melted butter, sifted flour, and beaten egg yolks. Mix well, fold in the beaten egg whites, and bake. Makes 5 7-inch waffles.

*Mary A. Saeger*

## WAFFLES II

½ cup melted butter
5 eggs
2½ cups flour, approximately

2 teaspoons baking powder
¼ teaspoon salt
2 cups milk

Mix the butter with the beaten eggs, sift in the flour, baking powder, and salt, alternating with the milk. Beat until smooth. Makes 6 7-inch waffles.

*Mrs. Victor Boyer*

## CREAM WAFFLES

1 heaping teaspoon soda
2 cups sour milk
1 cup sour cream

1½ tablespoons melted butter
3-3½ cups flour
½ teaspoon salt

2 eggs

Dissolve the soda in the sour milk. Place in bowl with sour cream, melted butter, sifted flour, salt, and beaten egg yolks. Fold in the beaten egg whites last. Makes 7 7-inch waffles.

*Helen B. Bailey*

## SALLY HOFFMAN'S WAFFLES

2 beaten eggs
½ cup shortening
3 teaspoons baking powder

½ teaspoon salt
3 cups sifted flour
2 cups milk

Cream the eggs and shortening, add the baking powder and salt, sifted with the flour, alternating with the milk. Beat well together. Makes 6 or 7 7-inch waffles.

*Mrs. Susan Laudenslager*

## CORN FRITTERS

3 eggs
2 tablespoons flour
Salt and pepper

1 teaspoon baking powder
6 ears corn, grated
(or 1 can corn)

Beat the eggs lightly, add sifted flour, seasoning and baking powder, stir together, and add the grated corn. Season and drop from a spoon into deep fat. Fry quickly to a golden brown. Drain on brown paper and serve at once. Makes 20.

*Mrs. Victor Boyer*

## APPLE FRITTERS

1 heaping cup flour
1 heaping teaspoon baking powder
Pinch of salt
3 beaten eggs

1 cup milk
1 rounded cup chopped apples
3 tablespoons sugar
1 teaspoon cinnamon

Sift the flour, baking powder, and salt and add to the beaten eggs. Alternate with the milk and add apples. Drop from a spoon into deep, hot fat and fry a golden brown. Do not prick with a fork, for they will absorb fat. Drain on brown paper, dust with sugar and cinnamon. Makes about 30.

*Mrs. Philip B. Woodroofe*

# Meats

*Pennsylvania smokehouse*

YOUR Pennsylvania Dutchman is a meat-eater and he prefers it three times a day. He comes by his preference honestly, for his forebears were meat-eaters too. Of course, during their early days in Pennsylvania, Dutchmen had to make do with rabbit, wild fowl, and venison—at least until their herds were established. They hadn't many cows at first, and certainly it was quite a while before they could afford to butcher a steer. They had to turn their swine into the woods for foraging in the beginning, and when they were rounded up and butchered in the fall the pork was likely to be tough and stringy. But whatever the meat, wild or let-to-run-wild, the *Hausfrau* found a way to cook it. She knew how to neutralize a gamey flavor with onions and how to tenderize coarse meat with spiced vinegar. Her *Hassenpeffer* was so good that her method of cooking rabbit has continued down the generations. She had such a way with pork that it is still the favorite farm meat. And, since beef is a primary source of the farmer's income, it is sold in the market place rather than kept for family use.

Cattle have always received devoted care from the Pennsylvania Dutchman. In the early days while the family still lived in its primitive log house, the farmer built a great barn for his cattle. Not until his increasing herds were properly housed did he give thought to a substantial stone house for himself. For cattle represented sustenance and financial security. Moreover, the farmer *liked* his cattle. From the Rhineland he had brought many superstitions about domestic animals and he half believed them. . . .

Cattle could become homesick—therefore the calf must not be permitted to see where it was going when it was bought or sold. It would return to its

55

former home unless its eyes were covered. Moreover, the cow must not know that her calf was being taken away. It would be best to cover her eyes too.

Hay must be left outside the barn on Christmas Eve, so that the dews of the Holy Evening could fall upon it and bless it. Each farmer tried to be the first in the neighborhood to feed his stock on New Year's Eve. If he succeeded, he would be rewarded with sleek, healthy cattle. He knew that the animals in the stable talked aloud during the last hour on Christmas Eve. He knew it just as surely as he knew that the water in his well turned to wine for the same period. No Pennsylvania farmer ever reported finding his herds in animated conversation on Christmas Eve, nor did he succeed in drawing wine from his well. But he believed these things could happen, so he adhered to the tradition.

The first Friday of the new moon was set aside as butchering day. Then everyone on the farm was kept busy from dawn to dark in one way or another. The farm became a factory, and, as on a belt, roasts, steaks, chops, liverwurst, sausage, bologna, scrapple, head cheese, pickled pigs' feet, and the like rolled off the farm assembly line. It is much the same today, and, except for the actual slaughtering, the farm wife bears her full share of the work. She must cook the meat for the liverwurst and she must save the water in which it has cooked to make her scrapple. This is sometimes called *Pannhaas*, meaning pan rabbit—probably for the same reason that melted cheese becomes Welsh rabbit elsewhere, and just as logically!

Butchering on the farm by no means ends with meat and meat products. There are also the by-products: lard, tallow, hides, and soap. Homemade soap! What satisfaction the creation of these solid white squares must have given the early farm wife who kept the soap kettle always ready in the yard! Nowadays civilization spares her hands, her labors, and her time. But as she unwraps the commercial products from their fancy coverings she must miss, a little, the satisfaction of a job well done.

At any rate, the butchering proceeds through the making of brine and the preparations for smoking certain of the meats. Hams are smoked and sides of bacon, beef tongues, some sausage and bologna. After their immersion in the brine, the hams are hung from hooks in the smokehouse ceiling. A fire of green wood burns slowly in the fireplace and is replenished to keep the same even temperature. Time passes, and gradually the mingled odors of hickory smoke and meat-delights-to-come pervade the countryside. Since the smoking process goes on for days upon days and is repeated year after year, smokehouse walls have a way of acquiring a patent-leather patina—as anyone who has ever been inside a smokehouse remembers. The aroma lingers long in the solid walls, and even an abandoned smokehouse retains some of it. A smokehouse can be a nostalgic sort of place!

## SAUERBRATEN
### (Sour Roast)

| | |
|---|---|
| 4 pounds beef, chuck or roast | 2 tablespoons sugar |
| Salt and pepper | 10 whole cloves |
| 3 cups vinegar | 3 tablespoons flour |
| 3 cups water | 2 tablespoons lard |
| 4 sliced onions | ¼ teaspoon ginger |
| 1 bay leaf | ¼ teaspoon allspice |
| 1 teaspoon peppercorns | ½ cup raisins |

Rub the beef with salt and pepper; place in a large bowl. Heat the vinegar, water, onions, bay leaf, peppercorns, sugar, and cloves together, but do not boil. (If vinegar is too strong for your taste, substitute a dry cooking wine.) Pour the heated mixture over the beef to partially cover. Cool, then cover securely and place in refrigerator for several days, turning each day. Melt the lard in a heavy kettle over a hot fire. Dredge the beef with flour and sear quickly in the hot lard, turning to brown all sides. Pour over the beef the vinegar mixture in which it has been standing, diluting a little if the vinegar seems too sour. Reduce heat, cover the kettle, simmer for 2 or 3 hours. By that time the meat should be tender and the vinegar mixture pretty well cooked down. Remove the beef, keep warm. Strain the liquid and return to the kettle. Thicken with flour to make a smooth gravy. Add the ginger, allspice, and raisins. Serve with *Grumbera Knepp*. Serves 8.

*Mrs. Abram Samuels III*

## GRUMBERA KNEPP I

| | |
|---|---|
| 4 potatoes | 2 tablespoons milk |
| ½ cup bread crumbs | ½ teaspoon salt |
| 1 egg | 1 tablespoon flour |

Boil the potatoes and cool in their jackets. Peel and rice. Mix the bread crumbs with the egg and milk, add riced potatoes and salt. If batter is too stiff add another egg. Mold into balls the size of walnuts, flour them very lightly, drop gently into boiling salted water. Cover and boil 10 minutes. Serve at once.

*Mrs. Abram Samuels III*

## ROAST BEEF WITH ONION SAUCE

1 2-inch sirloin roast
Flour to dredge
Butter
4 onions

1 tablespoon flour
1 tablespoon butter
1 cup scalding milk
Salt and pepper

Dredge the meat in a very little flour, place butter in frying pan, and, when hot, sear the meat in it, turning to brown both sides. Preheat oven to 350°, place pan in oven, and roast the beef for 25 minutes; lower heat to finish roasting (250°). Just before roast is ready chop the onions and simmer in a little butter until transparent and golden brown. Blend the flour and butter to a smooth paste and stir in the hot milk over a low flame. When sauce is thick and smooth add 2 or 3 tablespoons of drippings from the roasting pan to flavor and color. Season, add onions, and serve.

*Mrs. Abram Samuels III*

## BROWN BEEF STEW I

4 or 5-pound beef rump
1 pound pork, cut in small pieces
Pepper and salt
Pinch of cloves
Pinch of nutmeg
1 tablespoon flour
4 sliced onions

1 sliced lemon
2 carrots, sliced
1 bay leaf
1 crust bread
2 cups vinegar or dry wine
2 cups water or beef stock
½ cup sour cream

With a sharp knife cut deep gashes in the roast and lard with slivered pieces of the pork, which have been rolled in pepper, salt, cloves, nutmeg, and flour. Line the bottom of a large kettle with the rest of the pork pieces, add lemon and onion slices, carrots, and bay leaf. Place the roast on top of these and the bread crust on top of the roast. Pour the vinegar and water over the meat. It should be half covered. Cover the kettle securely and simmer on top of the stove about 3 hours, or until meat is tender. Remove roast to a hot platter and place in warming oven. Rub the crust through a sieve, skim the fat from the liquid, pour through the sieve, and return this to the kettle. Thicken with a little flour and simmer for 10 minutes. Add the sour cream. Pour over the beef. Serves 8.

*Mrs. Herman Kilpatrick*

## BROWN BEEF STEW II

4 pounds boiling beef
Salt, pepper, and paprika
Flour to dredge
2 tablespoons butter

Water to cover
6 chopped onions
½ cup chopped carrots
2 stalks celery, chopped

1½ cups tomatoes

Rub the seasoning into the beef, dredge lightly with flour, sear in a hot frying pan with the butter. Place beef in kettle, add the water gradually, simmer. Brown the vegetables together in the pan in which the beef was browned, add to the meat in the kettle. Simmer for 2½ hours, adding more water if needed. Thicken the liquid with a little flour after the roast has been removed to a hot platter. Serve with *Grumbera Knepp,* pour the gravy over beef and dumplings. Serves 6.

*Mrs. Rose Preschman*

## GRUMBERA KNEPP II

| | |
|---|---|
| 4 or 5 grated raw potatoes | 1 tablespoon flour |
| 1½ cups bread crumbs | 2 teaspoons chopped parsley |
| 2 teaspoons grated onions | Salt |
| 2 eggs | Pepper |

Milk to moisten crumbs

Grate the potatoes, moisten the bread crumbs with a little milk or water, mix with the onions. Add beaten eggs, flour, parsley, salt, and papper. Form into walnut-sized balls with floured fingers. (Make sure that the mixture is not too moist, or it will require too much flour to bind and make heavy dumplings.) Dust very lightly with flour and drop into bubbling salted water—or drop them into the stew before the meat is removed and the gravy made. Cover kettle tightly and boil about 15 minutes. Serve with brown beef and gravy. Serves 6.

*Mrs. Arthur J. McShane*

## ROLLED POT ROAST

| | |
|---|---|
| 1 good-sized beefsteak, cut thin | 2 tablespoons lard |
| 8 slices bacon | 1½ cups chopped green peppers |
| 2 large onions, diced | ½ cup chopped celery |
| Salt and pepper | ½ cup diced carrots |
| Flour | 2 teaspoons chopped parsley |

Cut the steak in 5-inch squares. Cover each piece with bacon and onion. Sprinkle with salt and pepper. Roll and tie each piece. Dredge lightly in a little flour. Melt 2 tablespoons lard in a kettle and when it is hot sear the rolls of beef in it, turning and browning. Reduce heat, add 2 cups boiling water and the peppers, celery, carrots, and parsley. Simmer about 1½ hours, or until the meat is tender and the vegetables well cooked down. Remove the rolls, thicken the stock with a little flour to make gravy, and serve with *Grumbera Knepp.*

*Mabel E. Mulock*

## BOOVASHENKEL I
### (Boys' Legs)

| | |
|---|---|
| 3 pounds beef | 6 potatoes |
| Salt and pepper | 2 or 3 onions |
| 6 cups water | 1 tablespoon butter |
| 2 cups flour sifted with | 2 teaspoons chopped parsley |
| 2 teaspoons baking powder | 3 eggs |
| 1 tablespoon lard | 1 cup bread crumbs |
| 2 tablespoons butter | ½ cup milk |

Rub the beef with salt and pepper, place in large kettle, cover with water, simmer for about 2 hours on top of stove. Skim the fat from the surface and save for the gravy. Make a paste of the flour, baking powder, lard, and 2 tablespoons butter. Roll out thin on a floured board. Cut into 8-inch circles. Slice the potatoes and onions very thin, boil quickly in salted water until tender. Mix with 1 tablespoon butter, parsley, and beaten eggs. Spread this mixture on the dough circles, roll them up as for jelly roll, press the edges tightly together. Drop the rolls into the boiling stew with the beef. Cover kettle tightly and steam for about ½ hour, when the dumplings should be thoroughly cooked. Pour the fat saved from the stew into a frying pan, adding lard if needed. Brown the bread crumbs in this, add the milk, stir as the gravy thickens. Place beef and dumplings on hot platter, pour gravy over them. 6 portions.

*Dorothy Glessner*

## MEAT LOAF

| | |
|---|---|
| 1½ pounds ground beef | ½ cup minced onion |
| ½ pound ground pork | ½ cup catsup |
| 2 slices bread | 2 eggs |
| ¾ cup milk | Salt and pepper |
| Pinch of summer savory | |

Mix the beef and pork in a bowl. Soak the bread slices in the milk and shred. Mix with the meat, onions, and most of the catsup (reserving 2 tablespoons), break in the eggs and season. Mix well together, form into a loaf, and place in a greased baking dish. Spread the remaining catsup over the top to form a crust. If you like, 6 slices of bacon may be placed over the top. Bake in 350° oven for 1-1½ hours.

## CABBAGE ROLL-UPS

Use the ingredients for meat loaf. Drop 6 or 8 cabbage leaves in boiling, salted water and cook until tender. Remove, fill with meat loaf mixture, roll up, and fasten with toothpicks. Place in greased casserole, cover, and bake in 400° oven for 1-1½ hours.

## BEEF WITH ONIONS

2 pounds boiled beef
3 large onions
2 tablespoons lard
2 tablespoons flour

2 cups beef stock or bouillon
1 tablespoon vinegar
1 teaspoon salt
¼ teaspoon pepper

Peel and slice the onions, chop fine. Brown in the hot lard over quick heat. Add flour, blend smoothly, simmer gently, thinning with stock and vinegar. Season, bring to a boil. Add beef, simmer until beef is hot. Serves 4.

*Mrs. C. C. Helffrich*

## POOR MAN'S TURKEY

1 4-pound beef flank, with pocket
2 cups diced, raw potatoes
1 onion, chopped

2 teaspoons chopped parsley
3 eggs
Salt and pepper

Have your butcher cut a pocket in the beef. Mix potatoes, onions and parsley with beaten eggs. Season. (Add prepared poultry seasoning if you like.) Stuff the pocket with this dressing. Roast in 325° oven, basting frequently, just as though it were turkey. Should take about 1¾ hours. Serves 6.

*Mrs. Victor Boyer*

## POOR MAN'S DINNER II

3 heaping tablespoons flour
½ teaspoon salt
¼ teaspoon pepper

¼ teaspoon sweet marjoram or thyme
1 pound cubed beef
3 tablespoons shortening

Combine flour and seasonings and dredge beef with the mixture. Put shortening in frying pan and heat. Brown the beef cubes in this, then turn into a kettle.

2 large onions
2 stalks celery

4 carrots
2 cups beef stock or bouillon

Brown the onions in the fat the beef was browned in, transfer to kettle. Add chopped celery and carrots, stock, and a little water. Cover and when stew is boiling turn down heat and simmer for about ½ hour.

1 cup flour
2 teaspoons baking powder
½ teaspoon salt

1 tablespoon shortening
½ cup milk
½ teaspoon caraway seeds

1 teaspoon minced parsley

Sift together the flour, baking powder, and salt. Soften the shortening and cut into the dry mixture. When well blended add milk and stir together. Add caraway seed and parsley. Drop dumplings from teaspoon into the bubbling stew. Cover and don't peek. Simmer 15 minutes. Serves 4.

*Helen B. Bailey*

## POOR MAN'S DINNER III

Use same ingredients as in recipe above, except that there should be 1½ pounds of the cubed beef. Proceed until dumplings. Make those with:

| | |
|---|---|
| 3 potatoes | ¼ teaspoon salt |
| 1 slice bread, soaked in | 2 eggs |
| a little milk or water | 1 tablespoon flour, heaping |
| | 1 pinch anise seed |

Boil, peel, and rice the potatoes. Press moisture from the bread, add potatoes and beaten eggs, salt and sifted flour. More flour may be added if needed, but care should be taken not to add enough to make dumplings heavy. Shape with floured fingers into balls the size of walnuts. Drop into bubbling stew, cover tightly, and cook 10 minutes. Then, if dumplings have risen to the top of the stew, they are ready to serve. (The anise flavoring is optional but very little should be used; the flavor is penetrating.)

*Mrs. Rose Preschman*

## BEEF AND POTATO PIE

| | |
|---|---|
| 1 pound cubed beef | 3 tablespoons shortening |
| 1 teaspoon salt | 1 cup onions, sliced |
| ¼ teaspoon pepper | 2 cups boiling water |
| 3 tablespoons flour | 2 potatoes, diced |

Dredge the beef with mixed salt, pepper, and flour. Reserve left-over flour; heat the shortening in a pan, sauté the onions in it until tender and golden brown. Remove from pan. Sear the beef in same pan, turning until well browned. Add any seasoning or flavoring sauce you prefer. Turn the beef into a kettle, add onions and left-over flour, simmer 1 hour. Add raw, diced potatoes, cook 15 minutes longer, while you make the pie crust:

| | |
|---|---|
| 1 cup sifted flour | ⅓ cup shortening |
| ½ teaspoon salt | 1 egg |

Sift the flour and salt into a bowl, cut in the shortening with a spatula. Add slightly beaten egg. Blend lightly into dough, roll out on floured board. Make 2 crusts. Place first on bottom of deep baking dish, mix meat mixture with onions, and pour into the crust. Slash a small vent in the center of the second crust, cover pie with it, and seal and crimp the edges together. Bake ½ hour in 425° oven. Four portions.

*Mrs. Floyd Siegfried*

## NO-CRUST BEEF PIE

2 tablespoons chopped onions
2 tablespoons shortening
2 cups mashed potatoes
1 pound ground beef

¾ cup beef bouillon or gravy
Salt and pepper
2 eggs
1 tablespoon minced parsley

Sauté the onions in the shortening until tender and golden brown. Mix with the mashed potatoes, ground beef, and bouillon or gravy. (If gravy is used, thin it with a little milk.) Add salt and pepper and any other seasoning or flavoring sauce you prefer. Add beaten egg yolks and parsley and mix well. Fold in the stiffly beaten egg whites. Spoon the mixture into a greased baking dish and bake at 350° for about an hour. The "pie" will be light and puffy. Four portions.

*Helen B. Bailey*

## FLANK STEAK WITH DRESSING

1 flank steak
½ teaspoon sugar

½ lemon
Salt and pepper
1 onion, sliced

### *Stuffing*

¾-1 cup bread crumbs
Salt and pepper
¼ teaspoon beef seasoning
2 tablespoons minced onion

3 tablespoons melted butter
¼ cup milk
1 beaten egg
3 strips bacon

Score the steak on both sides, use the lemon half to rub in the sugar and a little lemon juice. Sprinkle with salt and pepper. Combine the crumbs, seasoning, minced onion, butter and milk. Add the beaten egg and, if you like, 1 teaspoon minced parsley. Mix well and spread thickly on the steak. Roll up the meat and tie with a cord. Fry the bacon, remove it, and brown the steak roll in the hot fat. Place roll in roasting pan, pour in 1 cup water, and spread the sliced onions over the top of the meat. Cover tightly and roast at 350° for 2 hours. Serves 4.

*Mrs. Abram Samuels III*

## SWISS STEAK

| | |
|---|---|
| 1 round steak, about 2 pounds | 3 tablespoons bacon fat |
| ½ teaspoon sugar | 2 onions, chopped |
| ½ lemon | 1 green pepper, chopped |
| ½ cup flour | 3 stalks celery, chopped |
| 1 teaspoon salt | 2 cups stewed tomatoes |
| ¼ teaspoon pepper | ½ cup catsup |

Rub both sides of the steak with sugar and lemon. This helps to break down the fibers. Mix the flour, salt, and pepper and pound into the meat with the side of a saucer. Heat bacon fat in a skillet, sear the steak in it on both sides, remove, and place in a baking pan or casserole. Sauté onion, pepper, and celery in the skillet. When they are partly cooked, add tomatoes and catsup. Cook sauce a little longer until blended, then pour over the steak, cover, bake 1½ hours in 275° oven. Serves 4-6.

*Mrs. W. H. Miller*

## BAKED SHORT RIBS

| | |
|---|---|
| 4 pounds short ribs of beef | 2 tablespoons brown sugar |
| 4 tablespoons flour | 2 tablespoons vinegar |
| 1 teaspoon salt | ½ teaspoon dry mustard |
| ½ teaspoon pepper | ½ cup chili sauce |
| 4 tablespoons bacon fat | 2 teaspoons Worcestershire sauce |
| 2 chopped onions | 1 cup beef bouillon |
| ½ cup chopped parsley | ½ cup water |
| Tiny onions | |
| Small carrots | |

Mix the flour, salt, and pepper and rub into the short ribs. Brown them in the bacon fat in a skillet, turning as they brown. Add chopped onions and parsley. When they have sautéed pour off all but a little of the fat remaining, add balance of ingredients, except onions and carrots. When the sauce has come to a boil, cover skillet and place in 350° oven. Bake for 1½ hours. Then add as many onions and carrots as you like and bake for another hour. Serves 4-6.

*Mrs. Karl L. Lubrecht*

## BOILED BEEF TONGUE

| | |
|---|---|
| 1 beef tongue | 3 stalks celery |
| Water to cover | 1 cup water |
| 2 cups salt | ½ cup vinegar |
| 1 small pod red pepper | ¼ cup sugar |
| 1 onion, sliced | ½ teaspoon cloves |

Wash the tongue, cover with cold water, add salt and red pepper, onion and celery. Boil slowly in the brine for 2½-3 hours, adding water as needed. When tongue is tender take it out, remove the skin and root, and place it in a saucepan with 1 cup of water, the vinegar, sugar, and cloves. Simmer until the liquid is evaporated. Serve hot with a sauce or cold, sliced.

*Mrs. Herman Kirkpatrick*

## BAKED TONGUE

1 boiled beef tongue
1 small jar currant jelly

Juice of 1 lemon
2 teaspoons grated orange rind
1 teaspoon grated lemon rind

Melt the jelly in a saucepan, add other ingredients, blend, and cook until mixture thickens. Coat a beef tongue with the syrup, place in 425° oven until tongue is glazed. Serve hot.

## BEEF LIVER AND ONIONS

1½ pounds beef liver
Flour
Salt and pepper

¼ cup bacon drippings
4 cups sliced onions
¼ cup bacon drippings

Dredge the liver with mixed flour, salt, and pepper. Heat ¼ cup bacon drippings, brown the liver in it quickly on both sides. Remove to hot platter and keep warm. Sauté the onions in second ¼ cup drippings until golden brown. Pile on top of the liver and serve. 6 portions.

## STUFFED BEEF HEART

1 beef heart
1 tablespoon butter
1 tablespoon flour
¾ cup milk
1 cup bread crumbs

1 chopped onion
1 teaspoon minced parsley
½ teaspoon salt
¼ teaspoon pepper
Juice of ½ lemon

Wash the heart and let it stand in ice water for ½ hour. Remove any tough sections, wipe dry. Blend soft butter, flour, and milk to make a smooth paste, add half the bread crumbs with the onion and parsley. Season, using a little beef seasoning or sage or thyme, as you prefer. Stuff the heart with this dressing and pin the opening together with toothpicks. Place heart in a kettle, cover with water, and boil briskly for 10 or 15 minutes. Turn down heat and simmer for 2 hours. Remove from kettle, roll in a mixture made of the remaining bread crumbs, salt, pepper, and lemon juice. Add a little water if needed to make a smooth coating. Bake in 350° oven about ¾ hour, basting occasionally with a little water or wine. (Wine-basting is not typically Pennsylvania Dutch, but in this case it's a good idea!)

*Elizabeth Sanders*

## GREAT-GREAT GRANDMOTHER WAGNER'S
## KIDNEY STEW

2 beef or veal kidneys
Cold water
1 small onion
¼ teaspoon salt
½ cup milk

½ cup cream
Butter, size of walnut
Salt and pepper
Flour
1 tablespoon minced parsley

Hard-boiled eggs

Cut kidneys into small pieces, removing fat and membrane. Soak in cold water for several hours, then put in colander and run cold water over them. Place kidneys in top of double boiler and just cover with cold water. Add the small whole onion and very little salt. Cover the pan and bring to a simmering boil. Simmer 4 hours, replacing water in bottom of boiler as needed. Remove the onion and put in milk, cream, butter, and salt and pepper. Thicken with a little flour to consistency of thick soup. Add parsley. Do not serve until next day, then reheat, pour into tureen, and sprinkle mashed hard-boiled eggs on top along with a little more parsley. "Known in the family as 'Grandmother's kidlies.'!"

*Elizabeth Nimmo*

## WIENER SCHNITZEL I

6 slices bacon
2 veal steaks
Flour, salt and pepper
Plenty of paprika

1 small onion
¾ cup chicken stock
1 tablespoon tomato paste
¼ cup sour cream

1 teaspoon minced parsley

Fry the bacon, remove from the pan. Mix flour, salt, and pepper, cut the veal into serving portions and roll in the seasoned flour. Sprinkle paprika into the bacon fat until it becomes pink, sauté the veal in the hot fat, turning once, until it becomes golden brown. Remove veal. Mince the onion, crumble 2 pieces of the bacon, and add them to the fat in the pan. Dredge the veal pieces very lightly with a little more flour and let stand while you add bouillon and tomato paste to the mixture in the pan. Blend and simmer a few minutes. Stir in the sour cream. Return veal to the pan, cover, and let simmer for about 20 minutes until veal is tender. Sprinkle with parsley and serve. About 6 servings.

*Marilyn Buckner*

## WIENER SCHNITZEL II

| | |
|---|---|
| 2 pounds veal steak | 1 cup bread crumbs |
| 2 eggs, beaten | ¼ cup bacon fat |
| ½ cup milk | ½ lemon |
| Salt and pepper | 2 teaspoons chopped parsley |

Cut the veal into serving-size pieces. Mix beaten egg with milk, salt, and pepper. Dip the pieces of veal in this, then in bread crumbs. Heat the bacon fat, place the veal in the pan, brown quickly, turn down the heat, and simmer, covered. After about 10 minutes uncover, turn the pieces, and repeat the process. Sprinkle with lemon juice and parsley and serve. 4-6 servings.

*Mrs. Abram Samuels III*

## VEAL POTPIE

| | |
|---|---|
| 1 pound boiled, cubed veal | 1 scant tablespoon shortening |
| 1 diced onion | 1 egg |
| 1 cup flour | 2 teaspoons chopped parsley |

Seasoning

Boil the veal for about an hour with the onion. Make a paste of flour, shortening, and egg, adding a very little water if needed. Season. Roll out on a floured board, making 2 crusts. Use the left-over dough to make small, square noodles. When the veal is cooked, pour off water, add:

1 cup left-over vegetables

Mix the veal, vegetables, noodles, and pour into a deep pie dish lined with crust. Add the parsley and whatever seasoning you prefer. This could be sweet marjoram, summer savory, or rosemary—a very little. Put on the top crust, seal, and crimp the crusts together. Bake in 375° oven for about 20 minutes until crust is browned. Serves 4.

*Mrs. Victor Boyer*

## PRESSED VEAL

| | |
|---|---|
| 1 veal knuckle | Pepper, salt, and paprika |
| 1 pound lean veal | 6 hard-boiled eggs |
| 1 onion (sliced) | 1 tablespoon chopped parsley |

¼ teaspoon summer savory

Have the butcher saw through the bone of the veal knuckle. Separate into pieces and place in a kettle with the lean veal, cut in pieces, and the onion. Cover with boiling water and simmer 2-2½ hours until veal is tender. Season. Cover the bottom of a mold with hard-boiled egg slices and chopped parsley, then add a layer of shredded veal. Alternate until mold is filled. Cover with a plate, place a heavy weight on top, and press. Chill several hours. Slice to serve.

*Mrs. Herman Kilpatrick*

## TZITTERLE
### (Souse)

| | |
|---|---|
| 1 veal shin | 1½ cups vinegar |
| 1 pound pork shoulder | Salt and pepper |

Cook veal and pork in a kettle in water to cover until the meat leaves the bone. Remove meat, cool, cut into small pieces. Return to the broth, which is pretty well cooked down by this time, add vinegar, salt, and pepper. Simmer together a few minutes. Pour into mold and let stand overnight in refrigerator. Next day it should be nicely jellied. Slice to serve.

*Mrs. Victor Boyer*

## VEAL WITH SOUR SAUCE

| | |
|---|---|
| 1 veal rump | 1 cup vinegar |
| Flour | 1 tablespoon sugar |
| Salt and pepper | 1 minced onion |
| Bacon fat | 1 cup hot water |

Dredge the veal with a little flour, sprinkle with salt and pepper, melt some bacon fat in a skillet, put the veal in it, sear quickly on both sides. Remove to kettle, add water to cover, and pot-roast for 2 hours. When the veal is tender and the water is cooked down, add the vinegar (or cooking wine), sugar, onion, and hot water. Cook 45 minutes longer at low heat. Remove veal to serving platter, pour the sauce over it, and serve. Serves 6-8.

*Mrs. Abram Samuels III*

## ROAST LAMB WITH MINT SAUCE

| | |
|---|---|
| 1 6-pound leg of lamb | 1 cup cold water |
| Flour | Butter |
| Fat | Salt and pepper |

Dredge the lamb with a little flour, place in pan with hot fat, and sear quickly. Roast it in a 350° oven, adding the cold water to the roasting pan and basting frequently with butter, as lamb needs fat. Roast 3 hours, season toward the end of the roasting, and serve accompanied by mint sauce:

½ cup chopped mint leaves          ¼ cup brown sugar
¼ cup vinegar                      ¼ cup water

Chop the mint and mix with the vinegar. Boil the sugar and water for a few minutes, to make a syrup. Add the mint and vinegar.

*Mrs. Edward S. Shepherd*


## CROWN ROAST OF LAMB

1 lamb crown                       ½ cup minced onion
3 cups day-old bread               ½ cup mushrooms
½ cup chicken stock                4 tablespoons butter
½ cup chopped celery and leaves    Salt and pepper
                1 pinch of summer savory

Have your butcher prepare the crown roast. Place upright in roasting pan. Soak the cubed bread in the chicken stock, mix with other ingredients. Fill the crown with the stuffing. Butter a slice of bread and place it face down on top of the stuffing. Roast 35-40 minutes for each pound of lamb in 325° oven. A half hour before roasting is finished remove the crust from the top of the stuffing and allow it to brown on top. (The ends of the lamb bones may be protected by wrapping in pieces of bacon. Remove bacon when ready to serve.) Serve with currant jelly.


## LAMB STEW

2 pounds lamb shoulder, cubed      1 pound mushrooms
¼ cup bacon fat                    1 cup sour cream
Sprigs of fresh dill               ½ teaspoon lemon juice
                Salt and pepper

Brown the lamb pieces in hot bacon fat, then place in kettle. Cover with water, add dill, simmer 1-1½ hour until meat is tender. Remove lamb and dill. Place lamb on platter in warming oven. Add mushrooms to bacon fat in the original pan and sauté. Add the sour cream and lemon juice, salt and pepper. Thicken with a little flour stirred to a paste in water. Cook together over low heat a few minutes until sauce is blended.

## HUGUENOT STEW

| | |
|---|---|
| 2 pounds lamb shoulder | 2 pounds tomatoes, or 1 large can |
| 2 pounds onions | Salt and pepper |
| 2 pounds sweet potatoes | 2 tablespoons flour |

2 teaspoons chopped parsley

Have the lamb cut into 2-inch squares. Place in kettle with water to cover and cook about 1 hour, or until lamb is tender. Quarter the onions and cut sweet potatoes into 2-inch sections. Add to stew and simmer 20 minutes. Add tomatoes and simmer 10 minutes. Add salt and pepper. Make a paste of the flour and a little cold water, mix with a cup of the stew, and add carefully to the stew in the kettle, stirring to avoid lumps. Simmer a few minutes longer, sprinkle with parsley, and serve.

(We have eaten this dish in my family for generations. My grandparents called it French Stew, which may interest those who are curious about the mixed strains that go into the making of a Pennsylvania Dutchman. We children called it pink soup when it came to the table the second day, minus most of the meat and thinned a little. Really, it tasted better the second day than the first! It makes a wonderful one-dish meal, accompanied by a bowl of *Schmierkase* and a loaf of crusty bread.)

## HOLLAND HOUSE HAM IN BLANKET

| | |
|---|---|
| 1 12-14-pound hickory-smoked ham | 2 cups sifted flour |

2 tablespoons water

If you use a real country ham that has been hung, you will need to scrub it thoroughly and rinse it well. Soak overnight in cold water to cover. Simmer in water to cover on top of the stove for about 4½ hours. The ham will be partially cooked. Drain, remove skin. Make a paste of the flour and water and roll it out on a floured board, very thin. Cover the ham with the blanket, wrapping it completely so that all the natural juices are retained. Add nothing else. Bake at 425° for 20 minutes, lower the heat to 350°, and bake for 1 hour. Take ham from the oven, peel off the blanket, and serve. If you have a ham that does not need boiling, proceed with the blanket in the same manner but bake at 350° for 1 hour, then lower the heat to 325° and bake about 3½ hours longer—or until tender when a sharp-tined fork is stuck into the ham.

*Gertrude Rickert Holland*

## BAKED HAM

| | |
|---|---|
| 1 smoked ham | 2 tablespoons flour |
| ½ cup brown sugar | 2 tablespoons vinegar |
| 1 teaspoon dry mustard | Whole cloves |

Scrub the ham, rinse well, and bake slowly in 325° oven. Allow ½ hour for each pound of ham. An hour before it is done, remove ham from the oven, drain, and remove skin. Mix the brown sugar, mustard, flour, and vinegar into a paste, spread it over the fat side of the ham. Score the ham in diamonds, dot with cloves, and return to the oven. Finish baking, increasing the heat to 400° for the last 15 minutes.

*Mrs. Thomas B. Keck*

## BOOVASHENKEL II

| | |
|---|---|
| 2 slices ham | 1½ cups mashed potatoes |
| 2 eggs | 1 egg, beaten |
| 1 scant cup flour | 2 onions, chopped |
| ½ teaspoon salt | 1 tablespoon minced parsley |

Salt and pepper

Make a soft noodle dough by beating the eggs, working in as much flour as they will take, adding salt. Roll out on a floured board, very thin, let stand to dry. Cut into large-sized circles. Mix the mashed potatoes, 1 beaten egg, onion, and parsley for filling. Season. Place a heaping tablespoonful on each round, fold over, wet the edges, and pinch together. Drop into boiling, salted water to cover and simmer gently, uncovered, for 12 minutes. Fry the ham and serve on a platter surrounded by the dumplings. Should be accompanied by dandelion salad.

*Mrs. Harry Brown, Quakertown*

## SCHNITZ UN KNEPP I
### (Apples and Dumplings)

| | |
|---|---|
| 2 cups dried, sweet apples | 3-4 pounds ham hock |

*Knepp*

| | |
|---|---|
| 1 egg | 2 cups flour |
| 2 tablespoons butter | 3 teaspoons baking powder |
| ¼ (scant) cup milk | ½ teaspoon salt |

Soak the *Schnitz* (dried apples) in water overnight. Next day scrub and dry the ham and simmer it in water for about 3 hours. Add the soaked *Schnitz* and the water in which they have been standing. Boil together for another hour while you make the *Knepp*.

Beat the egg, add the butter and milk. Sift the dry ingredients and add to the first mixture. Use just enough of the milk to make a fairly stiff batter. Drop by spoonfuls into the fast-boiling stew, cover the kettle tightly, and steam the *Knepp* for 12-15 minutes. Serve on a hot platter, placing the ham in the center, the *Schnitz* circling it and the *Knepp* arranged round the edge. Serves 6-8.

*Mrs. Harry Hess Reichard*

## SCHNITZ UN KNEPP II

1 ham butt, or 1½ pounds
   smoked sausage

2 cups dried sweet apples
½ cup brown sugar

*Knepp*

1 beaten egg
1 cup flour
2 teaspoons baking powder

¼ teaspoon salt
⅓ to ½ cup milk
2 tablespoons butter

Soak the *Schnitz* overnight in water. Simmer the ham for several hours. Add *Schnitz*. (If using smoked sausage, they may be merely cooked together.) Add brown sugar. Mix the beaten egg with the sifted flour, baking powder, and salt to make the *Knepp*. Add the butter and milk, mixing very lightly; drop mixture from a spoon into the bubbling stew. Cover tightly and boil for about 15 minutes. Serve in circles on a large platter with the meat in the center. Serves 6.

*Mrs. Ira F. Zartman*

## SCHNITZ UN KNEPP III

1 small piece smoked pork
2 cups dried, sweet apples

2 tablespoons sugar
1 teaspoon salt

*Knepp*

1 cup flour
1 level teaspoon baking powder

Pinch of salt
A little cold water

1 egg

Boil the pork until tender, add the apples and water in which they have soaked overnight. Simmer together until apples are soft, add sugar and salt. Make *Knepp* by sifting the flour, baking powder, and salt together, mixing with the beaten egg and just enough water to make a batter that can be stirred with a spoon. Drop the *Knepp* in small spoonfuls between the apples in the stew. Cover and let boil briskly for 10 minutes. Serves 4.

*Kaye Schneitman*

(This is heresy—but try dried apricots sometime instead of dried apples.)

## HAM BAKED IN MILK

1 slice ham
2 teaspoons horseradish

Bacon fat
1 cup milk

Trim the edges of the ham slice, rub both sides with the horseradish, and sear quickly in a little bacon fat. Cover and bake in 350° oven, basting with milk and adding more from time to time if needed. Bake 1 hour covered, then uncover and bake 10 minutes or until ham is tender.

*Mrs. W. H. Miller*

## ROAST PORK

| | |
|---|---|
| 5 pounds rib pork | 1 cup water |
| Salt and pepper | 2 stalks chopped celery |
| Pinch of ginger | 3 chopped onions |
| 1½ tablespoons flour | 8 medium potatoes |
| 2 tablespoons fat | 1 tablespoon brown sugar |

Rub salt, pepper, and ginger into the pork. Let stand in refrigerator for a few hours. Dredge with flour, place in roasting pan with the fat, place pan on top of the stove, and sear the pork quickly on all sides. Add water, celery, and onions. Roast in oven at 350° for about 3½ hours, basting frequently. Peel the potatoes and place around the roast. Sprinkle brown sugar on top of pork. Baste pork and potatoes frequently until potatoes begin to brown. Roast ½ hour longer. Strain off some of the fat into a skillet, add flour to thicken and cold water to make gravy. Serve with applesauce or fried apples.

*Mrs. Karl L. Lubrecht*

## ROAST YOUNG PIG

One doesn't hear much nowadays about roast young pig, but if anyone yearns to know how it was done long ago here is a blow-by-blow description from an old cookbook:

| | |
|---|---|
| 1 freshly killed month-old dressed pig | 1 big red apple |

### Stuffing

| | |
|---|---|
| 1 cup stale bread crumbs | 1 teaspoon salt |
| 1 heaping tablespoon chopped suet | ¼ teaspoon ground pepper |
| 1 tablespoon chopped parsley | 2 tablespoons chopped onion |
| 1 teaspoon sage | ¼ cup cold water |

Mix stuffing thoroughly, stuff the pig, sew up and truss. "Place a stone or corncob in his mouth, to keep it open." Rub well with melted butter—all over—dredge lightly with flour, sprinkle with salt and pepper. Roast in a moderate oven (350°), baste frequently with salted water, then baste with butter. In 2½ hours the pig should be roasted. If it is large, roast for another ½ hour. Brush with melted butter to make it glossy, remove the stone and replace with the apple, surround with a wreath of parsley, and serve with applesauce to which 1 tablespoon of horseradish has been added.

## STUFFED PIG'S MAW

1 pig's stomach                          Brown butter

### Stuffing

Raw, diced potatoes                      1 pound lean pork
1 minced onion                           1 pound smoked sausage
                    Salt and pepper

Wash the stomach and remove membranes. Stuff tightly with dressing and sew up.
Boil in water to cover until soft. Then brown in oven at 375° about 2½ hours, or
until done. Pour brown butter over top, slice, and serve.

*Mrs. Victor Boyer*

## PIG'S STOMACH WITH SAUSAGE

1 fresh pig's stomach                    Brown butter

### Stuffing

Raw, diced potatoes                      1 pound smoked sausage
1 onion, chopped                         Salt and freshly ground pepper

Clean the stomach thoroughly, removing membranes. Mix potatoes, onion, sausage,
and seasoning to make dressing. Use spareribs instead of sausage if you prefer. Stuff
the stomach as tightly as you can and sew up. Boil or bake in moderate oven for
3 hours. Brown uncovered in oven for last 10 minutes. Melt butter in hot, small pan
until it smokes and darkens. Pour over top of pig's stomach just as it is served. Slice.

*Mrs. John Baer Stoudt*

## ROAST SPARERIBS I

3 pounds spareribs                       2 cups water
                    Salt and pepper

### Dressing

2½ cups bread crumbs                     Salt and pepper
3 tablespoons butter                     Pinch of sage or thyme
2 eggs                                   1 tablespoon chopped parsley

Trim rough edges of the spareribs, crack across the middle, rub with salt, and
sprinkle with pepper. Mix ingredients for dressing. Fold over the spareribs and stuff
with the dressing, sew up tightly, place in roasting pan with 2 cups water, baste
often, turn once. Roast at 450° for about 1 hour, or until meat browns. Serves 6.

*Mrs. Herman Kilpatrick*

### ROAST SPARERIBS II

2 sections spareribs  
½ pound salt pork  
⅓ cup chopped onion  
½ cup chopped celery  

1 sliced apple  
¼ cup brown sugar  
1 cup bread crumbs  
2 tablespoons minced parsley  

Salt, pepper, and flour

Fry the salt pork (or use 8 slices bacon) until crisp. Remove from pan and put in onion, celery, and sauté until soft and golden brown. Remove, put apple slices in the pan, sprinkle with sugar, and sauté. Add bread crumbs, parsley, crumbled salt pork or bacon, onion, and celery. Season. Place one section spareribs in baking pan, spread with stuffing, place second section on top, sprinkle with salt, pepper, and flour. Bake at 350° for 1½ hours.

### BAKED PORK CHOPS

6 pork chops  
6 slices onion  

6 2-inch squares cheese  
Salt and pepper  

Fry the chops until brown on one side. Turn over and top with onion. Cover pan and place in 375° oven for ½ hour. Uncover, place cheese squares on top of onion, bake about 15 minutes longer, or until chops are tender.

*Mrs. W. H. Miller*

### STUFFED PORK CHOPS

6 rib chops  
1 cup bread crumbs  
¼ cup chopped onions  
1 tablespoon minced parsley  

¼ cup milk  
Pinch of summer savory  
¼ teaspoon salt  
⅛ teaspoon pepper  

With a sharp knife cut pockets in sides of chops. Mix ingredients for dressing, fill the pockets, and sew up. Place in hot skillet and sear on both sides. Add a little water, cover the pan, and place in oven. Bake at 350° for ¾-1 hour. Serves 6.

*Mrs. W. H. Miller*

### OVEN PORK CHOPS

6 lean pork chops  
½ cup catsup  
1 teaspoon salt  
1 teaspoon celery seed  

⅓ cup vinegar  
1 cup water  
¼ teaspoon pepper  
1 bay leaf

Sear the chops on both sides in hot fat. Combine other ingredients and pour over chops. Cover and bake in 325° oven for 1-1½ hours.

*Quakertown Grange*

## SAUERKRAUT WITH DUMPLINGS

3 pounds pork shoulder                    3 pounds sauerkraut
                            Pepper

*Dumplings*

2 beaten eggs                            ¼ cup milk, scant
½ cup sifted flour                        Salt

Boil the pork until tender, add sauerkraut, and pepper. Cook together uncovered for ½ hour, until flavors are blended. Mix the dumplings, using as little milk as possible, to keep batter stiff. Drop in spoonfuls on bubbling sauerkraut. Cover tightly, cook 10 minutes. These are not light dumplings, but the kind that blend with the sauerkraut, absorbing its flavor. Serve with mashed potatoes and a side dish of dried apples, stewed with sugar and lemon juice. Serves 6-8.

*Ida Altemus Anewalt*

## BAKED SAUERKRAUT

Pork                                    Fat
Salt and pepper                          Brown sugar
Flour                                   Sauerkraut
                        Mashed potatoes

Boil a piece of pork in water until tender. Remove from water, rub with salt, sprinkle with pepper, dredge with flour, place in a pan on top of the stove and sear quickly in a little fat. Place in a roasting pan, sprinkle with a little brown sugar, smother in sauerkraut, and bake for ½-¾ hour, or until sauerkraut is well cooked down. Remove from oven, place pork on a large platter, ring with sauerkraut, and, using a spoon or a pastry tube, make a circle of mashed potatoes all around the edge. Place platter in oven and brown the potatoes very slightly. Serve piping hot.

*Mrs. W. H. Anewalt*

## PANNHAAS
### (Scrapple)

1 calf's liver                            Cornmeal
½ kidney (optional)                       ½ teaspoon sage
Pork scraps                              Salt and pepper

The correct way to make scrapple is to boil a lot of pork scraps in the water in which liverwurst has been made. Since this can occur only at butchering time on a farm, the way to get around that is to boil the liver and kidney until tender, remove them from the water, and chop the liver. Shred pork into fine pieces and place in the water with the liver. (Skip the liver if you do not care for its decided flavor.) Simmer until scraps of meat cook to pieces. Then dribble the cornmeal into the mixture, stirring constantly. When you have the consistency of mush, stop! Add sage, salt, and pepper. Simmer 15 minutes longer, constantly stirring. Pour into pans about 3 inches deep. Cool, slice, and fry lightly.

*Mrs. Arthur J. McShane*

## PHILADELPHIA SCRAPPLE

2 pounds pork shoulder
1½ quarts water
2 cups cornmeal (approximately)
1 teaspoon summer savory

1 teaspoon salt
¼ teaspoon pepper
½ teaspoon thyme
Salt and pepper

Boil the pork in water with salt and pepper, until meat comes from the bone. Remove meat and strain liquid. There should be 4 cups. Shred the meat, return to kettle with liquid, add seasoning and cornmeal, stirring constantly as the cornmeal goes in to prevent sticking. Simmer about 15 minutes, or until mixture is the consistency of mush. Pour into pans, cool; slice and fry lightly.

*Mary Louise Lewis*

## HASSENPEFFER

2 rabbits, cut up
3 cups vinegar
3 cups water
1 large onion, sliced
¼ teaspoon red pepper

½ teaspoon ginger
1 teaspoon salt
¼ teaspoon cloves
2 slices lemon
Butter and/or fat, for frying

Flour

Skin and clean the rabbits. Cut in pieces, place in a large bowl, cover with vinegar and water. Let stand a day or two, adding sliced onion, red pepper, and spices. On the third day place the rabbit in a kettle, cover with fresh water, add the lemon slices. (Lemon keeps the flesh white.) Boil until the meat is tender (about 1 hour) and remove from the kettle. Dip the pieces of rabbit lightly in flour and fry in hot fat, browning quickly. Cover and steam gently until thoroughly cooked.

When you have done all this, you will have as good an idea as anyone why this dish is called *Hassenpeffer*. There's an old Pennsylvania Dutch saying that *Do is's wo d'r Haws im pef'r sits* (Here is where the rabbit sits in the pepper.)

# Poultry

*Pennsylvania farm*

It is understandable that a folk who believed their cattle could talk on Christmas Eve may have been reluctant to dine on roast beef next day. If their Quaker neighbors sighed for the roast beef of Merrie Olde England, the Pennsylvania Dutch were content to feast on wild turkey—and glad to get it. And as the years passed, and their own farms produced chickens and turkeys, they still preferred poultry for holiday meals. Their folklore attributed no wisdom or special "gifts" to fowls, so Pennsylvanians could go right ahead popping chickens into pots without a qualm. There were usually plenty of them on the farm, and as an immediate source of good food chickens met any emergency.

One of the old Pennsylvania Dutch songs dwelt hilariously upon the joys of farming:

*"Ich fang 'n neie fashun aw,"* it says—

A new fashion I'll begin,
The hay I'll make in winter;
When it's hot I'll stay out of the sun
And eat the cherry pies.

I'll get a white, smearkase cow,
A yard full of guinea-hen geese,
A mighty high red-beet tree,
And a patent-leather fence.

The chickens I'll keep in the kitchen—

—but this funny fellow knew
perfectly well that the only chickens his wife would permit in the kitchen

78

would be those that went into the pot! Chicken is always good eating, and with proper care even an old hen can be turned into a delicious potpie before you can say Jack Robinson in Pennsylvania Dutch.

Chicken and waffles, chicken and biscuit, fried chicken, chicken potpie . . . roast chicken, roast turkey with stuffing . . . how good they are in Pennsylvania! It may be true, as the old saying goes, that "Roast pigeons will not fly into your mouth," but roast turkey and dressing, Pennsylvania style, seem to do just that.

## FRIED CHICKEN I

| | |
|---|---|
| 2 spring chickens | ¼ cup flour |
| Salt | ½ teaspoon salt |
| 1 egg | 1 cup crumbs |
| ¼ cup cream | Fat and butter, mixed |
| | Parsley |

Split the chickens and rub with salt. Mix beaten egg and cream, dip the halves first in this and then in a mixture of flour, salt, and crumbs. Heat butter and fat in deep frying pan. When hot but not smoking, fry the chicken in it to a light, golden brown. Remove the chicken, pour off most of the fat, and return chicken to the pan. If necessary, change to a pan large enough to hold all 4 pieces at once. Cover tightly and steam, either over a low flame on top of the stove or in a 350° oven. Cook until tender, drain, and serve, garnished with parsley. Serves 4.

*Elizabeth Schramek*

## FRIED CHICKEN II

1 broiler, cut in pieces                Butter for frying

*Batter*

| | |
|---|---|
| 1 beaten egg | Pinch of salt |
| 1 cup cream | ¼ teaspoon baking powder |
| | Sifted flour |

Dip the chicken pieces in the batter and fry in butter in a deep frying pan. When golden brown (about 20 minutes), cover tightly and steam over low flame. Simmer until thoroughly cooked and tender. Thin the balance of the batter with a little milk if necessary, add some of the butter in which the chicken was fried, and blend for cream gravy. Serves 4.

*Elizabeth Sanders*

## BAKED CHICKEN

2 spring chickens
1 tablespoon lard
1 tablespoon butter
2 cups hot water

Salt and pepper
Chicken giblets
½ small onion
1 tablespoon flour

Split the chickens, wash and dry. Put the butter and lard in a baking pan, add hot water. Put in the chicken and bake in 400°-425° oven for about ½ hour, until lightly browned, turning and basting frequently. Season with salt and pepper. Cover and bake 10 or 15 minutes longer at 325°. Serve with gravy made by boiling the giblets with the onion in a little water until giblets are tender. Brown the flour in the baking pan, blending with the fat already in the pan. Smooth by adding water in which the giblets were boiled. Add chopped giblets and stir. Serves 4.

*Mrs. Herman Kirkpatrick*

## STEWED CHICKEN

1 stewing chicken
Water to cover
2 small onions

2 stalks celery
3 slices lemon
Salt and pepper

1½ tablespoons flour

Wash the chicken, cut up, and place in water in kettle with skin side up. Add onions, celery, and lemon and simmer until chicken is tender, probably 2½ hours. Season with salt and pepper. Thicken the broth with a little flour rubbed through a sieve. Serve with waffles or biscuit. If biscuit, place chicken in center of a hot platter, arrange split biscuit in a circle around it, and pour gravy over all.

*Ida Altemus Anewalt*

## CHICKEN POTPIE I

1 stewing chicken
2 small onions
1 teaspoon salt
¼ teaspoon pepper
Chicken giblets
4 tablespoons flour

4 tablespoons butter
2 cups chicken stock
¼ cup diced celery
2 tablespoons chopped parsley
1 onion, minced
Biscuit dough

Stew the cut-up chicken in water to cover, with 2 small onions, until chicken is tender (about 2½ hours). Season, remove from the broth, take all the meat from the bones. Cook the giblets in salted water until tender, drain and mince. Brown the flour in a frying pan with the butter, thin with a little of the broth. Add the celery, parsley, and seasoning. Add the minced onion, giblets, more chicken stock, and cook all together for a few minutes. Butter a baking dish, line with the chicken, pour the sauce over all, and drop teaspoonfuls of biscuit dough on top, not too close together, to make the crust.

### Biscuit dough

1½ cups flour, sifted with
1½ teaspoons baking powder

Pinch of salt
1 scant tablespoon butter

¼ cup milk, scant

Sift the flour, baking powder, and salt 3 times. Cut the butter into the flour, mix, stir in the milk. Roll out lightly on floured board, cut in shapes.

Bake the potpie in 450° oven for 15 minutes, or until biscuit crust has browned.

*Mrs. Thomas B. Keck*

## CHICKEN POTPIE II

2 young chickens, cut up
Hot water to cover
1 small onion

Butter
Salt and pepper
20 tiny new potatoes

6 newly laid eggs

### Biscuit

2 cups sifted flour
2 teaspoons baking powder

½ teaspoon salt
2 tablespoons lard

½ cup milk

Cut up the chicken, wash, and simmer in hot water to cover. Add water if needed, to be sure of enough broth. Simmer for about 1½ hours with a small onion. Season, remove from broth, take all meat from bones, reserve the broth. Roll biscuit dough lightly on a floured board. Line a deep casserole with the dough and cut some tiny biscuits from the rest of it, making sure to leave enough for the top crust. Fill the casserole with alternate layers of chicken, potatoes, and biscuit. At the top, just before the crust goes on, place the raw eggs, making sure not to break them. Fill the dish three-quarters full with broth, put on top crust, gashed to form a vent at the center. Bake about 20 minutes or until crust browns, pouring more broth through the vent when potpie is half baked. Thicken the balance of the broth with a litttle flour rubbed through a sieve. Serve this gravy with the potpie.

*Mrs. Herman Kirkpatrich*

## BERKS COUNTY CHICKEN POTPIE

### Noodles

1 heaping tablespoon butter
2 cups flour

½ teaspoon salt
2 beaten eggs

⅛ cup milk or water

Mix the butter, flour, and salt together. Add the well-beaten eggs, then milk. Mix lightly. Roll out as thin as possible on floured board. Let stand for ½ hour. Cut in 1½-inch squares.

| | |
|---|---|
| 2 medium-sized potatoes | Minced parsley |
| 2 medium-sized onions | 3 cups cooked chicken |
| Salt and pepper | 2 cups thick chicken stock |

Slice the potatoes ¼-inch thick. Line the bottom of the kettle with them. Add a layer of noodles, then one of onions, sprinkle with salt, pepper, and parsley, add a layer of chicken. Repeat until all of the chicken has been used. The top layer should be noodles with spaces between them. Pour 2 cups of boiling chicken stock over all. Cover tightly, do not uncover, and simmer for 20 minutes. Serves 4.

*Mary Huyett*

## CHICKEN WITH DUMPLINGS

| | |
|---|---|
| 1 stewing chicken | Water to cover |
| 2 small onions | Salt and pepper |
| | 1 tablespoon flour |

### Dumplings

| | |
|---|---|
| 1 egg | ⅔ cup flour |
| 3 tablespoons milk | ¼ teaspoon salt |
| | 1 teaspoon baking powder |

Wash the chicken, cut up, place skin side up in kettle with water enough to cover. Add onions and stew about 2½ hours, or until chicken is tender. Season with salt and pepper, thicken with flour pressed through a sieve. To make the dumplings, beat the egg until light, add milk, and mix. Sift the flour, salt, and baking powder. Mix with eggs and milk to form a heavy batter. Drop from a teaspoon into the rapidly boiling stew. Turn down the heat to simmer, cover tightly, and boil for 15 minutes. Serves 4.

*Ida Altemus Anewalt*

## CHICKEN AND CORN PIE

| | |
|---|---|
| 1 young chicken | 3 eggs |
| Water to cover | 2½ cups milk |
| 1 small onion | ½ cup cream |
| 4 cups fresh, green corn | Salt and pepper |
| | Butter |

### Pastry

| | |
|---|---|
| 1 cup flour | 1 egg yolk |
| ½ teaspoon salt | 5 tablespoons butter |
| | 2 tablespoons ice water |

Wash and cut up the chicken, stew in water to cover, with a small onion, for about 1½ hours. Season. Make pastry by sifting flour and salt into a bowl and working the butter into it with 2 knives. Beat egg and water into it lightly and mix. Chill. Roll out on a floured board to thickness of ⅛-inch. Line a deep pie dish with the crust. Take all chicken meat from the bones, grate the corn from the cobs (be sure the corn is very fresh), beat the eggs lightly, mix these with the milk and cream. Season and pour into the crust. Dot with butter. Gash a large cross in the top crust and place on the pie. Turn back the corners of the crust at the center of the pie and pour chicken broth through the opening, filling the dish three-quarters full. Bake in 375°-400° oven for about ½ hour, adding broth as pie bakes. Thicken the balance of the broth with a little flour pressed through a sieve for gravy. Serves 6.

*Mrs. Donald L. Helfferich*

(When the first edition of this book was published, it was the recipe for Chicken and Corn Pie that caused a lot of the fan mail. People were fairly ecstatic about it. Not only did they like the dish but there was a good measure of nostalgia for Mother's kitchen, too!)

## ROAST CHICKEN

| | |
|---|---|
| 1 roasting chicken | Seasoning |
| Melted butter | Stuffing |
| Salt | Chicken giblets |
| Flour | Small piece of onion |

Clean the chicken, singe it if necessary, then "plump" it by plunging quickly 3 times in boiling water, then 3 times in ice water. Dry, stuff, and truss, having rubbed the cavity with melted butter before stuffing. Rub the whole chicken with melted butter, sprinkle with salt, and dredge very lightly with flour. Place on rack in roasting pan, breast side down, and roast in 350° oven for about ½ hour. Turn chicken breast side up and roast 2½ hours longer, turning heat to 325° if chicken browns too fast. Test for tenderness by pushing a steel fork into thick part of drumstick. If it turns easily the chicken is done. Baste frequently while baking. If there are not enough drippings, add a little water while roasting. Cook the giblets with a small piece of onion in water until tender. Mince and save with the water in which they were boiled for gravy. Smooth a little flour and water into paste and brown in the roasting pan after the chicken is removed to a hot platter. Thin with broth, add the giblets, season, and serve with the chicken.

*Mrs. Henry Dinkelspiel*

## ROAST TURKEY

| | | |
|---|---|---|
| Turkey | Melted butter | Salt and pepper |
| Flour | Seasoning | Stuffing |
| Giblets | | ¼ onion |

Clean the turkey and rub the cavity with melted butter. Stuff loosely and sew up the opening. Tie the legs down firmly, skewer the wings close to the body. Put a little water in the bottom of a large roasting pan, place the turkey on a rack in the pan, having rubbed it all over with melted butter, sprinkle it with salt, and dust lightly with flour. Turn the turkey on its side. Cover and steam for 1½ hours at 350°. Uncover, turn bird on other side, baste and roast uncovered for 45 minutes. Turn with breastbone up, baste and roast until tender, turning down heat to 325° if browning too fast. A 10-pound turkey will take about 3½ hours by this process, a 15-pound bird about 4½ hours. Test for tenderness with steel fork stuck in thick part of drumstick. If it turns easily, the turkey is done. While it is roasting, boil the giblets in a little water with the piece of onion. Mince and save for gravy with broth. Slide the turkey onto an old platter and place in warming oven. Put the roasting pan on top of the stove over low heat. If there is too much liquid in the pan, boil some of it away. There should be about 5 tablespoons. Add 4-5 tablespoons flour and brown, scraping drippings into gravy from the sides and bottom of the pan. Add 2 cups cold water and smooth. Add giblets and enough of the broth to make a smooth gravy. Season and serve with the turkey and cranberry sauce.

*Mrs. Henry Dinkelspiel*

## ROAST DUCK

| Duck | Dressing | Flour |
| Salt | Apple | |

Wash and singe the duck. Sprinkle the cavity with salt and stuff. Rub skin lightly with salt, dredge with a little flour. Truss. Place in roasting pan, pricking the skin so that fat will drain off. Roast uncovered in 325° oven for 15 minutes, breast down. Turn on its side, prick, and baste. Place an apple in roasting pan to absorb fat. Roast, turning and basting, for 2-2½ hours for a 5-pound duck. For final browning, turn with breastbone up, increasing heat to 350°. The duck can be basted with drippings, stock, or orange juice. When roasted, throw away the apple, remove duck to hot platter, and place in warming oven. Make gravy by browning a little flour in the drippings and adding stock or cold water. If orange juice has not been used for basting, grate a little orange skin over the duck. Instead of the usual poultry stuffing, duck may be stuffed with apples, celery, or prunes. When making the gravy be sure to skim off excess fat. Serve with currant jelly.

*Mrs. Henry Dinkelspiel*

A favorite Pennsylvania Dutch stuffing for roast duck is made of sauerkraut with a little onion mixed in and brown sugar added. It is packed loosely into the bird.

## ROAST GOOSE

Goose

Salt

Celery stalks

Quartered onions

Flour

Salt and pepper

¼ teaspoon ginger

Dressing

1 cup diced apples

3 tablespoons currant jelly

or ¼ cup currants

An old cook book is explicit about roasting goose: "It should be not more than 8 months old, should be killed at least twenty-four hours before roasting, the neck should be cut close to the back and the breastbone should be beaten flat with a rolling-pin. . . ." After that the goose gives up (or perhaps the cook) and is duly cleaned, stuffed, and trussed. Stuff with the usual poultry stuffing, to which add 1 cupful of diced apples and either 3 tablespoons currant jelly or ¼ cup currants. One old recipe calls for a "handful" of mixed raisins, currants, and crumbs added to the dressing, along with 1 large potato, cooked and mashed, and 1 tablespoon butter. Stuff loosely. If the goose is very fat, be sure to sew the opening tightly, to keep the fat out of the stuffing. A crust of bread, put in last, helps too: it is thrown away later. If by any chance the goose is not fat, skewer some slices of bacon across the breast. Sprinkle with salt, dredge with flour, roast in an open pan in 325° oven about ½ hour to the pound. Place celery stalks and onion quarters in the pan. Baste every fifteen minutes, pricking to drain off the fat. An apple in the pan will absorb some of it. After the goose has roasted an hour season with salt, pepper, and ginger. When roasted, transfer to a warm platter, place in warming oven. Put the roasting pan on top of stove, drain off excess fat, add 2 or 3 tablespoons flour, brown, and scrape with drippings, add 2 cups water and smooth. Add more seasoning to the gravy if needed.

## ROAST SQUABS

2 pairs squabs

Cooked chestnuts

Cooked potatoes

2 tablespoons butter

*Sauce*

1 cup raisins

1 cup cooked chestnuts

2 cups sherry

1 tablespoon flour

1 tablespoon butter

2 tablespoons "fine" sugar

1 pinch mace

Prick, singe, and dress the squabs. Fill with chestnuts and potatoes in equal measure, mixed with the melted butter. Roast, after brushing with melted butter and dredging with flour, in 325° oven for about 45 minutes. Baste while cooking. Use bacon fat, if needed. Make sauce by cooking the raisins in a little water for a few minutes, until plump. Mix raisins, chestnuts, and sherry and let stand overnight. Blend flour, butter, and wine from the raisin mixture, add sugar and mace and simmer together. When syrupy add raisins and chestnuts. Simmer while squabs roast.

*From* The Pennsylvania German, *1908*

The note accompanying this recipe said that it was very old, even then. I found myself wondering whether it could be traced back to beechnut and passenger pigeon days. But the sherry didn't seem indigenous.

## POTATO STUFFING

8 potatoes
½ cup minced onions
½ cup chopped celery
2 tablespoons butter
1 beaten egg

¼ cup flour
1½ cups milk
1 teaspoon salt
Pepper
1 teaspoon chopped parsley

Poulty seasoning    Thyme    Marjoram

Boil and mash the potatoes. Simmer the onions and celery in the butter. Beat the egg lightly, blend with the flour, mix both with the potatoes. Add milk and the celery, onion, and butter mixture. Salt and pepper to taste; add parsley, a little poultry seasoning, and/or pinch of thyme and marjoram.

*Phyllis Wunder Sieger*

## BREAD FILLING

1½ loaves bread, diced
½ cup cold water
1 teaspoon salt
½ teaspoon black pepper
¼ teaspoon poultry seasoning

1 teaspoon grated onion
1 teaspoon minced parsley
2 tablespoons melted butter
1 beaten egg
¼ cup milk

Mix, adding the fowl's cooked, chopped giblets if desired. Rub the cavity with salt and stuff the bird lightly.

*Mrs. Abram Samuels III*

## POULTRY STUFFING

Giblets, cooked and minced
1 minced onion
1 cup bread crumbs
2 stalks diced celery
1 diced apple

¼ cup raisins
1 teaspoon salt
¼ teaspoon pepper
½ teaspoon poultry seasoning
2 tablespoons butter

Mix ingredients lightly and stuff the bird lightly. Add currants and nuts if desired.

*Mrs. Abram Samuels III*

## CHESTNUT STUFFING

| | |
|---|---|
| 3 cups Italian chestnuts | 3 cups stale bread crumbs |
| 3 cups diced celery | ⅓ cup cream, scant |
| 2 tablespoons butter | ¼ teaspoon mace |

1 teaspoon salt

Boil the chestnuts, peel, and blanch. Break into small pieces. Brown the celery in butter, add chestnuts and crumbs, and mix. Moisten with the cream, sprinkle with salt and mace, stuff the bird loosely.

*Mrs. A. A. Fenstermacher*

## OYSTER FILLING

| | |
|---|---|
| 1 loaf stale bread, crumbled | ¼ teaspoon pepper |
| Liquor from 1 quart oysters | 1 egg |
| 1 cup melted butter | ¼ cup milk |
| 1 teaspoon salt | 1 quart oysters |

Pour the oyster liquor over the bread to moisten—it should have been heated and skimmed—add butter, seasoning, and beaten egg. Mix together, and if filling is too dry add milk. Add oysters last, being careful not to break them. Stuff the bird loosely, with care, handling stuffing lightly.

*Mrs. Herman Kirkpatrick*

## MUSHROOM FILLING

| | |
|---|---|
| 1 loaf stale bread, diced | ½ teaspoon pepper |
| ½ cup milk | 3 cups mushrooms |
| 1 cup melted butter | 3 tablespoons butter or fat |
| 1 teaspoon salt | ½ teaspoon nutmeg |

Mix the diced bread with melted butter and milk. Add salt and pepper. Sauté the mushrooms in butter or fat, sprinkle with nutmeg, mix well with the filling. Stuff loosely.

*Mrs. Henry Heffelfinger*

## APPLE STUFFING

| | |
|---|---|
| 3 cups diced bread | 1 teaspoon salt |
| ¾ cup butter | 1 cup chopped sour apples |
| 1 tablespoon lemon juice | 1 teaspoon chopped mint |

Mix the bread, butter, and lemon juice, moistening with a little water if needed. Add salt, apples, and mint. Mix. Stuff loosely.

*Mrs. Anna Keiser*

## PRUNE STUFFING

3 cups diced bread
½ cup melted butter
1 cup dried prunes
1 cup cold water

2 tablespoons lemon juice
1 tablespoon brown sugar
½ teaspoon salt
½ cup blanched almonds

Mix bread and melted butter. Place the prunes in a pan with the water, lemon juice, and brown sugar. Bring to a boil, then simmer for 5 minutes. Save any liquid that may remain and mix with the bread. Stone the prunes, chop, and sprinkle with salt. Blanch the almonds, chop, and mix all together. Stuff the bird loosely.

*Kate Weaver*

*Pennsylvania stone barn*

# Eggs

"NEVER take eggs with you when you move," runs the Pennsylvania adage, "for if you do and any break, it will bring you bad luck." "Set hens between eleven and twelve on Sunday, when the preacher is pronouncing the benediction," says another. And, "Set hens on an odd number of eggs." This helpful hint may have been the one that so baffled the hapless serving-maid, who was, in local folklore, "so dumb she couldn't tell eleven from even."

The Rhinelanders always crushed their eggshells to prevent witches from using them as boats. It was safest, really, to burn the shells to keep the witches from "putting spells on the hens." Eggs laid on Good Friday would never spoil, but spring would be delayed until the last Easter egg was eaten. To the forebears of the Pennsylvania Dutch, the egg was the symbol of life, and the egg and the rabbit (for fertility) became in time a part of Pennsylvania's Easter observance, just as the Christmas tree became part of Christmas. There are said even to have been Easter egg trees, decorated with brightly painted eggs.

Eggs were of great importance to the farmer, both as food and as a source of revenue. In the year 1910 Horne's *Pennsylvania German Manual* listed eggs as the top "crop." Certainly for years eggs have meant much more on the farm than just the farm wife's "pin money." Nevertheless, no housewife in Pennsylvania stints with eggs. "Dutch" cooks have always had a lavish hand with them, have used them by the dozens in cakes, turned out great varieties of dishes using eggs, and added them where they were least expected. As for eggs pickled in beet juice—Pennsylvania soldiers are said to have carried the news of them right across to California during the last war, demanding them with their beer. It is said that nowadays jars of ruby-colored eggs adorn many a California bar, although the Pennsylvania soldiers have long since returned

89

home to the joys of *Schnitz un Knepp* and shoofly pie. It seems fitting that the pickled eggs should join the pretzels on bars.

## POACHED EGGS

Bring water to a boil in a saucepan, salt liberally, drop in a small lump of butter. Stir the water with a spoon to make an eddy and drop in the egg. This will keep it in shape. Turn down the heat and simmer until egg is cooked. Poach eggs one by one, serve on buttered toast with a little bit of butter and salt and pepper on top. Sometimes Pennsylvanians add a tiny bit of thyme.

## EGGS POACHED IN MILK

Half fill a saucepan with milk and bring just to a boil. Add salt, stir into an eddy, drop in the egg. Simmer until egg is cooked; serve on buttered toast. Pour the milk over the egg, adding butter and seasoning.

## EGGS POACHED IN VINEGAR

The Pennsylvania Dutch poach eggs in water to which a little vinegar has been added. The vinegar keeps the egg in shape and cannot be tasted. Nowadays people sometimes substitute a little dry wine for the vinegar but either will do. Season and serve on buttered toast.

## SQUARE EGGS

| | |
|---|---|
| 6 or 8 eggs | Salt and pepper |
| 1 lump butter | Paprika |

Select a skillet so small that the eggs must be crowded almost yolk to yolk. Melt the butter in the pan, break the eggs into a bowl, and slide them into the pan, being careful not to break the yolks. Cover and cook over a low flame until the eggs begin to set. Uncover, baste with butter until the tops begin to become opaque. When eggs are firm cut in squares between the yolks, using a sharp knife. They will be 2-inch cubes, white on all sides, the yolks hidden in the center. Season and serve with bacon curls. Serves 3 or 4.

*Philip B. Woodroofe*

## BAKED EGGS

| | |
|---|---|
| 4 eggs | Salt and pepper |
| 1 tablespoon butter | 4 slices toast |

Beat the egg whites until stiff. Melt the butter in a hot pan, arrange the egg whites on it in four "nests" by swirling with a spoon. Slide the egg yolks one at a time into the centers of the nests. Place the pan in a 350° oven and watch carefully to prevent scorching. When egg whites have begun to color and the yolks are set, season and serve on buttered toast with a little butter on top. Serves 4.

*Dorothy Bassler*

## SCRAMBLED EGGS

Eggs should be scrambled in a heavy pan or, better still, in a fire-resistant glass or earthenware dish. Heat about 2 tablespoonfuls of milk for each egg, add a lump of butter, pepper, and salt. Just before the milk comes to a boil, break the eggs one at a time into a saucer, gently breaking the yolks with a spoon. Slide the eggs into the hot milk, mix, and keep scraping the eggs from the bottom and sides of the dish as it cooks. Stir and keep heat low and even until eggs are cooked.

*Mrs. Herman Kirkpatrick*

## SCRAMBLED EGGS WITH CELERY

Eggs
1 tablespoon milk for each egg
1 tablespoon butter

1 cup diced celery
1 teaspoon chopped parsley
Paprika, salt, and pepper

Proceed as for scrambled eggs above, adding the cooked celery. Sprinkle with parsley and season.

*Mrs. Herman Kirkpatrick*

## SCRAMBLED EGGS WITH HAM

Run pieces of cooked ham through food chopper. Melt a lump of butter in a frying pan, put in the ham. Beat the eggs, pour them over the ham, and heat, stirring together gently. Season with salt and pepper. When the eggs are cooked, simmer without stirring until brown on the bottom. Turn in one piece, if possible, and brown the other side.

*Mrs. Herman Kirkpatrick*

## CRUMB OMELET

1 cup milk
1 cup bread crumbs

6 eggs
Salt and pepper

Bring the milk to boil in a saucepan. Place bread crumbs in a bowl and pour the hot milk over them. Let stand a few minutes while you break the eggs into another bowl. Stir (do not beat) until well mixed. Add milk and crumbs. Season. Melt a lump of butter in a heated pan, pour the mixture into the pan, and cook slowly until the eggs are golden brown. Cut in squares and serve garnished with parsley.

*Mrs. Herman Kirkpatrick*


## TOMATO OMELET

6 slices bacon
½ cup chopped celery
1 tablespoon grated onion
1 tablespoon minced peppers

6 eggs
3 tablespoons water
Salt and pepper
1 tablespoon butter

1 cup cooked tomatoes

Fry the bacon, drain, and break into bits. Brown the celery, onion, and peppers in bacon fat and remove, leaving the fat in the pan. Beat the egg yolks 12 beats (because that is the proper number of beats for eggs) and add water. Beat the egg whites stiffly with salt. Mix all ingredients, adding egg whites last, and pour into bacon fat in heated pan. When omelet is set, turn down the heat and cook gently until finished. Fold and serve. Serves 6.

*Robert Butz Keck*


## BAKED OMELET

6 eggs, beaten separately
1 scant cup milk

1½ tablespoons sifted flour
Salt and pepper

Parsley

Stir the egg yolks into the milk. Mix the flour with a little milk and add to the mixture. Add stiffly beaten egg whites. Place in buttered baking dish and bake in 375° oven for about 15 minutes. Fold as the omelet is taken from the oven. It will not fall.

*Mrs. Abram Samuels III*


## CREAMED EGGS

6 eggs
2 tablespoons butter
1 tablespoon flour
½ cup milk

Salt and pepper
Chopped parsley
Paprika
6 slices toast

Let eggs stand outside refrigerator for a time before boiling. Hard-boil and shell. Make sauce with butter, flour, and milk. Season. Dice the hard-boiled egg whites and stir into the sauce. Heap the mixture on toast slices, put the yolks through a sieve, and sprinkle over the creamed egg whites. Dust with chopped parsley and paprika. (If you like, slices of baked ham, very thin, may be browned in a skillet and placed on top of the toast before the creamed eggs are added.) Serves 4.

*Mrs. Thomas A. Wright, Jr.*

## STUFFED EGGS

| | |
|---|---|
| Hard-boiled eggs | Mayonnaise |
| Mustard | Salt and pepper |
| | Paprika |

Slice the eggs lengthwise and remove yolks. Mix crumbled yolks with mustard and mayonnaise to taste, season, and stuff egg whites with the mixture. Sprinkle paprika on top.

## STUFFED EGGS WITH CELERY SAUCE

| | |
|---|---|
| Hard-boiled eggs | Bread crumbs |
| Minced onion, ham, or any | 1 beaten egg yolk |
| desired filling | Salt and pepper |

*Sauce*

| | |
|---|---|
| 1 cup diced, cooked celery | 1 chicken bouillon cube |
| 1 cup celery water | 1 tablespoon chopped parsley |
| Salt and paprika | 2 tablespoons cream |

Slice the eggs in two lengthwise and remove yolks. Mix the filling with the crumbled yolks, seasoning as preferred. Stuff the egg halves, dip in the beaten egg yolk, and stick halves back together. Dip whole eggs in beaten egg yolk and then in bread crumbs. Fry in deep fat until golden brown. Serve with celery sauce: Cook the diced celery in a little water with salt. Melt the bouillon cube in the measured cup of water the celery has cooked in. Combine ingredients, adding cream last. Simmer together until sauce has thickened. Makes about 1½ cups. Pour over the eggs.

*Mary Huyett*

## PICKLED EGGS

| | |
|---|---|
| 1 cup beet juice | ¼ teaspoon allspice |
| 1 cup vinegar | ¼ teaspoon mace |
| ¾ teaspoon salt | 1 or 2 small, cooked beets |
| ½ teaspoon cloves | Shelled, hard-boiled eggs |

Mix the beet juice, vinegar, salt, and spices and simmer together for 10 minutes. Pour into a wide-mouthed jar, put in one of the beets, then the eggs. Add the second beet. Let stand until the eggs are colored. They can be sliced lengthwise and served on lettuce or eaten as appetizers.

*Mrs. John Joseph Stoudt*


## EGG BREAD

3 beaten eggs                          2 slices bread
½ cup milk                             Lard to fry
Pinch of salt                          Pepper

Melt the lard in a heated pan, mix the eggs with the milk and pour into the pan. Place the slices of bread in the pan and scramble the eggs around and on the bread, making sure that the bread is browned. Season and serve. Serves 2.

*Mrs. John Kistler*


## MENNONITE EGG BREAD

3 beaten eggs                          8 thick slices bread
2 cups milk                            Lard to fry
Pinch of salt                          Powdered sugar
Butter                                 Jelly

Mix the eggs and milk, adding salt. Remove crusts from the bread, dip in mixture. Fry quickly in hot fat until a delicate brown, turning. Spread lightly with butter, sprinkle with sugar, place a spoonful of jelly on each piece. Serves 4.

*Dorothy Glessner*

*Springhouse*

# Cheese

You will find in this section the three ways to make the three Pennsylvania Dutch cheeses. And you will find here recipes for what are pretty much the only indigenous recipes that are made with cheese—Cheese Cake and Cheese Pie. (You may or may not be able to tell them apart!) The Pennsylvania Dutch love cheese, but they are disposed to keep it where it belongs and there is very little adding of cheese to vegetable and meat dishes in Pennsylvania kitchens.

Ball Cheese, Cup Cheese, and Schmierkase take time and patience in the making—time, patience, and space to store the crock or cheese board and a place to hang the cheese bags. Consequently, cheese is made nowadays chiefly on the farms. But when it is taken to the large city markets, it is eagerly snapped up by people who remember how good it tasted when they were young. Someone told me not long ago that he could remember as though it were yesterday the cheesemaking in his boyhood home, as well as the time the cheese was ruined. It seems that he and his mother heard strange popping sounds coming from the attic and, when they investigated, there was little brother, carefully poking a finger into each and every cheese, saying "pop" as he did so and licking his finger between the cheeses. . . .

I have a German cookbook published in this country in 1879 *fur die Deutschen in Amerika*. Although it is otherwise rather elaborate, it lacks cheese cookery. However, in this book was found the method of making Ball Cheese that is given here. The recipe was not in the body of the book—it was written in pencil on the back flyleaf. For detail, it rivals the cookbook itself; if reproduced here in all its ramifications, it might well deter one from cheesemaking forever. But it is an interesting recipe for all that. You are supposed to "heat the milk long enough so it sings," add coloring matter "the size of an apple-kernel" and "when it is thick nice, that which is in the boiler, you set on the stove." Then you proceed with the cheese:

## BALL CHEESE

Use thick, sour milk, bring to a careful boil, and drain off the whey. Pack in a crock and salt. Add fresh curds every other day, salting each time. When the crock is three-quarters full, take out the cheese and knead it into balls. Spread the balls on a board and place in a warm place to dry. Next day move to a warmer spot, and the day after that to a place still warmer. On the fourth day roll the balls in bicarbonate of soda, wrap in cheesecloth (or paper), and return to the crock. Cover and let stand all winter. When spring comes get out the crock, scrape the mold from the cheese, and it will be ready to use. Coloring matter may be added but is not essential.

*From an old cook book*

## CUP CHEESE

Three-quarters fill a wide pan with thick, sour milk and place in the oven. Set the gauge at about 300°, making sure of a mild, steady heat. Oven heat makes a tough curd and that is what you want for cup cheese. When the curds and whey have separated, drain off the whey and pack the cheese in a crock. Salt. Add more curds prepared in this manner every day for a week. At the end of the week, take the cheese from the crock, place in a kettle, and melt over low heat. Then bring slowly to a boil and add:

| | |
|---|---|
| 1 cup cream | 1 teaspoon soda |
| 1 cup butter | 1 beaten egg |

Boil together slowly for a few minutes, then pour into cups and cool. The Pennsylvania Dutch save their old cups for this purpose and the cheese is taken to market in them. This is a softer cheese than Ball Cheese.

*From an old cook book*

## SCHMIERKASE
### (Cottage Cheese)

| | |
|---|---|
| 6 cups thick, sour cream | Pepper and salt |
| 1 cup cream, scant | 1 tablespoon cream |

Heat the milk to moderate temperature. This is to be a soft cheese, so do not allow the curds to scald or they will toughen. When curds and whey have separated, pour off the whey and place the curds in a cheese bag, hung to drip over a pan in a warm place. (In the old days this was the back of the stove.) Hang until the curds have drained but are not dry. Place in a large bowl and mix with cream, pepper, and salt. Just before serving float a little cream on top, sprinkle with salt and freshly ground pepper and perhaps a little cup-up chives.

When I was a child I knew that one of my favorite old ladies made cottage cheese every Saturday morning, just after the wide boards of her kitchen floor had been scrubbed. At just about that time I had reached the mountain ash tree flaming at the top of the hill and was turning into her lane. The kitchen floor was still damp, but I wiped my feet carefully before I went in. She had geraniums in her kitchen window and peacock feathers tucked back of the clock on the shelf. An elaborately featherstitched "housewife" hung unfolded on the wall by the window, and as I poked my fingers into its many pockets, searching for buttons for my strings, her wooden spoon clattered in the yellow cheese bowl. We had a routine. I looked everywhere except at the round cherry table—until she asked me casually if I would like to "polish the bowl." It always seemed odd to me that so frugal a person would leave so much good cheese in the bowl! As I cleaned up the cheese she would be adding that final tablespoon of cream to the white mound transferred to a cutglass bowl—and that is how I never forget the technique of floating cream on top of cottage cheese. I remember too how pretty I thought the freshly ground black pepper looked as she flaked it on the cheese. After that we would go to the little parlor organ in the other room. She would sit down and pump away as she sang my favorite song in a quavering falsetto—"He'd fly through the air with the greatest of ease. . . ." She liked to sing and I liked cheese.

## CHEESE PIE I

*German Pastry*

1 cup sifted flour
½ teaspoon salt
1 tablespoon sugar
3 tablespoons butter
1 egg yolk
1 tablespoon lemon juice
1 tablespoon cold water

*Cheese Filling*

12 ounces cottage cheese
1 cup sugar
2 rounded tablespoons flour
1 rounded tablespoon butter
2 eggs
3 cups milk

Sift the flour into a bowl with the salt and sugar. Cut in the butter, stir together. Stir in the egg yolk lightly, add lemon juice and water. Chill in refrigerator for ½ hour. Roll out on a floured board. Line a deep 9-inch pie dish with the pastry and chill again. Mix the ingredients for the filling, beating the eggs separately and adding the egg whites last. Pour into the pastry shell and bake in 350° oven for about 45 minutes, or until filling is firm and golden brown. Makes 1 large pie.

*Mrs. Victor Boyer*

## MRS. HOLLENBACH'S CHEESE CUSTARD PIE (II)

*Pastry*
1 cup flour
½ teaspoon salt
2 teaspoons sugar
4 tablespoons butter
2 tablespoons ice water
1 tablespoon lemon juice

*Filling*
1 package cream cheese
3 eggs
Salt
½ cup sugar
1 cup milk
½ cup cream

Sift the flour, salt, and sugar into a bowl, cut in the butter, add ice water and lemon juice. Stir together and chill in refrigerator. Roll out the dough on a floured board, line a deep 7-inch pie dish with pastry and chill again. Beat together the ingredients for the filling, adding beaten egg whites last. The mixture should just about fill the crust. Bake in 450° oven for 15 minutes. Lower the heat to 350° and finish baking—about ½ hour. Makes 1 pie.

*Mrs. Donald L. Helfferich*

## CHEESE CAKE I

*Crumb Crust*
16 graham crackers
¼ cup sugar
¼ cup soft butter

*Filling*
8 ounces cream cheese
8 ounces cottage cheese
2 eggs
¾ cup sugar
1 teaspoon lemon juice
1 teaspoon vanilla
1-2 cups sour cream

Roll crackers to crumbs on a board, mix with sugar and butter. Pat the mixture firmly on the bottom and sides of a glass pie dish to form a crust. Chill in refrigerator. Mix all the ingredients except the sour cream, adding beaten egg whites last. Bake at 375° for 20 minutes. Remove from the oven, spread with the sour cream to which a little vanilla and sugar have been added. Sprinkle more graham crumbs on top. Return to oven and bake at 475° for 5 minutes.

*Polly Leinbach*

## CHEESE CAKE II

*Crumb Crust*

1½ cups graham cracker crumbs
½ cup melted butter
½ cup sugar
½ teaspoon cinnamon

*Filling*

3 cups cottage cheese
3 eggs
¾ cup sugar
⅔ cup evaporated milk
1½ tablespoons flour
¼ teaspoon salt
1 tablespoon lemon juice
½ teaspoon grated lemon rind

Mix the graham cracker crumbs with the melted butter, sugar, and cinnamon. Pat the mixture firmly on the bottom and sides of a deep pie dish to form crust. Chill in refrigerator. Mix cheese, beaten eggs, and sugar. Add milk, flour, salt, lemon juice, and grated rind. Pour mixture into shell. Sprinkle any left-over crumbs lightly over the top of the cake. Pineapple may be placed in the bottom if desired, or almonds (blanched and chopped) may be sprinkled over the top. Bake in 350° oven for 45 minutes. Makes 1 large cake.

*Mrs. P. A. Meixell*

# Fish and Seafood

*Trout Hall, Allentown, Pennsylvania*

PHILADELPHIA is the only Pennsylvania city having direct traffic with the sea, so that leaves the Pennsylvania Dutch pretty much dependent upon Philadelphia for ideas about seafood. Indeed, in the old days they were dependent upon Philadelphia if they got any at all. The Dutch like fish but do nothing particularly unusual in fish cookery. They are extremely fond of lobster and crab as well as oysters and clams, but rather more inclined to eat seafood in restaurants than to prepare it at home.

My own most vivid impression of Pennsylvania seafood cookery is the memory of my grandfather invading the kitchen to fry oysters as they should be fried. He was pledged to a method he had learned in a Philadelphia club, maintaining that he had paid the chef five dollars (no mean sum in those days) to teach him how. So—for the rest of his life—he taught all his family how to fry oysters whenever he did it himself! It became rather wearying and the family would have evaded his dinner invitations gladly if the oysters had not been so superb. The hubbub in the kitchen while he held forth was terrific, and everyone who could fled the spot. But how they devoured those oysters! I can hear my grandfather shouting as though it were yesterday, his opinion of "the damn fools who wipe dry an oyster and ruin it! It takes away the natural goodness. Dip them dripping, do you hear me? Dripping! That's the way they fry oysters in Philadelphia." It is not recorded that he had any other culinary skills.

100

## GRANDFATHER SHEPHERD'S FRIED OYSTERS

| | |
|---|---|
| 50 prime oysters | 3 cups cracker crumbs |
| 3 or 4 beaten eggs | 1 teaspoon salt |

Take the oysters right out of their liquor without draining, dip first in the crumbs, then set aside on a board in a cool place. (Make sure never to pierce the oysters with a fork. Lift them on a flat, slotted spoon.) Dip in the egg, then in the crumbs, and set aside again. Fry quickly in deep, hot fat. Drain on brown paper. Serve at once with catsup or pepper hash.

## OYSTER PIE

| | |
|---|---|
| 2 cups oysters | ¼ teaspoon pepper |
| 2 tablespoons butter | 2 hard-boiled eggs, cut fine |
| ½ teaspoon salt | 2 tablespoons flour |

Cream

Line a deep, 7-inch pie dish with puff paste:

| | |
|---|---|
| ½ teaspoon salt | 2 cups sifted flour |
| 1 teaspoon baking powder | ½ cup butter, or butter and lard |

2 tablespoons ice water

Sift the salt and baking powder with flour, cut in the shortening, handling lightly as ice water is added. Chill. Roll out quickly on floured board, very thin.

Pour the oysters onto the crust, filling up the measure with cream if there is not enough liquor with the oysters. Dot with butter, sprinkle with salt and pepper. Add the hard-boiled eggs. Sprinkle lightly with the flour. Roll out the top crust, score a cross in its center, place on the pie, seal and crimp edges. Fold back corners of the cross at the center to pour in more liquid or cream if needed as the pie bakes. Bake ½ hour, or until crust is nicely browned, in 375° oven. Serves 4-5.

*Marilyn Buckner*

## OYSTER PATTIES

| | |
|---|---|
| 2 cups oysters without liquor | 2 tablespoons butter |
| 1 cup milk | 2 tablespoons flour |
| 1 cup cream | Salt and pepper |

Puff paste

Make patty shells of puff paste, using recipe as in oyster pie. Heat the milk and cream in double boiler just to the boiling point. Add butter. Rub the flour smooth with a little cold milk, stir into the hot milk to thicken. Set aside. Heat the oysters in water until they are plump. Salt to taste and add dash of white pepper. Add the hot milk mixture, pour into patty shells. Bake in 375° oven for ½ hour, or until crust browns. Makes 8.

*Elizabeth Schramek*

## PANNED OYSTERS

| | |
|---|---|
| 8 rounds bread | Salt |
| 2 tablespoons butter | Pepper |
| 2 cups oysters and liquor | Chopped parsley |

Fit the rounds of bread into greased patty tins. Moisten with teaspoons of oyster liquor, dot each with butter, place under broiler. Partially brown, then remove from broiler. Moisten and dot again. Fill with oysters, sprinkle with pepper, dot with butter on top. Cover. Place in oven this time. Steam at 375° for 7 or 8 minutes. Sprinkle with salt, bake 1 more minute. Serve with chopped parsley. Makes 8 patties.

*Jeanette Heimbach*

## CRAB PATTIES

| | |
|---|---|
| 2 cups crabmeat (backfin) | 1 cup milk |
| 1 tablespoon chopped parsley | 1 tablespoon butter |
| ¼ teaspoon mace | 2 tablespoons flour |
| 1 scant teaspoon salt | 2 egg yolks |
| ⅛ teaspoon pepper | Bread crumbs |

Flake the crabmeat with a silver knife. Add parsley, mace, salt, and pepper. Put milk in a pan, blend the butter and flour, warm the milk and add the blended butter and flour. Stir until smooth and thickened. Add beaten egg yolks; cook a minute longer. Remove from stove and stir in the crabmeat. Cool. Shape into patties and let stand until firm. Dip into beaten egg, then in bread crumbs. Let stand. Fry in deep, hot fat, one at a time, until golden brown. Drain on brown paper, garnish with parsley, serve with tartare sauce. (Make a quick tartare sauce by adding to 1 cup mayonnaise: chopped pickles, capers, pepper, salt, and ¼ teaspoon dry mustard.) Serves 8.

*Elizabeth Schramek*

## DEVILED CRABMEAT

| | |
|---|---|
| 1 pound backfin crabmeat | ½ cup milk |
| ½ cup chopped green peppers and onions | 1 hard-boiled egg, chopped |
| ¼ cup soft butter | Salt and pepper |
| 2 tablespoons flour | ½ teaspoon Worcestershire sauce |
| | Paprika |
| Bread crumbs | |

Remove all pieces of shell from crabmeat, taking care to keep crab in as large pieces as possible. Sauté pepper and onion in half the butter until tender. Mix remaining butter with flour, stir in milk to make a smooth paste. Simmer and stir until it thickens. Add pepper, onions, crabmeat, egg, salt and pepper, Worcestershire sauce. Grease 6 crab shells and fill with the mixture, sprinkling crumbs and paprika over the tops. Bake in 350° oven for 20-25 minutes until nicely browned. Serves 6.

## DEVILED CLAMS

2 cups milk, scalded
2 tablespoons buttter
1 egg, beaten
½ cup cracker crumbs
1 dozen large clams
2 hard-boiled eggs, chopped

1 tablespoon chopped onion
1 tablespoon parsley, minced
1 tablespoon Worcestershire sauce
Salt, pepper, celery salt
4 tablespoons bread crumbs
2 tablespoons butter

Mix the first four ingredients, mince the clams and add. Add egg, onion, parsley, Worcestershire sauce, and seasoning. Pour into a greased baking dish. Brown the breadcrumbs in 2 tablespoons butter and scatter over the top. Bake in 400° oven for ¾ hour.

*Mrs. Bryce Mayes*

## BOILED FISH WITH PARSLEY SAUCE

Old recipes for boiled fish always talk about a fish kettle and then go on to say that if you're so unfortunate as not to have one you may sew the fish in a cloth. If you draw a cord through the wrapping we are told that you can shape the fish into a letter "S"—"so it will fit the kettle good," besides looking nice. A big fish, say the old cookbooks, should be put to boil in cold water, a small one in hot water. That is because when a small one touches the water it "cooks so fast that it is done yet." Anyhow, boil the fish, uncover, place on a heated platter, and serve with parsley sauce. To make the sauce, wash the parsley in cold water, toss for a minute in boiling water, then chop fine. Combine 2 tablespoons minced parsley with 1 cup drawn butter.

*From an old cook book*

## BAKED FISH

1 3-pound fish
Salt and pepper
Lemon juice
Flour
Fine bread crumbs

2 tablespoons butter
Minced parsley
Paprika
Lemon quarters
Parsley

Place the fish in a baking pan or on a plank. Sprinkle with salt, pepper, and lemon juice, dredge lightly with flour and crumbs. Dot with butter. Bake covered in 350° oven for 20 minutes. Uncover, baste with butter and lemon juice. Finish baking, about 20 minutes, uncovered, basting frequently. When taken from the oven, sprinkle with more lemon juice, dot with more butter, sprinkle with minced parsley and paprika, garnish with lemon quarters and whole parsley. 6 portions.

## WALNUT CATSUP FOR FISH

| | |
|---|---|
| 1 cup English walnuts | ¼ teaspoon powdered ginger |
| 2 cups water to cover | ¼ teaspoon powdered cloves |
| 2 tablespoons salt | ¼ teaspoon nutmeg |
| 2 cups vinegar | Few grains cayenne pepper |
| ½ teaspoon white pepper | 1 teaspoon minced onion |

¼ teaspoon celery seed

Prick each walnut with a steel-tined fork, place in jar, cover with salted water. Allow walnuts to stand in brine for a week. Drain. Cover with vinegar that has been heated to the boiling point; let stand for a few hours. Drain off the vinegar and save it. Crush the walnuts to a pulp, combine with the vinegar. Place minced onion in a small bag with the spices and drop it in saucepan with the walnuts and vinegar. Bring mixture to a boil. When it boils, turn down heat and simmer for 1 hour. Cool and bottle. Makes 1 pint.

*Elizabeth Schramek*

## BAKED SHAD

Bone the shad by cutting it open along the backbone with a sharp knife. Remove the large bone with any small ones that are attached to it; it will come away easily. The small bones will cook away if the fish is baked for 1½ hours (for each pound) at 275° instead of 350° for one hour per pound, as is usually done. Place the shad on greased broiler rack, sprinkle with salt, pepper, and lemon juice. Dredge with a little flour. Place some water in the bottom of the broiling pan, put in the rack with the fish, cover, and steam in the oven. Baste frequently with butter, making small gashes across the fish to hold the butter. Remove the cover, slide the fish under the broiler for a few minutes, to brown lightly, transfer to heated platter, garnish with parsley and quartered lemons.

Place the shad roe in ice water with a little salt added, for a few minutes. Boil a little water in a saucepan, let the roe stand in it for a few more minutes, then dredge lightly with flour, place on a greased broiler, dot with butter, slide under the flame, and broil gently for almost 10 minutes. Turn once and baste. Serve with the shad.

## BREAKFAST MACKEREL

1 salt mackerel
Water to cover
1 cup milk

½ cup cream
1 large tablespoon butter
Paprika

Freshen the mackerel by soaking it overnight in water to cover with skin side up. In the morning steam in a skillet with 1 cup water, covered. When water boils, pour it off and add milk. Simmer a few minutes until cooked. Heat the cream, take the fish from the pan, place on hot platter, dot with butter, and pour cream over it. Sprinkle with paprika. Serve with whole, boiled potatoes.

# Of Hexel
# and Mummix

*Kitchen fireplace, Ephrata Cloisters*

So FAR this collection of Pennsylvania Dutch dishes has proceeded along fairly conventional lines. But this section is going to be more or less apocryphal. It will deal with *Hexel* and *Mummix*. You will not find these words in a dictionary—and probably not even in a Pennsylvania Dutch dictionary, if you are lucky enough to get hold of one. These words are decidedly regional and colloquial.

The Pennsylvania Dutch, you see, have a fine old time with their dialect. All conversations in Pennsylvania Dutch seem to be humorous—at any rate, the speakers tilt their sentences with laughter at the ends. The dialect can make a comic song or a funny story doubly hilarious and much is lost in translation. A folk that will gather together solemnly on Grundsou Day to report its observations of the groundhog casting his shadow, celebrate his awakening, and then ostensibly eat woodchuck at the dinner marking the occasion, must possess an incomparable sense of humor. Along these lines, when, gathering these recipes, I was told in Quakertown, "This is the best *Mummix* I ever made," and, in Collegeville, "This is for *Hexel*," I decided that a section devoted to *Hexel* and *Mummix* might be fun in a Pennsylvania Dutch cook book.

*Hexel* and *Mummix*, by the way, are words for whatever is left over, scrambled, and turned into—hash.

Here are some very good recipes for various kinds of hash—*Hexel* and *Mummix* to you. And, in addition, here are some recipes that do not seem to fit anywhere else. Since I cannot think what to do with them, I am taking a leaf from the dialect and turning them into this hashed-up section!

## MUMMIX

| | |
|---|---|
| 1 pound ground beef | 1 cup boiled potatoes, cubed |
| 1 egg | 2 tablespoons vinegar |
| 1 chopped onion | 1 tablespoon lard |
| Salt and pepper | 1 tablespoon butter |

Melt the lard and butter in a hot frying pan. Mix other ingredients and toss into the pan. Stir and turn until fairly well cooked. Sprinkle ½ teaspoon sugar over the top, cover, and let simmer. Season and serve with parsley. Serves 6.

*Jeanette Heimbach*

## HEXEL

| | |
|---|---|
| 2 cups chopped beef | 1 lump butter |
| 1 chopped onion | 1 tablespoon minced parsley |
| 1 cup boiled potatoes, cubed | Salt and pepper |

Heat the butter in a frying pan, mix other ingredients, fry until well cooked, stirring and turning. Season, garnish wih parsley, and serve. 6 portions.

*Mrs. William U. Helfferich*

## DUTCH HASH

| | |
|---|---|
| 2 cups left-over beef | ½ cup water |
| 2 medium onions, sliced | ½ cup vinegar |
| 1 tablespoon flour | 1 teaspoon sugar |
| 1 lump butter | Salt and pepper |

Brown the onions in butter, add beef and brown that. Mix other ingredients, add to onions and beef, cover, and simmer until well done. Season and serve. Serves 4.

*Mrs. Victor Boyer*

## MRS. GANSELEITER'S HOT MUMMIX

| | |
|---|---|
| 1 pound ground beef | ¼ teaspoon cayenne pepper |
| 1 beaten egg | ½ teaspoon salt |
| 1 pepper, chopped | 1 tablespoon lard |
| 1 onion, minced | 1 tablespoon butter |
| 1 tablespoon Worcestershire sauce | ½ teaspoon sugar |

Melt butter and lard in iron skillet. Mix other ingredients except sugar and fry in the pan, stirring and turning until fairly well cooked. Sprinkle the sugar over the top, cover, and simmer. Season, serve garnished with strips of red pepper or pimiento. Serves 4.

*Robert Butz Keck*

## MRS. WEAVER'S EGG HEXEL

6 slices bacon
3 onions, chopped
6 eggs
½ cup milk and cream

¾ cup baked ham, cut up
¼ cup blanched chestnuts
Salt and pepper
Pinch of thyme

Fry bacon and shred. Brown onions in bacon fat. Beat eggs lightly with milk
and cream. Add ham, bacon, and broken-up chestnuts. Pour off excess fat from
pan, add mixture, season, stir gently. Cover, cook well, serve with parsley garnishing.
Serves 4.

*William W. Meixell*

## MUSH AND CREAMED BEEF HEXEL

6 slices mush
1 egg yolk
2 tablespoons milk
1 cup crumbs

Butter or bacon fat for frying
1½ cups milk
2 tablespoons butter
2 tablespoons sifted flour

1 cup shredded dried beef

Slice the mush in ¾-inch thickness, dip in egg yolk mixed with milk, then in
crumbs. Let stand a few minutes before frying. Or, thin slices of plain mush
may be fried, if preferred. Make a sauce of the butter, flour, and milk, add dried
beef, and blend. Pour over the fried mush and serve. 6 servings.

*Mrs. Donald L. Helfferich*

## TOMATO MUMMIX

1 diced onion
2 cups ground beef or pork
1 can beans in tomato sauce

3 tablespoons vinegar
Salt and cayenne pepper
2 tablespoons butter and lard

Melt butter and lard in heated pan. Toss in the mixed ingredients and fry
lightly. Cover and simmer. Serve with catsup or chile sauce.

*Thomas B. Keck*

## NOODLE AND PRUNE MUMMIX

2 cups stewed prunes
1 lemon, juice and grated rind
4 tablespoons sugar
4 cups homemade noodles

Salted water
¼ cup butter
1 cup crumbs
2 tablespoons butter

Brown sugar

Cook prunes with lemon juice and sugar in water to cover. When cooked, chop
and sprinkle with lemon rind. Butter a casserole, mix prunes and noodles (that

have been cooked in salted water with the ¼ cup butter). Fill the casserole with the mixture, cover with crumbs, dot with butter, and sprinkle a little brown sugar over the top. Serves 6.

*Abram Samuels, III*

*And these are hereby tossed in:*

## FRIED MUSH

| | |
|---|---|
| 1½ cups cornmeal | 1 teaspoon salt |
| 1½ cups water | 5 cups boiling water |

Place boiling water in top of double boiler, mix cornmeal, water, and salt and add the mixture to boiling water little by little, stirring. Cook over high heat for 3 minutes, cover, steam for 15 minutes longer. Pour into greased breadpan, cool. Cut into ¾-inch slices.

| | |
|---|---|
| 6 slices mush | 2 tablespoons milk |
| 1 egg yolk | 1 cup crumbs |

Maple syrup

Dip mush slices into mixture of egg yolk and milk, then in crumbs. Let stand a few minutes before frying in butter or bacon fat in a hot pan. Turn carefully, fry other side. Serve with real maple syrup.

## ZWIEBACK

| | |
|---|---|
| 3 eggs | 1 yeast cake, dissolved in |
| 3 cups flour, scant | ½ cup lukewarm water |
| 2 cups milk, scalded and cooled | ¾ cup butter |

½ cup sugar

Beat the eggs lightly, form into paste with flour, milk, yeast-and-water, butter, and sugar. Let rise, covered, in a greased bowl. Knead, let rise again. Place on floured board, shape into long, narrow loaves. Let rise in pans until doubled in size. Bake in 350° oven for about 45 minutes. When loaves are cooled, cut in diagonal slices about ½-inch thick with sharp knife. Brown slices carefully in oven.

*Mrs. Victor Boyer*

## PRETZELS

| | |
|---|---|
| 1 cup milk | 1 yeast cake |
| ½ cup butter | ¼ cup lukewarm water |
| 1½ tablespoons sugar | 1 egg white, well beaten |
| ½ teaspoon salt | 3 ¾ cups flour |

1 egg yolk

Scald milk, add butter, sugar, and salt. When mixture is lukewarm, stir in yeast softened in warm water, and the egg white. Stir in flour gradually, enough to make soft dough. Knead dough on floured board for 3-4 minutes, cover, and let rise in warm place until doubled. Punch down, roll out on floured board. Cut into thin strips, finger width, shape into pretzels, pinching ends together. Let stand on board until they begin to rise. Fill a large, shallow pan half full of water. When very hot, not boiling, drop pretzels in, one at a time. Cook them under the boiling point on one side, turn and cook on other. Drain, brush with beaten egg yolk, sprinkle with coarse salt or caraway seeds. Bake on buttered baking sheet in 400° oven 15 minutes. The story goes that pretzels are twisted as they are because they represent angels with their arms crossed in supplication.

## TRIFLES

2 eggs                          Vanilla and almond flavoring, mixed
Pinch of salt                   Fat
Flour to make paste             Powdered sugar
                    Jelly

Mix the paste, roll out lightly on floured board, shape with biscuit cutter. Fry quickly in deep fat, sift the powdered sugar on the trifles while still hot. When cool, drop a spoonful of jelly into the centers. With currant jelly, these are good served with roast duck, or they can be eaten as dessert.

## HOT TOMATO COCKTAIL

Chopped celery tops             4 cups tomatoes
1 chopped onion                 1 tablespoon chopped parsley

Cook together until flavors are thoroughly blended. Strain and season sharply. Serve hot with breadsticks.

*Mrs. Victor Boyer*

## APPLE RINGS

2 tablespoons sugar             1 egg
1½ cups sifted flour            1 cup milk
1½ teaspoons baking powder      Apples
½ teaspoon salt                 Sugar and cinnamon

Sift together sugar, flour, baking powder, and salt. Beat the egg in a bowl, add milk and blend. Sift in the dry ingredients to make batter. Peel and core apples and slice in rings. Dip in the batter and drop in deep fat, frying quickly on both sides. Drain on brown paper. Sprinkle with sugar and cinnamon. Serve at once.

*Mary Rose McWilliams*

## HOMINY FRITTERS

¼ cup fine hominy
1 cup boiling water
¾ cup milk
1 tablespoon butter

½ cup flour
½ teaspoon baking powder
¼ teaspoon salt
Maple syrup

Steam the hominy with boiling water until water is absorbed. Scald milk in double boiler, add hominy, and steam until tender. Add butter. Cool. Sift flour with baking powder and salt, blend with hominy. Add more milk if batter is too stiff to drop from a spoon into hot fat. Fry quickly and serve with maple syrup.

## AUNT SUE'S RASPBERRY VINEGAR

4 quarts red raspberries
1 quart cider vinegar

2 pounds sugar for each pint of juice
Water

Place 2 quarts of raspberries in a large, cold crock or jar. Pour vinegar over them and let it stand for 2 days. Drain off the vinegar and pour it back over the rest of the raspberries. Measuring 2 pounds for each pint of juice will require about 12 pounds of sugar, depending upon the quantity of juice. Place the sugar, all the berries, and the vinegar in a large kettle and bring to a boil. If too strongly vinegar-flavored, add a little water and a pound of sugar for each cup of added water. Simmer for 10 minutes, strain, and bottle. "Make tight shut." To serve, take 1 part syrup to 3 parts water, add sliced lemon and ice. Makes 12 bottles.

*John Joseph Stoudt, who wrote* Pennsylvania German Folk Art

## MRS. SCHAEFFER'S DANDELION WINE

1 quart dandelion flowers, no stems
3 cups boiling water
1 yeast cake

3 pounds sugar
1 lemon, cut in small pieces
Water

Pour the boiling water over the flowers and let stand for 24 hours. Strain. Add yeast to the liquid and let stand another 24 hours. Strain again, add sugar, lemon, and enough water to make 1 gallon. Set aside in a crockery jug. "If water is added, or if it stands as long as a month, it will ferment."

*Mrs. Susan Laudenslager*

## AUNT SUE'S DANDELION WINE

| | |
|---|---|
| 3 quarts dandelion flowers, no stems | 2 pounds sugar |
| 2 quarts cold water | 1 yeast cake |
| | 2 slices lemon |

Pour the water over the flowers and let stand in a large crock for 3 days and 3 nights. Strain through a cloth, add sugar, yeast, and lemon. Let stand 4 days and 4 nights. Strain again and bottle. "Make it in a cool place, to prevent fermentation" but "the older it is, the better it is"!

*John Joseph Stoudt*

## GRAPE JUICE

| | |
|---|---|
| 4 pounds Concord grapes | 3 cups water |
| | 1 cup sugar |

Wash the grapes and remove stems. Drop in kettle with water and cook gently until grapes are tender. Drain, allowing the juice to return to the kettle. Add sugar and bring to a boil. Bottle at once.

## BLACKBERRY SHRUB

| | |
|---|---|
| 4 quarts, 1 pint blackberries | 6 cups water |
| 3 lemons | 2 cups sugar |
| 4 oranges | 2 cups rum |

Steam the blackberries until juice starts to flow. Strain in a cheesecloth bag until juice stops flowing. Add juice of the oranges and lemons to the blackberry juice, also water and sugar. Bring just to a boil, add rum, and bottle.

*And here, if anyone is interested, is the old-time method of making:*

## "A GOOD, HARD SOAP"

"Use a specially constructed barrel raised off the ground high enough to allow a tub to be placed underneath. The bottom of the barrel should be perforated with holes. Then filled with wood ashes. Now and then, toss a bucket of water on the ashes. As the water passes through the ashes it dissolves the potash and soda. Take the solution obtained, put in an iron kettle with a quantity of grease fat. Boil the mixture for an hour or longer. Add salt. As mixture cools, the soap will solidify on top of the water."

Or—take:

**5 pounds grease**               **3 gallons soft hot water**
             **1 pound concentrated potash**

"Boil these together for 5 or 6 hours, adding water as it boils away. When done, it is a dark, yellowish brown, like jelly, almost transparent. It should *taste* smooth and pleasant. If sharp and acrid, it is not done. Stir frequently. Pour into zinc-lined tin and let it harden. Will be white when hard. Cut in bars."

*From an old cook (!) book*

# Vegetables

*Whitfield House, Nazareth, Pennsylvania*

THE farms of southeastern Pennsylvania are among the finest in the world. Anyone who has seen this rolling countryside and admired the centuries-old houses, built of native stone and set so rightly among their orderly farm buildings, knows what rural charm can be. And anyone who has visited the markets —in Lancaster, for instance—has seen the fruits of Pennsylvania farming beautifully displayed. Here temptation is great and the unwary emerge staggering under the weight of unpremeditated purchases. Farm families tend the market stalls, and everything they sell has been raised and carefully prepared by themselves. They are justifiably proud of their wares.

Farm wives have their own kitchen gardens, distinct and apart from their husbands' large truck gardens. In these small gardens are grown the radishes, onions, carrots, greens, and herbs for household use. Transferred from earth to kettle in the space of a few minutes, they are so fresh and so good that they need little sauce or accompaniment. The gardens have rows of berry bushes, too, and often a strawberry bed. The flower garden is nearby, so it is not unusual to find mignonette growing among the onions or pansies with the parsley. Pennsylvania Germans love flowers so much that if the poppies do wander among the beets no one minds—just so there are no weeds!

Farther out in the fields the farmer grows the vegetables that require heavier cultivation. There he raises his potatoes, corn, squash, cabbage, and the like. Much care and science goes into his farming, but there is also a traditional list of do's and don'ts according to folklore:

Plant lettuce in the dark of the moon, plant beans when the horns of the moon turn upward, plant cabbage on Good Friday and cucumbers on the year's longest day. When you plant radishes, say "as long as my arm and as

114

thick as my leg." Never transplant parsley: it is bad luck. Begin sowing on Friday and end it on Friday. Spread ashes on Ash Wednesday. And so on. *But* —anything planted in the name of God will grow.

So much for the planting of vegetables. Now a rule or two about the eating of them: "Sauerkraut and bacon will drive all cares away." "Be sure to eat dandelions or greens on Maundy Thursday." "Raise your cucumbers carefully but if you make salad of them—throw it in the swill barrel."

If a crop failed, if the potatoes were blighted, if prolonged rain or drought spoiled the harvest, there used to be a phrase for it: "Just like Old Man Dietz's funeral."

Old Man Dietz lived years ago, but his memory lingers on in the farm country. Traveling was difficult in his day, but when he came to die his son was sent for and managed to get there in time. Young Dietz had been called from home in the midst of harvesting and it seemed that Old Man Dietz was taking his time about dying. The son decided that if the funeral was planned it would do no harm and save time later. So the arrangements were made, friends notified, and the funeral baked meats prepared. The mourners arrived early on the appointed day, coming from far and wide—only to find Old Man Dietz sitting up and feeling better. Now there would be no funeral, no eulogies, no reunions, no reminiscences, and no funeral pie. So everyone went home.

To this day, when the onions don't come up or when the corn crop fails, farmers sigh and say, "Ach, it came to nothing. Just like Old Man Dietz's funeral."

## RAW FRIED POTATOES

| | |
|---|---|
| 6 potatoes | Salt and pepper |
| 6 slices bacon | 1 teaspoon minced parsley |
| ½ teaspoon celery seed | Paprika |

Peel the potatoes, cover with ice water, and let stand a few minutes. Drain. Dice the bacon and fry quickly, then remove from the fat. Slice the potatoes very thin and drop into the heated pan with the bacon fat. Cover and fry, turning to prevent burning. Season, add bacon, and serve. Serves 4.

## FRIED POTATOES

| | |
|---|---|
| 6 boiled potatoes | Salt |
| 2 onions | Pepper |
| ½ teaspoon celery seed | 3 tablespoons butter or fat |

Slice the onions and potatoes. Heat the pan and melt the butter. Put in the onions and potatoes, cover until browned on one side, taking care not to let them burn. Uncover, turn and stir, cover again. When nearly ready, add seasoning, cover, and finish frying. If done in this manner, there should be a crust on the bottom. Serves 4.

## CREAMED POTATOES

6 boiled potatoes
1 diced pepper
2 tablespoons butter

1 tablespoon flour
3 cups milk
Salt and pepper

Parsley

Cook the pepper in water until tender, then chop. Make a sauce of butter, flour, and milk. Dice the potatoes and add to the sauce with the pepper. Season and let simmer. If a red pepper is used, sprinkle with minced parsley. If a green pepper, substitute celery seed.

## POTATOES SCALLOPED WITH HAM

1 small slice ham
6 or 8 potatoes
1½ cups milk
1 teaspoon minced parsley

4 tablespoons butter
2 tablespoons flour
Onion salt
Salt and pepper

Crumbs

Butter a baking dish, cover the bottom with small pieces of the ham. Slice the potatoes thin, add a layer to cover the ham. Sprinkle with flour, dot with butter, season, and pour in milk to cover. Add another layer of ham and a layer of potatoes. Dredge with flour, season, add milk. Add more layers of potatoes if needed to three-quarters fill the pan. Milk should just cover the potatoes. Sprinkle parsley and a dusting of bread crumbs over the top. Dot with butter. Place baking dish in a large pan with a little water in the bottom, to catch any overflow of milk as the potatoes cook. Bake in 350° oven until potatoes are tender. Serves 6.

## POTATO CAKES

12 strips bacon
¾ cup onions, chopped fine
3 eggs, beaten

4 cups mashed potatoes
½ cup milk
Salt and pepper

Fry the bacon and drain on brown paper. Pour off fat, measure 3 tablespoons, return to pan. Brown the onions lightly in bacon fat. Beat the eggs, mix with potatoes, add just enough of the milk to handle when shaping into cakes, season, add onion. Shape into oval cakes about ¾-inch thick. Brown lightly in the bacon fat in which onions were sautéed, turning to brown other side. Cover and steam over low heat for 5 minutes. Serve with the bacon. 4 servings.

*Wilhelmina Gerhardt Stinson*

## DUTCH POTATO "SALAD"

6 large potatoes, boiled and mashed    3 large onions, chopped
12 strips bacon    Salt and pepper

Fry the bacon, drain, and crumble. Brown onions in bacon fat. Mix onions, mashed potatoes, and bacon, salt and pepper, return to pan with some of the bacon fat, brown quickly, turn, as an omelet, and brown other side. Steam, covered, for a few minutes and serve at once. 4 servings.

*Quakertown Grange*

## HOT POTATO "SALAD"

2 tablespoons butter    1 green pepper
2 tablespoons flour    ¾ cup chopped celery and leaves
1 cup milk    1 cup chopped onions
Salt and pepper    ½ teaspoon prepared mustard
6 cups cooked potatoes    1 cup prepared salad dressing
1 red pepper    2 hard-boiled eggs

Make a white sauce with butter, flour, and milk. Season. Dice the cooked potatoes, add and simmer in the white sauce for a few minutes. Chop the peppers and add to mixture, with celery and onions. Just before serving mix the mustard with the salad dressing, drop in the chopped vegetables, combine with the potatoes in white sauce and serve at once, garnished with the chopped hard-boiled eggs. (Have potatoes and sauce hot, so dish can be served warm.) Sprinkle with chopped parsley and paprika. Serves 6-8.

*Mary Louise Lewis*

## POTATO PIE

4 cups raw potatoes    1 pound pork sausage or frankfurters
Butter    1½ cups milk
Salt and pepper    Minced parsley

### Pastry

1½ cups flour    5 tablespoons butter
¾ teaspoon salt    1 egg yolk
2 tablespoons ice water

Sift flour and salt and work in butter for pastry. Mix lightly. Beat egg yolk with ice water, add and mix. Roll into a ball and wrap in waxed paper and chill in refrigerator while preparing filling. Grate the raw potatoes or chop very fine. Cut sausage or frankfurters into small pieces. Roll out bottom crust and place on deep 9-inch pie dish. Dot crust with butter, put in ⅓ of the potatoes, sprinkle with pepper, salt, and parsley, make a layer of ⅓ of the sausage, repeat twice. Pour milk over top, saving some if dish is nearly filled. Roll out top crust, gash a cross in center, seal, and crimp on pie. Turn back corners of crust at center to permit pouring in of more milk as needed in baking. Bake in 375° oven for about 1 hour, or until potatoes are soft and crust is brown.

## SWEET POTATO BALLS

2 cups mashed sweet potatoes
2 eggs, beaten separately
1 tablespoon melted butter
1 teaspoon lemon juice

½ teaspoon salt
1 teaspoon minced parsley
Bread crumbs ⎫
1 beaten egg ⎭ for batter

Mix salt and bread crumbs and beat 1 egg lightly to dip the potato balls. Blend all the other ingredients and form into balls. Let stand a few minutes, then dip first into the crumbs, then into the egg, then in crumbs again. Fry quickly in deep, hot fat. Drain on brown paper. Makes about 10.

## BAKED LIMA BEANS

2 cups dried lima beans
6 slices bacon
1 teaspoon mustard
2 tablespoons brown sugar
½ cup boiling water

1½ teaspoons salt
½ teaspoon pepper
½ teaspoon ginger
3 tablespoons molasses

Cover the beans with cold water and soak overnight. In the morning pour off the water, cover with fresh water in a saucepan, and simmer until beans are tender. Drain, put in beanpot with the bacon. Mix mustard, sugar, salt, pepper, and ginger with a little water. Add molasses and mix. Pour over the beans to cover. Add the boiling water if there is not enough liquid. Bake in beanpot or earthen bowl, covered, for 4 hours at 250°. Add hot water occasionally if the beans seem too dry. Stir. Uncover and raise the heat to 300°, bake until beans are tender and brown on top. Serves 6.

*Mrs. Philip B. Woodroofe*

## PORK AND BEANS

2 cups small soup beans
4 pork chops
½ teaspoon salt

2 tablespoons molasses
1 tablespoon brown sugar
¼ teaspoon pepper

Soak dried beans overnight. Next day drain and place in kettle with boiling water to cover. Simmer until the beans swell and skins begin to crack. Select small chops, parboil quickly, and put in a beanpot with the beans. Take 2 cups of the water in which beans were boiled, add salt, molasses, brown sugar, and pepper, mix and pour over the beans. A pinch of powdered ginger will vastly improve the flavor. Cover and bake in 250° oven for 4 hours, adding bean water from time to time. Uncover beans and finish baking. Pork should be thoroughly done and beans browned on top. Serves 4-6.

## HOLLAND HOUSE BAKED BEANS

3 pounds dried lima beans
1 can corn syrup
1 quart canned tomatoes

1 large yellow onion (not Bermuda)
1 teaspoon dry mustard
2 pounds smoked ham

Soak the beans overnight and drain. Mix the other ingredients, cut the ham in small pieces, and put all together in large beanpot. There will be enough liquid to start the baking but hot water will have to be added from time to time during baking. Bake in 275° oven for about 6 hours. If you have less time, parboil the beans before baking and bake for 3 hours. This must be done very carefully and the slow method is better. This is a picnic-sized recipe and serves 25.

*Gertrude Rickert Holland*

## STRING BEANS

1 quart string beans
1 teaspoon salt

1 stalk fresh mint
1 tablespoon butter

⅛ teaspoon pepper

Cut the beans fine, lengthwise, as for French beans. Plunge into a panful of boiling water and cook quickly. Drain, add fresh boiling water, salt, and chopped mint. Cook a few minutes longer, until beans are tender. Drain, add butter, pepper, and salt and shake over the flame until piping hot. Serves 6.

## SOUR BEANS

1 quart fresh butter beans

1 sliced onion

Cook the beans in boiling water until tender, about ½ hour. Drain. Slice the onion and mix with beans. Make dressing:

| | |
|---|---|
| 1 cup sour cream | 2 tablespoons sugar |
| 1½ tablespoons vinegar | ½ teaspoon salt |

Pinch of cayenne pepper

Mix cream, vinegar, and sugar, add salt and pepper, and stir lightly. Pour over the beans and onion. Let stand ½ hour and serve. Serves 6-8.

## FRIED EGGPLANT

| | |
|---|---|
| 1 eggplant | 1 beaten egg |
| Salt | 1 tablespoon milk |
| Pepper | Bread crumbs |

Peel a medium-sized eggplant and slice thin. Salt each slice liberally, pile up, and top with a weighted plate. Drain for ½ hour. Dip the slices, first in egg mixed with milk and pepper, then in crumbs. Fry quickly in hot lard to a golden brown. Serve with homemade catsup. Serves 6-8.

## FRIED TOMATOES

| | |
|---|---|
| 5 tomatoes, not too ripe | Milk |
| 1 beaten egg | ½ teaspoon sugar |
| Bread crumbs | Salt and pepper |

Fat for frying

Slice the tomatoes crosswise into thick slices. Mix egg and bread crumbs to form batter, thinning with a little milk. Sprinkle tomato slices with a very little sugar, salt, and pepper, dip in batter and fry in deep, hot fat. Turn carefully and brown on both sides. Make a sauce from any broken tomatoes and crumbs left in the pan by stirring in a little milk and a sprinkling of flour, if needed. Pour the sauce over the tomatoes.

*Mrs. Donald L. Helfferich*

## DRIED CORN

| | |
|---|---|
| 1 cup dried corn | 1 tablespoon butter |
| 1 teaspoon sugar | ½ teaspoon salt |
| ⅓ cup cream | ¼ teaspoon pepper |

Dried corn is a famous Pennsylvania dish. It may be oven- or sun-dried, but the process is unnecessary nowadays because excellent dried corn can be bought already dried and packaged. Follow the directions on the package carefully, for cooking time varies with the brand. Home-dried corn can be prepared by soaking the corn overnight, draining, adding sugar, and simmering slowly for an hour or so in water to cover, stirring to prevent scorching. Add water as needed. Add cream, butter, salt, and pepper, reheat and serve. Dried corn always accompanies the Pennsylvania Thanksgiving turkey. Serves 6.

## CORN PIE I

Fresh corn                      ½ cup butter
Salt and pepper                 1½ cups milk

### Pastry

1 cup flour                     4 tablespoons butter
½ teaspoon salt                 1 egg yolk
                2 tablespoons ice water

Sift flour and salt into a bowl, work in butter with 2 silver knives. Beat the egg and mix with flour. Stir water in lightly and blend. Roll out dough on a floured board, ⅛-inch thick. Line a deep 7-inch pie dish with the pastry and set in refrigerator while grating fresh corn from the cobs. Fill the pastry shell with the corn, season with salt and pepper, dot with butter. Roll out the top crust, slash a cross in the center, and place on the pie, sealing and crimping the edge. Turn back the 4 triangles of the crust and pour enough milk through the opening to almost fill the lower crust. Bake in 375°-400° oven for 10 minutes to prevent crust from becoming soggy. Then lower heat and bake until crust is golden brown. Cooking time, about ½ hour. Serves 4.

*Mrs. Harry Hess Reichard*

## CORN PIE II

Fresh corn                      Butter
1 small raw potato              Salt and pepper
2 hard-boiled eggs              Whole milk

### Pastry

1½ cups sifted flour            6 tablespoons butter
¾ teaspoon salt                 1 egg yolk
                2½ tablespoons ice water

Sift flour and salt, work in butter, and mix lightly. Beat the egg yolk with water and add. Mix, chill in refrigerator ½ hour. Roll out dough on floured board to ⅛-inch thickness. Line a deep, 9-inch pie dish with pastry and chill again while cutting corn from cobs. This size pie requires about 8 ears of Golden Bantam corn to fill. Mince the raw potato (to bind) and add, with chopped hard-boiled eggs, to the corn. Pour mixture into pie shell. Season and dot with butter. Roll out top crust and gash a cross in the center. Put on pie, sealing edges tightly. Fold back the corners at the center and pour in milk to keep filling moist. Add more milk as baking progresses. Bake at 375° for 10 minutes, lower heat, and bake about 20 minutes longer. Serve with a pitcher of hot milk. 6 portions.

*Mrs. Ira F. Zartman*

## FRIED CORN

6 ears corn
6 slices bacon

¾ cup cream or milk, and water
Salt and pepper

Cut corn from cobs. Fry bacon and drain on brown paper. Pour off bacon fat, measuring ⅓ cup. Return this to the pan and heat. Pour corn into pan and fry lightly, stirring to prevent burning, for about 5 minutes. Add mixed cream and water, season. Simmer 15 minutes, or until thick and nicely browned.

*Mary Louise Lewis*

## OYSTER CORN FRITTERS

2 cups corn pulp
2 eggs, separated

2 tablespoons flour
Pepper and salt

Mix corn pulp with beaten egg yolks, flour, and seasoning. Add stiffly beaten egg whites and blend. Drop by spoonfuls into deep, hot fat and fry until golden brown.

*Quakertown Grange*

## CORN PUDDING

2 eggs
6 ears corn

4 tablespoons milk
1 tablespoon butter
Salt and pepper

Beat eggs, grate corn, mix with the egg yolks. Melt butter, add with seasoning and milk. Beat egg whites stiff, fold in. Bake in a buttered baking dish placed in a pan of hot water, in 350° oven for ½ hour. Serves 4.

## CREAMED CABBAGE

½ cabbage, sliced thin
½ cup cream

2 tablespoons butter
Pepper and salt

Slice cabbage as for coleslaw and place in deep, hot frying pan. Cover with 2 cups boiling water. Cover pan and simmer for 10 minutes. Pour off water, add cream, butter, and seasoning. Simmer 2 or 3 minutes longer. Serve hot. 6 portions.

*Jeanette Heimbach*

## RED CABBAGE

2 small heads red cabbage
1 tablespoon fat
3 tablespoons vinegar

1 teaspoon salt
1 onion
4 whole cloves

Slice cabbage very thin. Heat fat in large frying pan and toss in the cabbage. Add vinegar (to retain color of cabbage) and salt, stir gently. Stick cloves in medium-sized onion and bury it under the cabbage. Add water to cover, place a tight lid on the pan, and simmer very slowly for 25 minutes, or until cabbage is tender. Add water as needed while cooking. Serves 6-8.

*Jeanette Heimbach*

## STUFFED CABBAGE

1 head cabbage
3 tablespoons butter
½ cup bread crumbs

1 beaten egg
1-1½ cups cooked pork or chicken
Salt and pepper

Cut out the heart of the cabbage, mix crumbs, egg, and meat and season highly, as you prefer. Place cabbage in a small bag to keep leaves in place, and place in deep saucepan or a kettle. Cover with boiling water. Simmer until cabbage is tender, about ½ hour. Remove from water, take off bag, melt the butter on top of the cabbage, and serve. Serves 6-8.

*Kate Weaver*

## FILLED CABBAGE

1 small head cabbage
Seasoning
1 cup diced, cooked potatoes
½ cup bread crumbs

1 tablespoon minced onion
2 beaten eggs
1 teaspoon minced parsley
2 tablespoons butter

Drop the cabbage into boiling, salted water and cook slowly for about 10 minutes, or until leaves can be pulled apart. Remove from water, cut out the heart, fill center with mixed potatoes, crumbs, onion, egg, parsley, and seasoning. Tie a string around the cabbage to hold it together. Simmer in boiling water until tender, about 15 minutes. Brown the butter, untie the cabbage, pour butter over it, and serve. 6 servings.

*Mrs. Victor Boyer*

## CABBAGE WITH CARAWAY SEED

1 small cabbage
1 tablespoon fat
2 tablespoons vinegar

1 teaspoon salt
¼ teaspoon pepper
1 teaspoon caraway seed

Slice cabbage very thin. Melt fat in large frying pan, put in the cabbage, add vinegar, salt, and pepper. Add water to cover, place tight lid on pan and simmer slowly for 30-40 minutes. Sprinkle with caraway seeds and continue cooking 5 or 10 minutes until cabbage is tender. (Add more water while cooking, if needed.) Serves 4-6.

*Tim Palmer*

## BAKED ONIONS

Onions                          Butter
Milk                            Salt and pepper
Flour                           Paprika

Select medium-sized onions. Butter a baking dish and fill with whole onions crowded tightly together. Cover with milk, sprinkle lightly with flour, and dot with butter. Bake in 375° oven, covered, for 1 hour. Uncover and bake until onions are tender.

## ONION PIE

3 cups sliced onions            1 teaspoon sugar
4 cups water                    ¼ teaspoon salt
8 slices bacon                  2 cups milk
3 eggs                          Pinch of nutmeg or caraway seed

### Pastry

1 cup sifted flour              4 tablespoons butter
¼ teaspoon salt                 1 egg yolk
            2 tablespoons ice water

Sift flour and salt into a large bowl, cut in the butter with silver knives, and blend, add egg yolk, mix, add ice water, and pat lightly into a ball. Wrap in waxed paper and place in refrigerator for ½ hour (while you fry the bacon). Roll out dough lightly on floured board to ⅛-inch thickness. Line a deep 9-inch pie dish with the pastry, trim edge high, turn back and down, and crimp to build up the rim. Prick bottom with a fork and bake in 500° oven for 10 minutes. Remove from oven. When bacon is fried, drain on brown paper and reserve. Simmer the onions in water for 20 minutes and drain. Beat the eggs, add sugar and salt. Scald milk and add with the onions. Pour into pie shell, scatter crumbled bacon over the top, dust lightly with nutmeg or caraway seed, bake in 350° oven for about 30-40 minutes, or until a knife slipped into the custard comes out clean.

*Herbert Gerhardt Stinson*

In case you have an idea that Pennsylvania Dutch food is entirely farm cookery you might be interested to compare this recipe with one for *La Quiche Lorraine* in your French cookbook. Because if you do, and substitute the onions for Swiss cheese, you'll find the recipes are otherwise identical. There is no reason why Pennsylvania Dutch onion pie cannot be used as an appetizer just as is its French cousin!

## SUGAR PEAS

| | |
|---|---|
| 1 small piece ham | ½ teaspoon salt |
| 1 pound sugar peas | 2 tablespoons butter |
| 1 small onion | 1 teaspoon sugar |

Sugar peas are particular Pennsylvania Dutch favorites. They have to be snapped up where and when they can be found, as their season is short. Cook them in the pods and do not cut or sliver. Simply "string" them. Boil the ham until it is almost cooked. Then drop in the peas, add sugar and the tiniest onion you can find for flavoring. Tiny new potatoes may be cooked with the peas if you like. Or they may be cooked in meat stock without the ham. However you prepare them, when the peas are cooked (about 20 minutes or when tender), melt the butter with them and season. 4 servings.

## SOUR-SWEET BEETS

| | |
|---|---|
| 2 cups boiled beets | ½ teaspoon salt, level measure |
| ⅓ cup sugar | ⅓ cup cider vinegar |
| 1 level tablespoon flour | 2 cloves |
| 1 tablespoon butter | |

Select tiny beets. Cut off the tops, leaving a bit of stem, wash and put in saucepan, half covered with boiling water. Boil gently for ½-1 hour, adding water as needed. When beets are tender cool and skin. Place over boiling water in double boiler the sugar, flour, salt and vinegar. Stir and blend until smooth, add cloves, cook until sauce is clear. Add beets. Simmer ½ hour. Remove cloves, add butter, blend, and serve.

# SALADS

You won't find a tossed salad or a drop of olive oil in the lot of salad recipes that follow. And you can toss your idea of crisp, chilled greens out the window because you're going to get a lot of hot dressings and wilted greens if you're going to eat Pennsylvania Dutch salads. But before you decide to skip this section you might give thought to cucumbers languishing in sour cream and tender, young dandelions coated with delicious bacon dressing. And, surely, you're not going to forget coleslaw and potato salad—those Pennsylvania Dutch standbys! If you'll linger a few minutes, I have an idea you can be sold on Pennsylvania Dutch salads, after all.

## CENTER COUNTY DANDELION SALAD

| | |
|---|---|
| 2 quarts dandelion greens | ¼ pound bacon, diced |

### Dressing

| | |
|---|---|
| 2 eggs | ½ cup water |
| ½ cup sugar | ½ cup vinegar |

### Sliced, hard-boiled eggs

Wash and pick over the dandelions, cut fine. Fry the bacon until crisp. Beat eggs, add sugar, water, and vinegar. Stir this mixture with the hot, fried bacon. Stir over low heat until the dressing thickens, then pour over the dandelions. Mix well, garnish with hard-boiled eggs. (If dressing is too sweet, add vinegar; if too sour, add sugar.) Endive, lettuce, poke shoots, or any kind of greens may be substituted for dandelions.

*Mrs. Ora Cronister Yoder*

## DANDELION GREENS

| | |
|---|---|
| Dandelion greens | 4 slices bacon |

### Dressing

| | |
|---|---|
| 2 tablespoons bacon fat | 1 egg yolk |
| 3 tablespoons vinegar | 1 teaspoon flour |
| 2 tablespoons sour cream | ½ teaspoon salt |

### 1 tablespoon sugar

Select fresh, young dandelion greens, using about 1 pound. Wash and shake dry. Fry bacon, remove from pan, and crumble. Drain off bacon fat from pan, return 2 tablespoonfuls. Add vinegar and sour cream to fat. Add a little water to egg yolk and blend with flour. Stir into the mixture in the pan over low heat, stirring constantly as dressing thickens. Add salt and sugar. Bring to a quick boil and pour over greens at once. Scatter bacon on top.

*Mrs. Thomas B. Keck*

## GREENS WITH HOT SAUCE

Dandelions, endive, or lettuce     1 or 2 eggs
4 slices bacon     3 tablespoons sugar
½ cup vinegar     Pinch of salt
⅔ cup water     Pinch of dry mustard

Cut thin slices of bacon in 1-inch squares and fry. Mix the vinegar with half the water and slowly add to bacon and bacon fat. Beat the eggs, add them to the remainder of the water with sugar and salt. Heat. Turn to low heat under the bacon and slowly add the egg mixture. Stir constantly. Cook until sauce is smooth and slightly thickened. Pour over washed and drained greens. Serve immediately.

"This has been handed down from my grandmother by word of mouth. A Baltimore friend who ate dandelion greens this way for the first time said, 'Well, I daresay anything would taste good with *that* sauce.' "

*Mrs. Ira F. Zartman*


## GREENS WITH MUSTARD DRESSING

### Greens

2 tablespoons sugar     2 eggs
1 tablespoon flour     ¾ cup milk
1 teaspoon dry mustard     ½ cup vinegar
½ teaspoon salt     ½ cup water

Mix together the sugar, flour, mustard, and salt. Break the eggs into the mixture and blend thoroughly. Add milk, stirring constantly. When the dressing begins to thicken, add vinegar and water that have been heated together. Cook until thick, pour over washed, drained greens.

*Mrs. W. H. Anewalt*


## DUTCH SALAD

### Dandelion greens or endive

1 tablespoon flour     2 cups cold water
1 tablespoon sugar     4 slices bacon
2 tablespoons vinegar     Bacon fat
1 egg yolk     1 egg white

Wash and drain the greens. Mix flour, sugar, and vinegar with egg yolk. Add water. Fry the bacon, remove from pan, and set aside. Measure 2 tablespoons of the bacon fat, cool slightly, return to pan. Over low heat stir the flour mixture slowly into the fat. Cook until dressing thickens. Beat egg white and stir in. Stir the greens quickly into the boiling sauce and take out just as greens begin to wilt. Add bacon. Serve at once. If this dressing is used for lettuce, place lettuce in bowl and pour over it. Crumble bacon on top.

*Eleanor-Rose Roth*

## SPINACH WITH DRESSING

4 cups raw, chopped spinach,
  packed solidly

4 slices bacon,
  fried crisp

### Dressing

2 tablespoons bacon fat
2 tablespoons flour
1 teaspoon salt

2½ tablespoons sugar
1 cup milk
2 slightly beaten eggs

3 tablespoons cider vinegar

Fry bacon until crisp. Remove from pan and crumble. Measure bacon fat and return just 2 tablespoons to the pan. At low heat slowly add flour, salt, and sugar to bacon fat. Stir constantly while slowly adding milk. Bring to a boil and stir for 3 minutes. Remove from stove and slowly pour into a bowl with the beaten eggs. Add vinegar and blend. Place mixture in top of double boiler to keep hot. Wash the spinach carefully and drain. 15 minutes before serving, mix with the dressing and bacon. If this dressing is used with lettuce, proceed in the same manner but serve immediately after mixing.

*Gertrude Rickert Holland*

## POTATO AND ENDIVE SALAD

6 medium-sized potatoes
1 head endive
1 medium-sized onion, chopped
1 stalk celery, chopped
3 cups water
2 tablespoons sugar

2 tablespoons vinegar
1 teaspoon salt
1 beaten egg
4 strips diced bacon
½ cup flour
1 hard-boiled egg

Boil potatoes in jackets, peel, and dice. Wash endive, drain, and cut in small pieces. Add to potatoes with onion and celery. Combine water, sugar, vinegar, salt and egg, and set aside. Fry bacon slowly in large skillet. When almost done, add flour and stir until blended. Pour in egg mixture and stir until thickened. Pour sauce over potatoes and endive in a bowl, garnish with hard-boiled egg, and serve at once. Serves 6.

*Mrs. W. H. Miller*

## POTATO SALAD I

| | |
|---|---|
| 8 potatoes | 1 large onion, sliced |
| 2 stalks celery, diced | 2 hard-boiled eggs |

### Dressing

| | |
|---|---|
| 2 beaten eggs | ½ cup vinegar |
| 1 cup cream | ½ teaspoon salt |
| | ¼ teaspoon pepper |

Boil the potatoes in their jackets, peel while warm, and dice. Beat the eggs, mix with the cream, add vinegar and seasoning, bring to a boil. Mix potatoes, celery, and onion and pour dressing over them. Slice hard-boiled eggs over top and serve.

*Mrs. Victor Boyer*

## POTATO SALAD II

| | |
|---|---|
| 6 slices bacon | 1 cup celery, chopped |
| 4 beaten eggs | 4 hard-boiled eggs |
| 4 tablespoons sugar | 1 tablespoon grated onion |
| 3 tablespoons vinegar | 1 teaspoon celery seed |
| 1 tablespoon flour | 1 cup prepared salad dressing |
| 1 tablespoon bacon fat | 1 cup heavy cream |
| 8 boiled potatoes | 1 teaspoon salt |

Fry the bacon lightly, remove from fat and crumble. Mix beaten eggs, sugar, and vinegar. Smooth in the flour and cook the mixture in a saucepan over low heat, stirring until it thickens. Add bacon fat. Blend and cool. Dice the boiled potatoes, celery, and hard-boiled eggs and mix together. Add onion and celery seed. When the dressing has cooled, add prepared salad dressing, cream, and salt. Beat together well. Place other ingredients in a large bowl, add the crumbled bacon, pour dressing over all, mix well. This is a picnic-sized recipe and will serve a dozen people.

*Elizabeth Schramek*

## COLESLAW I

| | |
|---|---|
| 1 cabbage, sliced thin | 2 onions, sliced |
| 2 stalks celery, diced | 4 carrots, sliced fine |

### Dressing

| | |
|---|---|
| 2 tablespoons sugar | 2 tablepsoons vinegar |
| ½ cup cream | ½ teaspoon salt |
| | Pepper |

Slice cabbage and cut up other vegetables. Place in large bowl, pour ice water over all, and let stand in refrigerator 1 hour. Drain. Make dressing by combining other ingredients. Pour over vegetables and mix thoroughly. Serves 6.

*Mrs. John H. Adams*

## COLESLAW II

### 1 cabbage, shredded

| | |
|---|---|
| 1½ tablespoons vinegar | 2 tablespoons sugar |
| ½ teaspoon salt | 1 cup sour cream |
| ¼ teaspoon pepper | 1 tablespoon mayonnaise |

Shred cabbage very fine. Make dressing by combining vinegar, salt, pepper, sugar, cream, and mayonnaise. Pour over cabbage and mix well.

*Ida Altemose Anewalt*

## COLESLAW III

| | |
|---|---|
| 1 cabbage, shredded | 5 slices bacon |

### Dressing

| | |
|---|---|
| 1 beaten egg | ½ teaspoon salt |
| 1 tablespoon flour | 1 cup milk |
| 2 tablespoons sugar | 3 tablespoons vinegar |

Fry bacon and crumble. Mix dressing, add bacon, and place in small saucepan. Bring slowly to a boil, stirring constantly. Pour over cabbage and serve hot. Serves 6.

*Mrs. John Baer Stoudt*

## COLESLAW IV

| | |
|---|---|
| 1 small head cabbage | 1 teaspoon celery seed |
| ½ teaspoon salt | 1 hard-boiled egg |
| 3 teaspoons sugar | ¼ cup white vinegar |

### ½ cup sweet cream

Shred the cabbage finely, add salt, sugar, and celery seed. Mix well. Set aside for ½ hour. Slice the egg. Add vinegar to cabbage and stir well. Add cream and blend. Place slices of egg on top and serve. Serves 6.

*Mary Huyett*

## CUCUMBERS IN SOUR CREAM

| | |
|---|---|
| 3 cucumbers | 2 tablespoons sugar |
| 3 medium-sized onions | 1 cup sour cream |
| ½ teaspoon salt | 1½ tablespoons vinegar |

Peel cucumbers, slice and pile up, salting each piece. Let stand 10 minutes. Slice onions, combine with cucumbers. Beat sugar, cream, and vinegar together. Pour dressing over the cucumbers and onions. Serves 8.

*Mary A. Saeger*

## MRS. SHOLLER'S TOMATO SALAD

| | |
|---|---|
| 4 large tomatoes | Pepper and salt |
| 2 onions | Lettuce |

Slice sun-ripened tomatoes in thick pieces and garnish with thickly sliced onions. Serve on chilled lettuce, using salt, lots of freshly ground pepper and no dressing. Serves 4.

*Mrs. Susan Laudenslager*

## BALD EAGLE VALLEY TOMATO SALAD

| | |
|---|---|
| 4 large tomatoes | 1 tablespoon sugar |
| ½ cup vinegar | 1 tablespoon minced onions |
| ¼ cup water | Black pepper |

"This is a sweet-sour dish I have enjoyed every summer since I can remember. As my mother, Mrs. Jacob H. Yoder, made it: cut the ripe tomatoes in chunks to fill a dish. Dilute the vinegar with water, so it isn't too sour. Sweeten with sugar, mix with the onions, and pour over the tomatoes. Sprinkle with black pepper and eat!"

*Donald Herbert Yoder, co-author,* Songs Along the Mahantongo

## WILTED LETTUCE

| | |
|---|---|
| 1 head Boston or leaf lettuce | ¼ cup vinegar |
| 6 slices bacon | 1 teaspoon sugar |
| 2 tablespoons bacon fat | Salt and pepper |
| 1 tablespoon minced chives | |

Fry the bacon, drain on brown paper, and crumble. Pour off the bacon fat, measure 2 tablespoons, and return to the pan. Heat the fat, adding vinegar, sugar, salt, and pepper. Sprinkle chives over the lettuce in a bowl, pour the dressing on top, sprinkle with bacon, and serve at once. Serves 4.

*Mary Louise Lewis*

# Sweets
# and Sours

*Pennsylvania harvest*

THERE has been much pleasantry about the "seven sweets and seven sours" of Pennsylvania Dutch cookery. But any Dutch housewife limited to just seven would consider herself cruelly circumscribed. Sweets and sours should be eaten, not counted! Their spicy flavors and their infinite variety are so tempting that the only dispassionate appraisal they ever earn is at the county fair. There, if you *must* count them, you can wander through the array of blue-ribboned exhibits and add away! But the immediate result will be gastronomic frustration!

At the Allentown Fair or the Reading Fair you can obtain a good idea of the whole year's farm activity, for it is all spread out before you. You can admire the prize cattle and swine, poultry and grain, pumpkins and apples. You can see the handsome results of the long winter evenings on the farm: quilts, hooked rugs, and crocheted tablecloths. And you can see some fascinating old furniture: stenciled chairs, water benches, dough troughs—even an old cradle that winds up and rocks itself for fifteen minutes. The utilitarian objects of Grandfather's day are, of course, antiques now. The farmer knows this, for he has shown the same heirlooms at the fair year after year, just as his wife has gone on exhibiting her grandmother's "show towels" and woven counterpanes. It is all part of the fair routine.

After the farmer has made his careful comparisons in the exhibition building, inspected the new farm machinery, satisfied himself that his year's appraisal of crops and progress is a good one, he sallies forth to collect his family and enjoy the balance of their annual holiday. He finds them pausing to listen to the barkers along the midway, grinning at the heckling going on in broad Pennsylvania Dutch. Pushing and jostling good-naturedly, along with everyone else, they make their way to the nearest stand to buy the hot dogs smothered in sauerkraut. The youngsters beg for huge blobs of pink spun sugar on sticks and get them. The races are as exciting as ever, and tense crowds pack the grandstands. True, the side shows are the same old frauds they've always been but that is as it should be, part of the fun. The beer stand does a rushing business, with constant reunions of old friends come from far and near. Withal, it's been a heartening day, and when at last the family turns homeward, the exhausted children fall asleep in the back seat, Mother steals a quick look at the prize ribbons in her purse, and Father, gazing fixedly at the highway ahead, quietly plans his next year's triumphs.

But "the morning hours have gold in hand," his grandsire used to say, so next day the farmer is up before sunrise. He is going to give back to the farm the day he has stolen. His wife, however, is not ready to settle down to the year-long routine. She is still in a gregarious, if not garrulous mood. It is a fine, bright day. She begins to think about apple butter.

With a little persuasion the farmer loads his battered truck with apples and goes off to the cider mill, just as his father loaded the old two-horse wagon before him. Empty barrels for the cider are balanced on top of the apples, and he rumbles down the road in pleasant anticipation of the spicy odors that soon will be filling the fall air. While he is gone, the neighbors gather and the women and girls set to work peeling and cutting the huge quantity of apples that will be needed. The boys keep bringing apples and more apples in baskets and find time to gather wood for the fire. The great apple-butter kettle is brought out and set up in the yard. By the time the farmer comes back with the cider, the fire is burning brightly under the kettle and in goes the cider. A penny or a peach pit is dropped on the bottom to prevent burning, the cider is brought to a boil, and the apples are poured in. Then the stirring begins, for apple butter must be stirred constantly, even if there is a penny in the kettle. But stirring can be an agreeable occupation, especially if the right young people stir in combination. It can be distracting too—and burned apple butter is a dead giveaway!

So another day wears pleasantly into evening. The fair is gone over thoroughly, crops are catalogued, and neighborhood news is brought up to date. The young people stir the apple butter, and the "old folks" with the redolence of apples filling the air decide that yes, smokehouse apples do make the best applesauce, that pound sweets are best for dumplings, and Paradise apples make the finest *Schnitz*. Cider, they agree, can be made from almost any kind of apple—but here there is an interruption: the apple butter is finished!

## LATTWERK
### (Apple Butter)

2 quarts Schnitz
6 cups apple cider
1½ cups sugar (white or brown)

½ teaspoon allspice
½ teaspoon cloves
1 teaspoon cinnamon

¼ teaspoon salt

Peel and quarter the apples for "*Schnitz.*" Boil the cider in a large kettle until it has cooked down to half the quantity. Drop the apples in the cider and cook for 20 minutes, or until soft and pulpy. Stir constantly to prevent scorching. Put the fruit and liquid through a sieve, add sugar, spices, and salt and cook until mixture is thick and smooth. The old method was to put the apple butter in earthenware crocks, but this is a small recipe and will fill about 3 pint-sized jars. Pour apple butter into hot jars, fill within ½-inch of the top, partially seal, and place on rack at bottom of a large kettle half full of boiling water. Tighten the lids. Add more boiling water to top the jars by an inch or two. When water again comes to a boil, allow the jars to remain in water for 5 minutes. Seal. Makes 3 pints.

*Mrs. Arthur J. McShane*

## APPLESAUCE

8 sour apples
Water
½ teaspoon salt

3 whole cloves
1 cup sugar
Cinnamon

Wash, peel, and cut up apples. Place in pan, cover with water, add salt and cloves and simmer 5 minutes. Add sugar. Cook slowly until apples are soft. Remove cloves, strain applesauce, adding more sugar if needed. Cool. Sprinkle with a little cinnamon.

## BAKED APPLES

Apples
Cloves

1 cup sugar
Cream

Wash apples, core, and peel top halves. Crowd into a baking dish, pour in boiling water to cover to depth of one-third, cover, and place in oven to steam. When apples are fairly tender when tested with a toothpick, remove, pour off any water remaining and save it, stick a whole clove into each apple, sprinkle with sugar, and return to 425° oven uncovered. As apples bake baste with remaining water in which they were steamed. When they are crisp and golden brown take out of oven and cool. Remove cloves. Serve with cream.

## GOOSEBERRY BUTTER

4 cups gooseberries                    4 cups sugar

Wash and drain the berries, mash, and measure. Place pulp and juice in a pan and bring to a boil, stirring constantly. Add sugar; stir until sugar is dissolved. Simmer about 20 minutes, or until syrup threads when dropped from a spoon. Pour into glasses. Makes 6 6-ounce glasses.

## GRAPE BUTTER

1 pint grape pulp to                   1 pound sugar
                                       Salt

Skin the grapes, put pulp in one saucepan, skins in another. Scald the pulp. Cook skins until they are tender. Combine in one kettle. Simmer until seeds can be seen clearly. Rub through a sieve. Return juice to kettle and add sugar. Stir over low heat until sugar is dissolved. Add a pinch of salt. Increase heat and boil rapidly until mixture thickens, stirring constantly. Pour into hot jelly glasses. (If you find these proportions too sweet, enough more grapes may be added to make the proportion one pint to ¼ pound.)

## GRAPE CONSERVE

4 pounds Concord grapes               5 cups sugar
1 cup walnut meats                    ¼ teaspoon salt
2 oranges, juice and grated rind      1 cup seedless raisins

Wash and drain grapes. Separate pulp from skins. Place pulp in a saucepan and cook 10 minutes, or until seeds can be seen plainly. Rub through a sieve. Cool. Pour boiling water over the nutmeats, drain, and cut fine. Grate the orange skins. Add orange juice, grated rind, sugar, salt, and raisins to the grape pulp; stir over low heat until sugar is dissolved. Increase heat, boil until mixture thickens, stirring constantly. Add grape skins, boil 5 minutes longer, or until mixture is quite thick. Add nutmeats. Pour into hot jelly glases, cool, and seal with paraffin. Makes 8 6-ounce glases.

*Martha Twining*

## PLUM CONSERVE

3 pounds plums                        1 cup seedless raisins
2 oranges, juice and grated rind      4 cups sugar
                  1 cup  nutmeats

Wash plums, cut up and pit. Grate orange skin, squeeze juice. Chop raisins. Put plums, orange juice and grated rind, raisins in large saucepan. Add sugar and stir over low heat until sugar is dissolved. Raise heat and boil rapidly for about 20 minutes, stirring all the time, when mixture should have thickened. Add chopped nutmeats. Pour into hot jelly glasses. Cool and seal with paraffin. Fills 8 6-ounce glasses.

## QUINCE HONEY

4 large quinces                                    4 cups water
4 cups sugar                                       3 tablespoons lemon juice

Peel and chop the quinces. Place pulp in saucepan with water. Stir until mixture boils. Add sugar, simmer 20 minutes. Add lemon juice, increase heat, cook 10 minutes longer, until syrup is clear and threads when dropped from a spoon. Fills 4 ½-pint jars.

## RED RASPBERRY JAM

4 cups red raspberries          4 cups sugar          1 cup water

Boil sugar and water together until syrup threads. Wash and drain berries, crush, and measure. Add to syrup, cook rapidly while stirring for 20 minutes, when mixture should have thickened. Place in hot jars and cool. Seal with paraffin. Fills 6 6-ounce glasses.

## CHERRY HASH

4 cups cherries          4 cups shredded pineapple          1 cup sugar

Use sour cherries. Pit and run through food chopper, using medium cutter. If pineapple shreds are too large, grind these also. Mix and let stand until well blended, preferably overnight. This requires no cooking. Place in jars. Makes 2 quarts.

## PICKLED CHERRIES

5 pounds sour cherries          5 pounds sugar          Vinegar

It is best to do this recipe in the old-fashioned way, by weight. Pit the cherries, place them in a large earthenware bowl, cover with vinegar, and let stand, covered, for 24 hours. Drain off vinegar, put the cherries in a crock in layers, alternating with layers of sugar. Stir each day for a week. Place in jars. No cooking is required.

## SPICED CHERRIES

1 quart sour cherries
1 cup vinegar

4 cups sugar
½ tablespoon cloves

½ tablespoon cinnamon

Pit the cherries, put in saucepan with vinegar and sugar, cook over low heat for about an hour, stirring frequently. After ½ hour's cooking, add cloves and cinnamon. Finish cooking and pour into heated jars. Seal. Fills 3 or 4 ½-pint jars.

## SPICED CRABAPPLES

4 pounds ripe crabapples
4 pounds granulated sugar
2 tablespoons whole allspice

2 tablespoons whole cloves
10 small pieces stick cinnamon
1 quart white vinegar

1½ cups water

Use firm not overripe fruit. Pick over and wash, handling carefully to retain shape and color, and retaining any stems to add to appearance. Parboil crabapples whole in water until they can be pricked with a toothpick. Combine sugar and water and simmer over low heat to form syrup. Tie spices in cheesecloth bag and drop into syrup. Cook and stir until syrup threads from spoon. Pack crabapples in hot, sterilized jars. Pour syrup over them, filling jars until they overflow. Delicious with poultry. Fills 4 large jars.

*Gertrude Rickert Holland*

## APRICOT JAM

4 cups apricot pulp        3 cups sugar        4 tablespoons lemon juice

Use dried apricots. Heat them in a little water and simmer until tender. Mash and measure 4 cups pulp. Put apricots, sugar, and lemon juice in a saucepan, add a tiny pinch of salt, stir until sugar is dissolved over low heat. Increase heat and bring to a boil, stirring constantly until mixture thickens. Pour into hot jelly glasses, cool, and seal. Fills 6 6-ounce glasses.

## STRAWBERRY JAM

4 cups crushed strawberries        3 cups sugar

Wash berries, hull, and drain. Mash and measure 4 cups of pulp. Heat in saucepan with the sugar, stirring constantly. Simmer about ½ hour, or until syrup threads from spoon. Pour into hot jelly glasses, cool, and seal with paraffin. Fills 6 6-ounce glasses.

*Martha Twining*

## PEAR MARMALADE

4 cups pulp and juice of ripe pears        2 oranges, grated rind and juice
3 cups sugar

Peel and quarter the pears and run through food chopper. Measure pulp and juice to make 4 cups. Grate rind of oranges. Combine pear pulp, orange rind and juice with sugar and simmer all together for about ½ hour, stirring all the time. When the syrup threads from a spoon, pour into hot jelly glasses. Fills 10 6-ounce glasses.

*Mrs. Arthur J. McShane*

## SPICED PEARS I

5 pounds winter pears        3½ cups cider vinegar
Whole cloves        5 cups brown sugar
Small pieces stick cinnamon

Peel pears but do not core. Retain any stems. Stick 2 or 3 cloves in each pear. Make a syrup of vinegar and sugar, add cinnamon sticks, and simmer for a few minutes until sugar is dissolved, stirring. When syrup comes to a boil add the pears. Cook gently until the pears are tender. Place in two large jars, pour in syrup until the jars overflow. Seal.

*Mrs. Susan Laudenslager*

## SPICED PEARS II

7 pounds pears        1 teaspoon cloves
3 pounds brown sugar        1 teaspoon cinnamon
2 tablespoons vinegar

Peel and cut up the pears. Cook in water to cover until soft. Drain. Tie spices in cheesecloth bag. Add brown sugar, vinegar, and spices to the pears and simmer ½ hour, stirring and adding a little water now and then if needed. When mixture has thickened, remove spices and pour into jars.

*Quakertown Grange*

## GINGER PEARS

2 pounds hard, late pears        2 pounds sugar
1 lemon, juice and rind        ½ cup water
2 ounces ginger root or crystallized ginger

Peel and quarter pears, removing cores. (Be sure pears are not too ripe.) Slice thin. Squeeze lemon juice and cut rind in narrow strips. Combine water, lemon juice, lemon rind, and sugar in a kettle, add ginger and simmer about 45 minutes, until mixture becomes clear and syrupy. Add pears, simmer all together for 45 minutes, when the fruit should be transparent. When syrup is thick, pour into jars. Fills 2.

*Jennie Dietz*

## SPICED PEACHES

| | |
|---|---|
| 3 pounds peaches | ½ cup water |
| 1½ pounds brown sugar | ½ cup vinegar |
| | Whole cloves |

Select firm, perfect peaches. Do not peel. Cook sugar, water, and vinegar together, stirring, until syrup threads from a spoon. Stick cloves in the peaches and add to syrup. Boil gently until peaches are tender, stirring frequently but taking care not to break the skins. Add as much water while cooking as is needed to keep the peaches in a syrup. This will take about 45 minutes. When peaches are well cooked and syrup is thick, remove fruit and put in heated jars. Pour syrup over peaches to the very top of jars. This will fill 2 jars.

*Mrs. Abram Samuels III*

## PICKLED PEACHES

| | |
|---|---|
| 3 quarts firm peaches | 1 cup cider vinegar |
| 1½ pounds brown sugar | Whole cloves |
| | 2 cinnamon sticks |

Select firm, rather underripe fruit. Peel peaches and quarter. Place fruit and sugar in alternate layers in saucepan, cover, and let stand overnight. In the morning add the vinegar to peaches and juice, add cloves and cinnamon (broken into small pieces), and simmer together until soft. Stir carefully. Cook slowly until peaches are tender and syrup has thickened, about 45 minutes. Place the fruit in hot, sterilized jars, pour in syrup to the top. Seal. Fills 2 jars.

*Mrs. Edward S. Shepherd*

## PEACH MARMALADE

| | | |
|---|---|---|
| 3 pounds peaches | 1½ pounds white sugar | ½ cup water |

Peel and quarter the peaches. Place in saucepan with water and simmer slowly, stirring to prevent sticking until the fruit is reduced to a pulp. Mash the peaches, add sugar, simmer three-quarters of an hour, stirring constantly. When marmalade is clear and thick, pour into heated jars. Cool. Seal with paraffin. Makes 6 6-ounce glasses.

## ELDERBERRY JELLY

Green grapes                    Elderberries                    sugar

Use ripe elderberries and green grapes. Wash, stem, and put in separate saucepans with water to cover. Simmer until fruit is reduced to pulp. Then strain the juice and use 1 part sugar, 1 part grapes, and 2 parts elderberries. Combine, simmer until syrup thickens when dropped from spoon. Bring to a quick boil and remove from stove at once. Pour into scalded jelly glasses. Cool and seal with paraffin.

## CURRANT JELLY

3 cups currant juice                    3 cups sugar

Wash currants and put in kettle with a little water. Simmer over low heat until color has left currants and they are pulpy. Remove from stove and strain the juice. Combine juice and sugar and simmer slowly over low heat until the mixture threads from a spoon. Bring quickly to a boil, remove from heat at once, and pour into hot jelly glasses. Cool and seal. Fills 5 6-ounce glasses.

## LANCASTER COUNTY WATERMELON PICKLE

Watermelon rind, diced          1 cup sugar
Salted water                    3 drops oil of cloves
1 cup vinegar                   3 drops oil of cinnamon
                1 tablespoon lemon juice

Peel green from watermelon rind, leaving a little of the pink on the inner side. Dice into 1½-inch cubes. Boil in salted water to cover until tender. Drain. Combine other ingredients in a saucepan and simmer until it comes to a boil. When boiling fast, add watermelon. In a few minutes, lower heat and simmer for about 45 minutes, when syrup should be thick and watermelon rind transparent. Fill sterilized jars and seal.

*Mrs. Amos Shaub*

## WATERMELON PICKLE II

3 cups vinegar                  1 tablespoon mace
4 cups sugar                    Whole cloves
Stick cinnamon, broken small    3 pounds watermelon rind
1 tablespoon nutmeg             2 lemons

Boil vinegar and sugar, adding spices in a cheesecloth bag. Dice the watermelon rind, which has been cut with a little of the pink showing. Cook the syrup for a few minutes. Pour over the watermelon and let stand overnight. Next morning, boil spices and syrup again for a few minutes and pour over rind. Repeat this for the next 2 days, then boil the rind in the syrup for 5 minutes. Add lemon juice, cook 3 minutes. Seal, while hot, in sterilized jars.

*Mrs. Arthur J. McShane*

## WATERMELON PICKLE III

4 pounds watermelon rind
Lime water
4 pounds granulated sugar

4 cups white vinegar
2 tablespoons whole allspice
2 tablespoons whole cloves

10 small pieces stick cinnamon

Buy lime water at drugstore. Cook diced, trimmed watermelon rind in lime water at low heat for 2½ hours. Drain. Cover with fresh water, cook 1½ hours, or until fairly tender. Let stand overnight, then drain. Make a syrup of vinegar and sugar, adding 1 cup water, put spices in bag and drop in, bring to a slow boil, add watermelon rind, and simmer for 2 hours. Remove spice bag, pour into hot sterilized jars. Seal. Store in a cool place.

*Gertrude Rickert Holland*

## TOMATO MARMALADE

1 quart ripe tomatoes
1 lemon

2 oranges
2 pounds sugar

Peel tomatoes and measure, firmly packed. Place in saucepan and simmer. Peel lemon and oranges and add pulp to the tomatoes as soon as they have come to a boil. Cut rind in narrow strips and add to mixture. Add sugar. Stir constantly while simmering until fruit rinds become transparent. Pour into heated ½-pint jars. Cool and seal with paraffin.

*Mrs. Arthur J. McShane*

## TOMATO BUTTER

3 quarts tomatoes
1 pound sugar

½ lemon
Stick cinnamon

Scald tomatoes and remove skins. Place in a kettle with water to cover, boil down until they are thick, add sugar. Slice lemon with rind attached and add to tomatoes. Break up cinnamon and add. Cook slowly for 45 minutes when thick and smooth. Fill hot ½-pint jars. Seal.

*Anna Wessner*

## YELLOW TOMATO PRESERVE

2 pounds firm, yellow tomatoes
2 pounds sugar

1 large lemon, juice and
grated rind

Water

Make a syrup with the sugar and as little water as possible. Simmer until it comes to a slow boil. When syrup thickens when dropped from a spoon, add lemon juice and grated rind. Add tomatoes. Boil carefully for ½ hour, stirring, until mixture is thick and smooth. Pour into heated ½-pint jars. Cool and seal.

## CHILI SAUCE

15 ripe tomatoes
1 sweet red pepper
1 green pepper
1 onion
3 tablespoons sugar

1 tablespoon salt
3 tablespoons vinegar
1 tablespoon cinnamon
1 teaspoon allspice
1 teaspoon nutmeg

1 teaspoon cloves

Wash vegetables. Peel tomatoes and onion. Cut away the stem ends of tomatoes, remove seeds from peppers. Run all through a food chopper, using medium coarse cutter. Place in large saucepan with salt and sugar. Simmer until mixture thickens, then add vinegar and spices. Cook for about 1 hour, stirring to prevent scorching. Pour into hot, sterilized jars and seal at once. Fills 2 pint jars.

## MOTHER'S CATSUP

2 gallons tomatoes
1 quart vinegar
1 pound brown sugar
4 tablespoons salt

4 tablespoons dry mustard
3 tablespoons black pepper
1½ teaspoons paprika
1 tablespoon cinnamon

Boil tomatoes until pulped and press out juice. Boil tomato juice with vinegar and brown sugar. Simmer until reduced to half the quantity. Add spices and seasoning and 2 tablespoons whole allspice. Simmer 15 minutes longer. When mixture is thick and smooth, remove from stove and pour into sterilized bottles. Makes 8 pints.

*Mrs. Elda Keck*

## GRANDMA BERTELS' PICALILLI

1 head cauliflower
4 stalks celery
2 large onions
1 yellow pepper
1 green pepper
1 red pepper
4 cups green tomatoes
25 small cucumbers
2 cups lima beans

2 cups kidney beans
2 tablespoons salt
1½ cups brown sugar
1 tablespoon mustard seed
6 cups cider vinegar
1 teaspoon turmeric
2 tablespoons cloves
2 tablespoons cinnamon
1 tablespoon allspice

1 teaspoon nutmeg

Wash and drain the vegetables. Cut up cauliflower, celery, onions, peppers, and tomatoes. Slice cucumbers. Place them with the beans in a large bowl or crock and let stand overnight, sprinkled with salt. Next day add sugar, mustard seed, cover with vinegar, put in kettle, and bring to a boil. Place spices in a bag and simmer with vegetables. Cook gently for about 1 hour or until mixture thickens and vegetables are tender. Remove spice bag, pour into sterilized quart jars, cool, and seal. Fills about 2 jars.

*Mrs. Arthur J. McShane*

## GREEN CHOWCHOW

1 hot green pepper
5 small cucumbers
15 tiny onions
1 small head cauliflower
1 stalk celery
½ cup sugar

1 teaspoon salt
Vinegar to cover
1 teaspoon mustard seed
2 teaspoons celery seed
½ teaspoon dry mustard
1 teaspoon turmeric

Chop vegetables fine, scald with boiling water, drain. Add sugar and salt, cover with cider vinegar, and boil slowly for about 1 hour, when mixture should have thickened. Add spices to taste (cloves, cinnamon and/or nutmeg), mustard seed, celery seed, and turmeric. When relish is thoroughly cooked place in hot, sterilized jars. Here the old recipe tells us to "cover with dry mustard to make it keep nice," but processing and sealing will do the trick nowadays.

## MOTHER'S RELISH

2 quarts green tomatoes
1 small cabbage
6 medium onions
12 green peppers
¼ cup salt

3 tablespoons mustard seed
2 tablespoons celery seed
1 cup sugar
2 cups vinegar
1 tablespoon dry mustard

Chop tomatoes, cabbage, onions, and peppers, very fine. Sprinkle with salt. Let stand overnight. Next day, drain, add mustard and celery seed, sugar and vinegar (holding out 1 tablespoon). Bring to a quick boil, simmer 30 minutes, add dry mustard mixed with the tablespoon vinegar, mix well, and, while still boiling hot, pour into hot, sterilized jars. Seal. Makes 2 quarts.

## BIRD'S-EYE SAUCE

½ head cabbage
1 quart green tomatoes
2 onions
1 teaspoon celery seed
1 teaspoon mustard seed

1 cup sugar
1½ tablespoons salt
2 cups vinegar
1 cup water
½ teaspoon ginger

½ teaspoon cloves

Chop all the vegetables, using coarse cutter. Mix with mustard and celery seed, sugar, and salt. Place in kettle, add vinegar, water and spices, bring to a boil and then simmer 20 minutes or longer—until mixture is well cooked and has thickened. Fill hot, sterilized jars and seal. Makes 1 quart.

## PEPPER HASH

½ head cabbage
1 red pepper
1 yellow pepper
1 green pepper
1 onion

1 stalk celery
3 tablespoons salt
½ teaspoon mustard seed
½ teaspoon celery seed
1 tablespoon sugar

Vinegar

Chop the vegetables in food chopper with medium coarse cutter. Sprinkle liberally with salt and drain in colander overnight. Mix with mustard and celery seed, sugar, and enough vinegar to cover. Let stand 3 hours and serve uncooked, or seal in jars. Makes 3 pints.

## CORN SALAD

10 ears corn
1 green pepper
½ red pepper
2 onions

½ teaspoon celery seed
1½ teaspoons dry mustard
1⅓ cups vinegar
1⅓ cups sugar

⅓ teaspoon turmeric

Select fresh corn, grate from the cobs, mix with other ingredients, boil all together slowly for ½ hour. Seal in sterilized jars. Makes 3 pints.

*Mrs. Herman Oswald*

## QUAKERTOWN CUCUMBER PICKLES

| | |
|---|---|
| 3 quarts cucumbers | 4 pounds sugar |
| 3 quarts water | 4 tablespoons mustard seed |
| 3 cups salt | 2 tablespoons celery seed |
| 1 quart cider vinegar | 2 tablespoons whole cloves |
| 2 cups water | 10 small pieces stick cinnamon |

¼ pound ginger root

Scrub cucumbers. Make a brine of salt and water and, if you want a brine favored by the old cookbooks, you may have to add more salt. It should be "strong enough to float an egg." (But these proportions will be effective.) Cover the crock with a weighted plate "to keep pickles from popping" and let them stand 2 or 3 days in the brine. Drain, pour fresh, cold water over the pickles and pack in hot, sterilized jars. Turn jars upside down to drain. Make a syrup of vinegar, 2 cups boiling water, and sugar. Simmer together until thickened. Add celery seed, mustard seed; drop into each jar of pickles several whole cloves, 3 or 4 pieces stick cinnamon, and a bit of ginger root. Fill with cooled but not cold syrup. Seal. About 3 quarts.

*Mrs. Arthur J. McShane*

## SWEET PICKLES

| | |
|---|---|
| 100 tiny cucumbers | 2 cups sugar |
| 4 cups vinegar | 3 tablespoons salt |
| 1 cup water | 1 level teaspoon allspice |

1 level teaspoon cloves

Scrub and drain pickles. Pack into sterilized jars. Mix vinegar, water, and sugar, bring to a boil and simmer, adding salt and spices, until thickened to syrup. Fill jars to overflowing with syrup. Seal. Wait a month before using. Makes about 4 quarts.

## ADAMS COUNTY 14-DAY PICKLES

| | |
|---|---|
| 4 quarts small cucumbers | 1 tablespoon alum |
| 2 quarts cold water | 2 cups vinegar |
| ½ cup salt | 1½ pounds white sugar |
| Horseradish leaves | 1 tablespoon celery seed |
| Boiling water to cover | 1 teaspoon allspice |

Stick cinnamon

*First Day*—Wash cucumbers and immerse in brine made of the salt and water. Let stand 7 days.

*Eighth Day*—Remove pickles from brine. Place in crock, alternating layers of pickles with layers of horseradish leaves. Cover with boiling water.

*Ninth Day*—Remove pickles from leaves and water. Cover with 1 gallon of boiling water to which the alum has been added. (1 tablespoon alum to 1 gallon is the proportion.)

*Tenth Day*—Remove pickles from solution. Reboil alum and water in which pickles have been standing. Again pour over pickles.

*Eleventh Day*—Repeat procedure.

*Twelfth Day*—Slice each pickle into ½-inch pieces. If pickles are small, split them. Cover with boiling syrup made of vinegar and sugar, cooked until slightly thickened. Add celery seed, allspice, and cinnamon. Let pickles stand in syrup.

*Thirteenth Day*—Remove pickles from syrup. Reboil syrup and pour over pickles.

*Fourteenth Day*—Pack pickles in hot, sterilized jars, 1-quart size. Reboil syrup. Pour into jars to fill to top. Seal. Makes 4 quarts.

*Mrs. Margaret Eckert Garretson*

## BREAD AND BUTTER PICKLES

4 quarts cucumbers
8 small white onions
¼ cup salt
4 cups vinegar

4 cups sugar
3 teaspoons celery seed
½ teaspoon turmeric (optional)
3 tablespoons mustard seed

Peel onions, wash cucumbers. Slice cucumbers very thin without peeling. Slice onions, mix with cucumbers, add salt. Let stand overnight, covered. Next day pour off liquid and cover cucumbers and onions with ice water. Heat vinegar with sugar and spices to boiling point, then turn down heat and simmer a few minutes. Drain cucumbers and onions, add to spiced vinegar, stir over low flame until mixture boils, then simmer. Stir in turmeric. Pour into hot, sterilized jars and seal. Makes about 3 quarts.

*Mrs. Karl L. Lubrecht*

## MIXED PICKLES

1 head cauliflower
3 red peppers
4 green tomatoes
2 cups small, white onions
2 carrots
3 cucumbers

2 cups small, fresh lima beans
½ cup salt
3 cups cider vinegar
3 tablespoons mustard
½ cup sugar
½ cup flour

1 teaspoon turmeric

Put all vegetables except lima beans through food chopper, using medium coarse cutter. Add lima beans. Sprinkle with salt, cover with water, and let vegetables stand overnight in the brine, covered. In the morning, heat the vegetables and brine in a kettle, slowly bring to a boil. Drain. Mix flour, sugar, and turmeric with vinegar and cook together for a few minutes until a smooth paste is formed. Pour into the kettle with the vegetables and cook all together slowly until mixture thickens and vegetables are thoroughly cooked. Pour into hot, sterilized jars and seal. Makes about 3 quarts.

## GINGER PICKLES

| | |
|---|---|
| 12 medium-sized cucumbers | ½ teaspoon mustard seed |
| 8 small onions | 1 teaspoon celery seed |
| 2 cups vinegar | 1 teaspoon ground ginger |
| 1 cup sugar | 1 teaspoon salt |

Wash cucumbers, do not peel, slice very thin. Slice onions thin. Add vinegar, sugar, spices, and mix. Let stand in a bowl 3 hours. Place in a kettle and slowly bring to a boil. Place in sterilized jars. Fills 3 1-pint jars.

*Mrs. Herman Oswald*

## MUSTARD PICKLES

| | |
|---|---|
| 1 quart small green tomatoes | Salt |
| 1 quart small cucumbers | 2 quarts cider vinegar |
| 1 pint small, white onions | ½ cup flour |
| 1 cauliflower | ½ cup ground mustard |
| 1½ cups sugar | |

Quarter the tomatoes, slice but do not peel cucumbers, peel onions and slice thin. Cut cauliflower in small pieces. Mix and let stand overnight in salted water. Next morning, drain vegetables. (The old method was to cook each vegetable separately for better flavor.) Cook vegetables slowly in just enough water to keep from sticking and when they are tender place in a crock. Mix flour and mustard, smooth into the vinegar, add sugar, and cook slowly until syrup boils. Pour mixture over the vegetables. Mix and turn into sterilized jars. This pickle was warranted to keep a year without spoiling because of the large amount of mustard used. You may prefer to use half the amount of mustard.

## PICKLED BEETS

| | |
|---|---|
| 10 fresh beets | 1 teaspoon ginger |
| 1 quart vinegar | 2 tablespoons horseradish |
| 1 teaspoon mace | 1 tablespoon sugar |

Boil the beets without breaking the skins. If they are small, use about 15. Do not slice. If large beets are used, slice thin. Pack beets into sterilized jars. Heat vinegar with spices and sugar. When it comes to a boil, add horseradish and pour over the beets in the jars. Seal. May be cooled and eaten same day. Makes about 1 quart.

## MUSTARD BEANS

| | |
|---|---|
| 4 quarts yellow string beans | 1 pint vinegar |
| ½ cup prepared mustard | 1 pound sugar |

Wash, string, and drain the beans and boil in salted water until tender. Add mustard, vinegar, and sugar. (Use brown sugar if preferred.) Fill sterilized jars with the beans after they have cooked long enough to absorb most of the vinegar. Makes about 3 quarts.

*Mrs. Herman Oswald*

## PICKLED MUSHROOMS

| | |
|---|---|
| 1 basket mushrooms | 10 whole cloves |
| Vinegar to cover | 1 teaspoon dry mustard |
| 1 bay leaf | 10 peppercorns |

Wash the mushrooms, being careful not to break them. Steam for 15 minutes. Cool and pack loosely in sterilized jars. Heat vinegar, about 1 quart, adding bay leaf, cloves, mustard, and peppercorns. Bring to a boil, remove bay leaf, and pour over mushrooms. Seal. Makes about 2 quarts. These should not be kept too long.

## PICKLED ARTICHOKES

| | |
|---|---|
| Jerusalem artichokes | Bay leaf |
| Ice water | Mace |
| Vinegar | Cloves |

Use the native Jerusalem artichokes, which are really just the knobby roots of a variety of sunflower that grows like a weed in Pennsylvania. Pickled, they are splendid appetizers, and if properly prepared are crisp and crunchy. They should be scrubbed thoroughly and well picked over. Large artichokes can be cut into 2 or 3 pieces. Toss into ice water and let stand a while. Then drop into a brine of salt and water and let stand 3 hours. Pack into sterilized jars. Heat the vinegar, add bay leaf, mace, and cloves (powdered). Add a teaspoon of horseradish if you like a sharp flavor. Bring mixture to a boil and pour over artichokes in the jars. Seal. Do not open for at least a week.

## PICKLED WALNUTS

I've been tracking down this recipe for years but the closest I could get to it for a long time was to find people who remembered vaguely being given some pickled walnuts in childhood and not liking them much! They don't sound particularly like a delicacy for children. Finally, when I did get hold of the recipe there was a difference of opinion as to whether the walnuts were pickled in their shells or without them. I could not understand how a walnut shell could be pricked with a steel fork or a needle, and it was a long time before I learned that the walnuts were picked and processed in summer, before the woody shells were formed. So now we can go ahead with the walnuts:

| | |
|---|---|
| 100 walnuts | 2 tablespoons allspice |
| Salt | 2 tablespoons powdered ginger |
| Water | 1 tablespoon powdered cloves |
| 4 quarts vinegar | 1 tablespoon nutmeg |
| 4 tablespoons black pepper | 2 tablespoons mustard seed |

Select young, unripe walnuts before the shells have begun to form. Prick with a steel-tined fork or needle and drop into strong brine, made by putting so much salt in water that "an egg will float on top." Let stand in brine for 9 days, changing brine at the end of each 3 days. On ninth day place in a large, shallow pan and set out in the hot, summer sun. Do this for 3 days, when the walnuts will have turned black. Sterilize jars and while still hot, pack in the walnuts, leaving space at the top to fill. Mix vinegar and spices, using the spices you prefer and not necessarily all of them, except that pepper, ginger, and allspice are traditional, and simmer over low heat until mixture comes to a boil. Simmer 10 minutes longer. Pour syrup over walnuts, filling jars to the top. Seal and store 6 weeks before opening. If you want to pickle whole walnut *meats,* simply make a vinegar and spice combination that suits your taste and prepare in same manner (but smaller proportions).

# Pies and Pastries

*Half-timbered house, Lancaster Pennsylvania*

IT HAS been asserted that New England invented the fruit pie. Well, certainly pies were brought to this country by the English but the Pennsylvania Dutch stuck their fingers in the pie very soon thereafter. If they didn't invent the fruit pie, it is obvious that they got hold of it and developed it to the point of no return! In Pennsylvania the variety of fruit pies is limited only by the fruit available, for whatever it is the Dutch housewife will turn it into a pie. There is, and has always been, pie for breakfast in Pennsylvania—and pie for lunch, dinner, and a snack at bedtime. Pie in the Pennsylvania sky, for all I know. You must understand that the Pennsylvania Dutch have such a lien on pie-making that it covers any conceivable kind of pie and, in Pennsylvania, anything eatable can be tucked into pie crust and turn into a satisfactory pie. It can be meat, vegetables, fruit, milk, eggs, molasses—anything! And, once it's enveloped in pastry dough, that's that.

There are pies for special occasions, too, in Pennsylvania—and pies that perform special services. *Poor Man's Pies,* or *Flitche,* will make use of anything handy and satisfy the children while the major business of pie-making goes on. *Amish Half-Moon Pies,* or *Preaching Pies,* will not drip because they are stuffed with dried apples but they'll keep children quiet during long Sunday services. *Rosina Boi,* or *Raisin Pie,* bursting with the sweetness of raisins, will console mourners and satisfy their hunger. I could go on and on.

Old-timers in Pennsylvania provided a constant supply of pies by baking them by the dozen and storing them in their pierced-tin "pie cupboards." Safe in these ventilated interiors they were always available. As the Dutch art of pie-baking spread through the state, settlers in western counties went the

150

Pennsylvania Dutch one better and ate "stack pies" at their barn raisings. They simply piled up six or eight different pies, cut wedges down through the whole thing, and helped themselves to a stack of all kinds of pie. It saved having to make up their minds, probably. It's so difficult to choose between Pennsylvania pies!

## PLAIN PASTRY

2 cups flour                                ½ cup shortening
¾ teaspoon salt                             5 tablespoons ice water

Sift the flour into a bowl with the salt. Cut in the shortening by holding 2 knives in the hand like scissors. Mix lightly, stirring with a fork while adding water. Try to pour water on dry, floury parts of the mixture. Form into a ball with lightly floured hands. Chill before using. Roll out on floured board, lifting rolling pin instead of pushing, rolling away in one direction. Makes 2 8-inch shells.

## EASY PIE CRUST

⅔ cup lard                                  2 cups flour, sifted
⅓ cup boiling water                         ¾ teaspoon baking powder
                    ¾ teaspoon salt

Mix lard with boiling water, beat together until cool. Chill. Sift baking powder and salt with the flour and resift into the lard-and-water mixture. Combine all ingredients into dough and form into a ball. Cover and leave overnight in refrigerator. Roll out on floured board. Never fails. Makes 2 8-inch crusts.

## RICH PASTRY

1 cup sifted flour                          5 tablespoons butter
½ teaspoon salt                             1 egg yolk
1 tablespoon sugar                          1 tablespoon ice water

Sift flour into a bowl with salt and sugar. Cut in the butter. Mix together lightly. Stir in egg yolk and add water. Form into a ball and chill. Roll out lightly on floured board. (For fruit pies, 1 tablespoon lemon juice may be added.) Makes 1 9-inch crust. Chill again before filling.

*Mrs. Victor Boyer*

## SWEET DOUGH

1 cup sifted flour                          ¼ cup butter and lard, mixed
½ cup sugar                                 1 egg

Mix ingredients into dough, form into ball, and chill. Roll out lightly on floured board. Line pie dish with pastry and chill again. For pies with strips on top, reserve ⅓ of the dough and add to it:

| | |
|---|---|
| 1 teaspoon baking powder | 2 tablespoons milk |

Mix again and roll out. Cut in strips and place on top of pie, all in one direction. These strips may not be crossed because they puff up. Use for fruit and berry pies.

*Mrs. Donald L. Helfferich*

## POOR MAN'S PIE

| | |
|---|---|
| Butter, size of an egg | ½ cup cream |
| 2 tablespoons flour | Cinnamon |
| ¼ cup sugar | Nutmeg |

Line a pie dish with pastry. Spread butter over the bottom. Dredge with a little flour. Sprinkle with sugar. Pour cream over all. Sprinkle with cinnamon and nutmeg. Bake in 350° oven for 40-45 minutes. Makes 1 7-inch pie. Serve warm.

*Mrs. Donald L. Helfferich*

## VINEGAR PIE

| | |
|---|---|
| 1 egg | 1 cup cold water, scant |
| 1 heaping tablespoon flour | 1 tablespoon vinegar |
| 1 scant cup sugar | Nutmeg |

Line a pie dish with pastry. Beat egg lightly, mix with flour and sugar. Mix water with vinegar and nutmeg. Add to egg and flour mixture. Pour into pie shell and cover with top crust. Bake in 375° oven for about 45 minutes. Makes 1 8-inch pie.

*Mrs. Arthur J. McShane*

## TAFFY PIE

| Pastry | Molasses | Cream | Butter |
|---|---|---|---|

Line the bottom of a deep 8-inch pie dish with pastry, using recipe for Plain Pastry and cutting down proportions by one-fourth. Pour molasses over the bottom to half fill the pie. Pour cream over that, to two-thirds fill crust. Dot with butter, dredge lightly with flour. Bake in 350° oven until filling is set and edge of crust is browned. Makes 1 pie.

*Mrs. Donald L. Helfferich*

## MILK FLITCHE

(*Flitche* is a dialect word, considered untranslatable, but I like to think it means something put together casually with a flick of the wrist.)

| | |
|---|---|
| 1½ tablespoons sifted flour | ¾ cup milk |
| 1½ tablespoons sugar | 1½ tablespoons butter |
| | Cinnamon |

Mix flour, sugar, and milk. Line a 7-inch pie dish with plain pastry recipe, using half the amounts. Dot pastry shell with butter and sprinkle with cinnamon. Pour in mixture, dot with more butter, and sprinkle with cinnamon. Bake in 350° oven until filling is firm and crust brown. Makes 1 pie.

*Mrs. Herman Oswald*

## MOLASSES FLITCHE

| | |
|---|---|
| ¾ cup molasses | 1 heaping tablespoon flour |
| ⅜ cup cold water | 1 heaping teaspoon sugar |

Line a pie dish with pastry, using half the recipe. Mix ingredients and pour into unbaked shell. Bake in 350° oven for about 45 minutes, or until filling is firm. Makes 1 pie.

*Mrs. Herman Oswald*

## SCHLECK BOI
### (Lickin' Good Pie)

| | |
|---|---|
| 4 tablespoons light brown sugar | ¼ cup milk |
| 1 scant tablespoon flour | ½ teaspoon vanilla |
| 1½ tablespoons butter | Cinnamon to taste |

Use any pastry you prefer, half the recipe. Line a pie dish with pastry and chill. Mix sugar and flour and sprinkle over the bottom of the pie. Mix milk and vanilla and pour in. Sprinkle cinnamon over top. Bake in 350° oven for about ½ hour. Makes a rather thin but delicious pie—for a snack.

*Mrs. Arthur J. McShane*

## MRS. KRUSEN'S MONTGOMERY PIE

| *First Layer* | *Top Layer* |
|---|---|
| ½ cup molasses | 1 cup sugar |
| ½ cup sugar | ½ cup milk |
| Generous ½ cup water | ¼ cup butter |
| 1 beaten egg | 1 beaten egg |
| 1 lemon, juice and grated rind | 1 teaspoon baking powder |
| 1 tablespoon flour | 1¼ cups sifted flour |

Line 2 pastry tins with pastry, using recipe for Sweet Dough. Mix ingredients for first layer and pour into pastry shell. Mix second and pour on top. Bake in 350° oven for 45 minutes. Makes 2 8-inch pies.

*Mrs. Donald L. Helfferich*

## MRS. GOTTSHALL'S LEMON STRIP PIE

1 egg
1 cup sugar
½ cup molasses

1 tablespoon flour
1 lemon, juice and grated rind
1 cup cold water

Using entire recipe for Sweet Dough, line a pie plate with dough made of two-thirds of the mixture. Save one-third for making strips, as directed. Mix the beaten egg and sugar. Add molasses and flour, then lemon juice and grated rind. Add cold water, mix well, and place mixture in top of double boiler and cook and stir over boiling water until thick and smooth. Chill. When cool, pour into pastry shell. Roll out Sweet Dough for strips and place across the pie. Bake in 350° oven for 45 minutes, or until filling is firm and crust golden brown. Makes 1 8-inch pie.

*Mrs. Donald L. Helfferich*

## NOCHKUCHE
### (Abe's Have-Some-More Cake)

*Pastry*

¾ cup sifted flour
½ teaspoon salt

¼ cup shortening
¼ cup butter
2 tablespoons cold milk

*Filling*

½ cup sifted flour
4 tablespoons sugar

1½ cups cream
1 tablespoon butter
Cinnamon

Mix pastry very lightly, as it is very rich. Chill. Roll out one way on floured board to ⅛-inch thickness. Line a deep pie dish with pastry, dot with butter. Mix cinnamon, flour, and sugar and sift into the pie. Pour cream over this and again dot with butter. Sprinkle cinnamon across top. Bake at 350° for about 45 minutes. Makes 1 8-inch pie.

*Elizabeth Schramek*

## OSTERFLADEN
### (Easter Cake)

*Pastry*

| | |
|---|---|
| 2 cups sifted flour | 1½ tablespoons sugar |
| Pinch of salt | 2 tablespoons butter |
| | 1 egg |

*Filling*

| | |
|---|---|
| 3 eggs | 1 cup cream |
| 3 heaping tablespoons | 1 teaspoon vanilla |
| powdered sugar | Cinnamon |

Sift flour, salt, and sugar, cut in butter and add egg to make pastry. Chill. Roll out lightly on floured board, rather thick. Line 2 7-inch pans with pastry, building up around the rim and pinching top thickly, to hold custard. Beat eggs, add sugar, mix. Add cream and vanilla. Fill pastry shells with mixture. Sprinkle with cinnamon. Makes 2 small pies.

*From an old cook book*

## MRS. REINERT'S FUNNY CAKE

| *Lower Part* | *Upper Part* | |
|---|---|---|
| ½ cup cocoa | 2 cups sugar | 2 cups flour |
| 1 cup sugar | ½ cup shortening | 2 teaspoons baking |
| ½ cup boiling water | 1 egg | powder |
| | 1 cup milk | ¼ teaspoon salt |

Bake in pastry shell, using half recipe for Plain Pastry. Line pie dish with pastry and chill. For the lower part of filling, add boiling water to mixed sugar and cocoa. Use chocolate instead of cocoa if you prefer. Pour into pastry shell. Mix ingredients for upper part as you would cake batter and pour on top of chocolate mixture. Bake in 350° oven about 35 minutes until cake part is done. Makes 1 Funny-cake Pie. This is a "traditionally Pennsylvania Dutch" recipe, by permission.

*Virginia Thompson Smith, co-author,* Traditionally Pennsylvania Dutch

## CRUMB PIE

| | |
|---|---|
| 2 cups sifted flour | ⅓ cup lard and butter |
| 2 heaping teaspoons baking powder | 2 eggs |
| 1½ cups light brown sugar | ¾ cup milk |
| ¾ teaspoon salt | Vanilla or grated orange rind |

This is another of those pies that is eaten for breakfast! Line 2 pie tins with pastry, using recipe for Rich Pie Crust. Sift flour, baking powder, and sugar into a bowl, add salt, and butter and lard mix. Mix well together until crumbly. Reserve 1 cup of the crumbs. To the rest, add egg yolks, milk, and flavoring. Beat the whites stiffly and add. Pour into unbaked shells and sprinkle the 1 cup crumbs thickly over the tops of the pies. Bake in 350° oven for about 45 minutes. Makes 2 7-inch pies.

*Mrs. Arthur J. McShane*

## ROSINA BOI
### (Raisin Pie)

| | |
|---|---|
| 1 cup seeded raisins | 1½ cups sugar |
| 2 cups water | 4 tablespoons flour |
| 1 egg, beaten | Pinch of salt |

1 lemon, juice and grated rind

Soak raisins in water until soft and plump. Make pie crust, using recipe for Rich Pastry. Chill. Mix egg and sugar, add sifted flour, salt, raisins, lemon juice, and water. Place in top of double boiler, over boiling water, and cook gently for 15 minutes. Add grated lemon rind and stir. Cool. Line pie tins with pastry and fill shells with the mixture. Crisscross strips of pastry for the tops. Bake in 375° oven for about 40 minutes. This is the "Funeral Pie" that is traditional. Makes 2 8-inch pies.

*Amy Kerr*

## ROSINA KUCHEN
### (Raisin Tarts)

| | |
|---|---|
| ¾ cup melted butter | 1 cup seeded raisins |
| 1 cup sugar | Pinch of salt |
| 3 eggs | 1 wineglass sherry |

Cream butter and sugar with eggs. Flour food chopper and run raisins through it, using medium coarse cutter. Add to mixture with salt and sherry. Use recipe for Easy Pie Crust, roll out on floured board, cut in rounds with a large floured cup, line patty tins with the rounds. Drop a generous teaspoonful of filling into each shell and bake in 350° oven about 35 minutes, or until filling has puffed and is firm and crust lightly browned. Makes 20 tarts.

*Mrs. Edward S. Shepherd*

## BUTTERSCOTCH PIE

2 tablespoons butter
1 cup brown sugar
2 scant tablespoons flour
2 eggs

¼ cup water
1 teaspoon vanilla
Pinch of salt
2 tablespoons white sugar

Use half the recipe for Rich Pastry. Line a pie tin with pastry and bake the shell in 350° oven until medium brown. Cream brown sugar and butter, add flour. Place mixture in top of double boiler, over boiling water, bring to a boil. Beat egg yolks lightly, mix with water; add to mixture. Simmer together until thick and smooth. Pour the custard into baked pastry shell, having added vanilla when custard was taken from stove. Beat egg whites stiffly with salt, mix lightly with white sugar, and spread over pie. Bake in 350° oven for 15 minutes, or until meringue is golden brown. Turn off heat, let stand in oven a few minutes with door wedged partly open. Makes 1 pie.

*Mrs. Eva Dinkelspiel*

## LEMON PIE

1 lemon, juice and grated rind
2 eggs
1 tablespoon cornstarch

1 cup water
½ cup sugar
1 rounded tablespoon butter
Pinch of salt

To make pastry, use two-thirds recipe for Sweet Dough. Line a pie tin with pastry and bake in 350° oven until crust is light brown. Mix egg yolks, cornstarch, water, sugar, and butter. Cook together over boiling water in top of double boiler, stirring constantly until thick and smooth. Cool. Add lemon juice, grated rind, and salt to stiffly beaten egg whites. Stir this mixture into the cooled custard. Spread on baked pie shell. Top with meringue:

3 stiffly beaten egg whites          3 tablespoons confectioner's sugar

Heap meringue lightly on the pie and bake in 350° oven about 15 minutes, or until meringue is golden brown. Turn off heat, wedge oven door open a little, and let pie cool slowly in cooling oven. Makes 1 8-inch pie.

*Mrs. Victor Boyer*

## LEMON SPONGE PIE

3 eggs, beaten separately
1 cup granulated sugar
Butter, size of an egg

3 tablespoons flour
1 lemon, juice and grated rind
1 cup milk

Using recipe for Rich Pastry, take half the proportions and roll out one crust. Line a pie tin and bake the shell in 350° oven until crust begins to brown. Remove. Beat egg yolks lightly, cream sugar and butter, combine. Add sifted flour, lemon juice, and milk. Beat egg whites stiffly and add with grated lemon rind. Pour mixture into pie shell and finish baking at 400°, until filling is firm and meringue nicely browned. Makes 1 pie.

*Mrs. Elwood Shaub*

## CITRONENKUCHEN
### (Lemon Tarts)

| | |
|---|---|
| Butter size of walnut | 1 lemon, juice and |
| 1 cup brown sugar | grated rind |
| 6 egg yolks | Pinch of salt |

Use recipe for Rich Pastry. Roll out lightly and cut in rounds on floured board with coffeecup. Line patty tins with pastry. Mix filling by creaming butter and sugar, blending with beaten egg yolks, adding lemon juice, grated rind, and salt. Drop in heaping teaspoonfuls into patty shells. Bake in 350° oven about ½ hour, until filling is firm and crust golden brown. Makes 20.

*Mrs. Elda Keck*

## CUSTARD PIE

| | |
|---|---|
| 4 eggs, beaten separately | 1 large teaspoon butter |
| ½ cup sugar | 1 teaspoon vanilla |
| 2½ cups milk | 2 tablespoons confectioners' sugar |
| | Pinch of salt |

Use half the recipe for Rich Pastry. Line pie dish and chill crust. Beat egg yolks lightly, add sugar. Place milk in saucepan and bring just to a boil. Add butter. Pour milk and butter over egg and sugar mixture. Add ½ teaspoon vanilla. Stir together and cool. Pour mixture into crust and bake quickly in 400° oven, to prevent crust from becoming soggy. When crust has browned, turn off heat and let pie stand in oven for ½ hour, to set custard. Beat egg whites stiffly with pinch of salt and add confectioners' sugar. Add ½ teaspoon vanilla. Spread meringue lightly over the pie. Brown in 325° oven for about 15 minutes, when it should be a light golden color. Makes 1 9-inch pie.

*Sophie D. Driebelbies*

## APPLE CUSTARD PIE

2 heaping cups stewed sour apples    ¼ teaspoon salt
2 eggs, beaten separately    ¼ teaspoon nutmeg
1 cup sugar    Pinch of salt
½ cup butter    2 tablespoons confectioners' sugar
            Vanilla

Use recipe for Plain Pastry. Line pie dish with the crust. Chill. Stew and mash the apples. Beat egg yolks, blend butter, sugar, and salt, add the egg yolks. Stir in apples and nutmeg. Pour filling into crust, put on top crust, seal and crimp edges of pie, bake in 350° oven for about 45 minutes. Beat egg whites stiffly with pinch of salt, add confectioners' sugar and a little vanilla. Spread this meringue over the top crust, return to oven, and brown for 15 minutes at 300°-325°. Makes 1 9-inch pie.

*Mrs. Donald L. Helfferich*

## COCONUT PIE

1½ cups grated coconut    2 tablespoons cornstarch
3 eggs, beaten separately    2 cups milk
1 cup granulated sugar    1 teaspoon vanilla
¼ teaspoon salt    Pinch of salt
         3 tablespoons confectioners' sugar

Use half the recipe for Rich Pastry. Roll out crust, line pie dish, and bake shell until lightly browned. Beat egg yolks, add sugar and salt. Stir in cornstarch. Scald milk and pour over mixture (adding a lump of butter to hot milk if desired). Place in top of double boiler over boiling water, stir until thick and smooth. Reserve a scant ½ cup of coconut for top of meringue. Add remaining coconut to custard. Cool. Stir in vanilla and pour mixture into baked pastry shell. Beat egg whites stiffly with pinch of salt, stir in sugar. Spread meringue lightly over pie, sprinkle with coconut, bake in 300° oven for 15 minutes, or until meringue is lightly browned. Makes 1 8-inch pie.

*Sophie D. Dreibelbies*

## CHOCOLATE PIE

2 squares chocolate    2 cups milk
½ cup sugar    1 teaspoon vanilla
¼ cup cornstarch and flour, mixed    Pinch of salt
3 eggs    2 tablespoons confectioners' sugar

Use half the recipe for Rich Pastry. Line pie tin with pastry and bake shell until lightly browned. Melt chocolate, mix with sifted sugar, cornstarch, and flour. Beat egg yolks and add with milk. Place mixture in top of double boiler over boiling water, cook until smooth and thick. Cool. Add vanilla. Fill baked shell with custard. Beat egg whites stiffly with salt. Add confectioners' sugar. Spread lightly over pie and bake at 300° for 15 minutes until meringue is lightly browned. Makes 1 9-inch pie.

*Mrs. Arthur J. McShane*

## EBBELKUCHE
### (Apple Tart)

| | |
|---|---|
| 1 tablespoon flour | ½ teaspoon salt |
| 2 tablespoons sugar | ½ teaspoon cinnamon |
| 1½ tablespoons butter | ⅛ teaspoon nutmeg |
| Cored and halved apples | ⅛ teaspoon cloves |
| 3 tablespoons brown sugar | 1 tablespoon ice water |

Line a deep pie dish with rich pastry. Sift the flour and sugar over the bottom of the pie and dot with butter. Fill shell with apple halves. Put a little butter in each half-apple and sprinkle with brown sugar, salt, and spices. Add water (and a little lemon juice, if desired). Crisscross the top of the pie with strips of pastry. Bake in 450° oven for 10 minutes. Reduce heat and bake at 350° for about 40 minutes longer, when crust is lightly browned and apples soft. Makes 1 9-inch tart.

*Mary Rose McWilliams*

## BERKS COUNTY APPLE TART

| | |
|---|---|
| 2 tablespoons flour | Cinnamon |
| ¼ cup sugar | Butter |
| Apple halves and pieces | Light cream |

"This is the best pie between the Atlantic and the Pacific—and, while I'm at it, I'll include South America, Europe, Asia, Africa and Australia as well. . . . Use Yellow Transparent apples, which come into market in early July. . . . Line a pie dish with rich pastry. Cover bottom generously with flour and half the sugar. Place in the pie dish halves of apples, peeled and cored (face up), one half face down in the center, the other halves surrounding it. Fill in crevices between halves with smaller pieces of apple and sprinkle with rest of sugar and with cinnamon. Fill in with rich top milk or light cream till the apples are half-submerged and dot each half with butter. Bake in hot oven until apples are soft. Cool and eat with thanksgiving. . . . To my way of thinking this dish represents Pennsylvania Dutch cooking at its height."

*Fredric Klees, who wrote* The Pennsylvania Dutch

## AMISH HALF-MOON PIES

| | |
|---|---|
| 2 cups dried sour apples | 2 cups sugar |
| 2 cups cold water | 1 orange, juice and grated rind |
| Pinch of salt | 1 tablespoon cinnamon |

Roll out pastry (use recipe for Plain Pastry) and cut in 8-inch circles. Cook dried apples with water and salt. When they are soft and pulpy, add sugar, orange juice and rind, and cinnamon. Simmer until water is cooked away. Place generous portions of the mixture on half the pastry rounds, fold over the pastry, pinch the edges tightly together, and bake in 450° oven for 10 minutes. Reduce heat to 350° and bake about 40 minutes longer until nicely browned. These are the guaranteed dripless "preaching pies" that beguile Amish children during long Sunday services but I have eaten them at Buckhill Falls Inn with, I am sure, equal pleasure.

## SOUR CHERRY PIE

| | |
|---|---|
| 4 cups sour cherries | ¼ cup sifted flour |
| 1½ cups sugar | Pinch of salt |
| | 1 tablespoon butter |

Use recipe for Rich Pastry. Line a pie dish with bottom crust, dot it with butter, dredge very lightly with flour, sprinkle with a little sugar. Mix cherries with sugar and pour into the shell. Dredge with flour and salt, dot with butter. Roll out top crust, gash with leaf design for air holes, place on the pie and seal edges carefully, crimping. Bake in 350° oven for 30-40 minutes until crust is lightly browned. Makes 1 deep-dish 8-inch pie.

## KARSCHEKUCHE
### (Cherry Tart)

| | |
|---|---|
| 2½ cups black cherries | ⅔ cup sugar |
| 1 tablespoon flour | Pinch of salt |
| | 1 tablespoon water |

Use recipe for Sweet Dough. Line a pie dish with bottom crust. Mix cherries with flour, sugar, and salt. Pour into the pie, sprinkle water over the top, then sprinkle with more sugar. Dot with a little butter. Place strips of dough one way across the pie. Bake in 450° oven for 10 minutes, lower heat to 350°, and bake 30 minutes longer. Makes 1 8-inch tart.

*Ralph Kirschner*

## CHERRY CRUMB PIE

### Filling

| | |
|---|---|
| 2½ cups sour cherries | 2 tablespoons flour |
| ½ cup granulated sugar | 2 tablespoons butter |
| ½ cup light brown sugar | ½ cup water or cherry juice |

### Crumbs

| | |
|---|---|
| ¾ cup flour | ¼ teaspoon salt |
| ¾ cup sugar | ¼ cup butter |

½ teaspoon nutmeg or cinnamon

Use half of recipe for Sweet Pastry, roll out bottom crust, and line 9-inch pie dish. Dredge with a little flour and sugar and dot with butter. Mix flour, sugar, and water or cherry juice to a smooth paste. Cook in saucepan over low heat until mixture thickens. Add balance of butter and cook a minute longer. Remove from heat, mix with cherries, cool, then pour into pie shell. For crumbs, mix flour, sugar, and salt, blend with butter, add spice (or substitute vanilla or lemon juice) and when mixture breaks into crumbs sprinkle thickly over cherries. Bake in 350° oven for 35-40 minutes.

*Martha Twining*

## STRAWBERRY TART

| | |
|---|---|
| 1 tablespoon instant tapioca | 2 egg whites |
| 2 cups strawberries | Pinch of salt |
| ½ cup sugar | 1 tablespoon sugar |

Use half the recipe for Rich Pastry. Line a deep pie dish with crust and sprinkle tapioca across bottom. Add strawberries mixed with sugar. Bake in 400° oven for 40 minutes. Cool a little. Beat egg whites stiffly with salt, mix in sugar, spread lightly over top of tart. Return to oven long enough for meringue to brown lightly. Use same method to make raspberry tart. Makes 1 deep 7-inch tart.

*Mrs. Mahlon H. Rickert*

## STRAWBERRY PIE

| | |
|---|---|
| ¾ cup sugar | 4 cups strawberries |
| 1 tablespoon butter | ⅓ cup sifted flour |

Pinch of salt

Use Rich Pastry. Roll out bottom crust and line deep pie dish. Sprinkle a little sugar across crust and dot with butter. Mix strawberries with sugar and pour into shell. Dredge lightly with flour and salt, dot with butter. Roll out top crust and gash a design for air holes. Place on pie and crimp and seal. Bake in 350° oven for ½ hour. Remove, sprinkle a little powdered sugar on the crust, brush with a tiny bit of butter. Return to oven, bake 10 minutes longer, when crust will be golden brown. Makes 1 deep 8-inch pie.

*Mrs. Arthur J. McShane*

## GOOSEBERRY TART

*Sweet Dough*

| | |
|---|---|
| ½ cup sugar | ½ teaspoon baking powder |
| 1 cup flour | Milk |
| 1 tablespoon butter | 1 egg |

*Filling*

| | |
|---|---|
| 1 egg | 1 tablespoon flour |
| 1 cup sugar, scant | 2 cups green gooseberries |

"Another true masterpiece. . . . The contrast of the acid fruit and the sweet dough makes this one of the most delicious pies ever baked. For this, tail and top the gooseberries. Beat the egg well and add nearly a cup of sugar, the amount of sugar depending upon the ripeness of the berries. Mix sugar, egg and flour together and add to the berries. Stir and pour into pie dish lined with the dough. Make sweet dough by combining ingredients, using just enough milk to mix well. Roll out bottom crust and make a lattice-work over the tart. Bake in medium oven. Green currants or green fox grapes may be used instead of gooseberries." Makes 1 8-inch tart.

*Fredric Klees, who wrote* The Pennsylvania Dutch

## WALNUT PIE

| | |
|---|---|
| 2 tablespoons butter | 1 cup molasses |
| 1 cup light brown sugar | ½ cup water |
| 3 tablespoons flour | ½ cup milk |
| 3 eggs, separated | 1 teaspoon vanilla |

1 cup walnut meats

Cream butter with sugar and flour. Beat egg yolks and mix with butter and sugar mixture. Mix molasses, water, and milk, pour in and mix. Add stiffly beaten egg whites and vanilla. Line 2 pie dishes with pastry, sprinkle walnuts over the bottom, and bake 10 minutes at 450°, lower heat and bake ½ hour at 350°. Makes 2 8-inch pies.

*Mrs. Walter L. Batt*

## RASPBERRY PIE

Rich Pastry
4 cups red raspberries
¾ cup sugar
1 teaspoon cornstarch

1 cup milk
2 tablespoons sugar
2 egg whites
Pinch of salt

Line a deep pie dish with Rich Pastry. Pour in raspberries, cover with sugar, saving 2 tablespoons. Cook cornstarch, milk, and 2 tablespoons sugar together, stirring constantly until mixture thickens. Cool. Beat egg whites stiffly, with salt, pour over raspberries. Roll out top crust, cut air holes, place on pie, crimping and sealing edges. Brush crust with butter and sift a little powdered sugar over top. Bake in 350° oven for about 40 minutes until crust is nicely browned. Makes 1 deep 8-inch pie.

*Mrs. Arthur J. McShane*

## HUCKLEBERRY PIE

Pastry
4 cups huckleberries
½ cup sugar

1 teaspoon flour
½ teaspoon salt
Nutmeg

Line a pie dish with Plain Pastry, mix berries with sugar, and pour into pie. Sprinkle flour and salt over the huckleberries and add a pinch of nutmeg. Roll out top crust, cut a design in center for air holes, bake in 350° oven for about 40 minutes, or until crust is golden brown. Makes 1 8-inch pie.

## GRAPE PIE

Rich Pastry
4 cups Concord Grapes
1 cup sugar

1 teaspoon butter
2 tablespoons flour
Pinch of salt

Skin and mash the grapes to loosen seeds. Simmer in water to cover for ½ hour, stirring. Remove seeds from pulp. At the same time cook the grape skins in a little water until tender. Combine pulp and skins, add sugar and butter and cook together for a few minutes. Line a pie dish with Rich Pastry, dredge with half the flour and a little sugar. Dot with butter. Add grape mixture, dredge again with flour and sugar, and sprinkle with salt. Dot with butter. Roll out top crust, gash air holes in center, place on pie, seal and crimp. Bake 30-40 minutes in 350° oven. Makes 1 8-inch pie.

*Mrs. Arthur J. McShane*

## WINEBERRY PIE

Pastry
½ cup sugar
1½ tablespoons flour
⅛ teaspoon salt

4 cups wineberries
1 tablespoon lemon juice
1 tablespoon butter
Milk

Line pie pan with Rich Pastry. Combine sugar, flour, and salt. Sprinkle one-fourth of the mixture on bottom of pie shell. Pour in wineberries, sprinkle with remainder of dry mixture. Add lemon juice and dot with butter. Brush the rim of the bottom crust with milk. Cover with top crust, with air holes gashed in center, and seal edges carefully. Crimp. Bake in 450° oven for 10 minutes. Reduce heat to 350° and bake 20-25 minutes longer. Makes 1 9-inch pie.

*Mrs. Arthur J. McShane*

## RHUBARB PIE

Rich Pastry
1 heaping tablespoon butter
½ cup flour

1 cup sugar
3 cups rhubarb
Pinch of salt

Roll out Rich Pastry into 2 crusts. Line a pie dish with pastry and dot with butter. Mix flour and sugar and sprinkle some of it over crust. Skin the rhubarb, cut in 1½-inch pieces, and measure 3 cups. Mix rhubarb with remaining flour and sugar and pour into pie shell. Dot with butter. Put vents in top crust and seal on the pie, crimping edges. Bake in 450° oven for 10 minutes and in 350° oven 25-30 minutes longer, when crust should be golden brown. Makes 1 8-inch pie.

*Mrs. Victor Boyer*

## PUMPKIN PIE

2 cups cooked pumpkin
4 eggs, beaten separately
1 cup sugar
½ teaspoon cinnamon
¼ teaspoon ginger

¼ teaspoon cloves
1 tablespoon flour
2 tablespoons butter
½ cup evaporated milk or cream
¼ teaspoon salt

Pastry

Beat the egg yolks, mix with pumpkin, add spices and flour. Melt butter, add with cream. Add salt. Line pie dish with pastry, fill with mixture, bake in 400°

oven for 10 minutes to prevent crust from becoming soggy. Lower heat to 325° and bake 45 minutes longer, when pie should be firm and golden brown. Turn off heat and allow pie to stand in oven 15 minutes longer so the filling may set. Makes 1 9-inch pie.

## MINCE PIES

2 pounds chopped beef
1 pound chopped suet
4 pounds tart apples, chopped
1 cup chopped citron
1 quart cider
2 pounds seeded raisins
1½ pounds currants
1½ pounds sugar
1½ teaspoons mace
1 teaspoon cloves

1 teaspoon nutmeg
1 teaspoon salt
Juice of 2 oranges, grated rind of 1
1 lemon, juice and grated rind
½ cup candied orange peel
½ cup candied lemon peel
1 pound blanched, chopped almonds
1 cup candied cherries
1 cup brandy
Rich Pastry

Simmer beef in a little water until tender. Cool. Chop in bowl with suet and apples. Cut citron fine with knife dipped in boiling water. Place mixture in large kettle, with cider, raisins, currants, sugar, spices, and salt. Simmer for 1 hour, stirring. Add orange and lemon juice and grated rind. Remove from stove, add chopped orange peel, lemon peel, almonds, candied cherries, and brandy. The brandy will preserve mincemeat until used. Fill about 10 pint jars with mincemeat. Using Rich Pastry recipe, roll out 2 crusts for each pie, line pie pans with crust, fill with mincemeat, cut vents in top crusts, and seal on pies. Bake on lower rack in 450° oven for 10 minutes, on upper rack at 350° for 45 minutes. (If using commercial mincemeat, add apples, fruit, juices, grated rind, almonds, and brandy. If mincemeat lacks richness, add a lump of butter. Let stand overnight.)

*Frances Thompson*

## HUCKLEBERRY MERINGUE PIE

½ recipe Rich Pastry
3 cups huckleberries
2 egg yolks
1 cup sugar (scant)

2 tablespoons flour
⅛ teaspoon salt
1 tablespoon butter
3 tablespoons orange juice

1 teaspoon lemon juice

*Meringue*

2 egg whites
2 tablespoons sugar

Pinch of salt
½ teaspoon flavoring

Mix pastry, roll into ball, and chill. Roll out, line pie dish, double back the rim and crimp, bake in 350° oven until lightly browned. Wash and drain berries. Beat egg yolks, mix with sugar, flour, and salt, add berries and stir together. Place in saucepan over low heat, stirring, and bring slowly to a boil. Turn down heat and simmer 3 minutes. Take off stove, stir in butter, orange and lemon juice. Pour into baked pie shell. Beat egg whites until almost stiff, sprinkle in the sugar and salt, stir in vanilla or whatever flavoring you prefer, beat until stiff. Spread meringue over filling. Brown lightly in 325° oven for about 15 minutes. Makes 1 8-inch pie.

## BLACKBERRY PIE

Rich Pastry
3 cups blackberries
1 cup sugar

2 tablespoons orange juice
2 tablespoons flour
Pinch of nutmeg

1 tablespoon butter

Line a pie dish with pastry and chill. Cook berries over low flame with sugar, stirring, bring to a slow boil, simmer 3 minutes. Cool. Add orange juice. Sprinkle a little flour over bottom of crust, pour in berries, sprinkle with flour and nutmeg, dot with butter. Put on top crust, seal edges with a little milk, crimp. Cut air holes in center of crust. Bake in 450° oven for 10 minutes, lower heat to 350°, and bake ½ hour, or until crust is lightly browned. Serve with cream. Makes 1 8-inch pie.

*Marilyn Buckner*

*Ephrata Cloisters*

# Cake

WHEN it comes right down to it, the "typical" Pennsylvania Dutch cake is some kind of a coffee cake—probably crumb-topped, often encased in pie crust, sometimes rich with molasses, sometimes with cheese, sometimes adorned with apple quarters, sometimes with raisins or nuts. You know all that if you've been coming along with me. But all that, of course, is *Kuchen* and *Kuchen* can cover a lot of ground in baking. Pretty much everything that goes in the oven, is dropped in fat, or is fried on a griddle (if it's sweet), started out as *Kuchen* in Pennsylvania. So—*Kuchen* is cakes in Pennsylvania, and of all kinds. In this section are set forth the cakes made and liked by the Pennsylvania Dutch, that is, cake in the usual sense of the word. You can't stand up and say they're indigenous but you can't say they're not, because they've been baked in Pennsylvania Dutch ovens for generations. At any rate, these are Pennsylvania's favorite cakes. And they're all from old, tried and true recipes.

## POOR MAN'S CAKE

| | |
|---|---|
| 1 cup sugar | ½ teaspoon salt, scant |
| 2 heaping cups flour | 1 cup milk |
| 2 teaspoons baking powder | 1 teaspoon vanilla |

Since this cake is made without eggs or butter, the flour should be sifted several times to insure lightness, then sifted with baking powder and salt, then with sugar, and finally mixed with milk and flavoring. Bake in greased, floured layer cake tins in 375° oven for about 20 minutes. Put together with icing. Makes 1 8-inch cake.

*Mrs. Victor Boyer*

## AUNT SUE'S FEATHER CAKE

2½ cups sifted flour
2 teaspoons baking powder
¼ teaspoon salt
½ cup butter

2 cups sugar
3 eggs
1 cup milk
1 teaspoon vanilla

Sift the flour, baking powder, and salt. Cream butter with sugar. Beat egg yolks lightly and stir in. Sift in the flour mixture, alternating with milk. Add vanilla, beat for 1 minute. Fold in stiffly beaten egg whites. Bake in 1 9-inch loaf tin or 2 8-inch layer cake tins at 350° for 30-40 minutes, depending upon thickness. Cool and ice. Makes 1 cake.

*Mrs. John Joseph Stoudt*

## CHILDREN'S CAKE

½ cup butter
1 cup sugar
2 eggs, beaten separately
1¾ cups flour

2 teaspoons baking powder
⅔ cup milk
1 teaspoon vanilla
Pinch of salt

*Icing*

1 square chocolate
½ cup powdered sugar

1 teaspoon vanilla
1 egg white

Cream butter and sugar, stir in lightly beaten egg yolks. Sift flour and baking powder several times, add to mixture alternately wih milk. Add vanilla and egg whites, stiffly beaten with the salt. Bake in layer cake pans in 350° oven for about ½ hour. Cool. Melt chocolate, blend with sugar, add vanilla and stiffly beaten egg white. Spread between layers and on top and sides of cake. Makes 1 8-inch cake.

*Mrs. Susan Laudenslager*

## HURRY UP CAKE

1½ cups cake flour
2 teaspoons baking powder
1 cup sugar
¼ teaspoon salt

2 eggs
¼ cup soft butter
1 cup milk
1 teaspoon vanilla

Sift flour with baking powder, sugar, and salt. Mix eggs and soft butter. Add sifted flour and milk alternately. Add vanilla and beat hard for 3 minutes. Bake in 2 greased and floured 8-inch layer cake pans in 325° oven for 5 minutes. Raise heat to 350° and bake for ½ hour. Cool, spread with chocolate icing.

*Mrs. Victor Boyer*

## APPLESAUCE CAKE

| | |
|---|---|
| 1 cup brown sugar, closely packed | ½ teaspoon salt |
| ¼ cup melted butter | ¾ teaspoon cinnamon |
| 1 egg | ¼ teaspoon cloves |
| 2 cups cake flour | 1 teaspoon soda |
| 1 cup seedless raisins | 1 cup sour milk |

1 cup applesauce

Sift brown sugar, mix with butter. Beat in egg. Sift a little of the flour over the raisins and resift the rest of the flour with salt and spices. Sir into batter until smooth. Dissolve soda in sour milk, add with applesauce. Beat batter well. Bake in greased 9-inch loaf pan in 325° oven for a few minutes. Raise heat to 350° and bake for about 35 minutes longer. Makes 1 cake.

*Mrs. Donald L. Helfferich*

## SOUR MILK CAKE

| | |
|---|---|
| ⅓ cup butter | 1 cup sour milk |
| 1½ cups sugar | 1 teaspoon cinnamon |
| 2 cups sifted flour | ½ teaspoon cloves |
| 1 teaspoon soda | 1 cup chopped raisins |

1 egg

Cream butter and sugar, add flour, sifted several times. Dissolve soda in sour milk. Add spices, then sour milk and soda. Stir in raisins that have been dredged in a little flour. Beat in egg. Bake in 8-inch loaf pan at 325° for about 45 minutes. Makes 1 cake.

*Mrs. Victor Boyer*

## SPICE CAKE I

| | |
|---|---|
| 1 package seedless raisins | 5 cups sifted flour |
| 2 cups sugar | 1 teaspoon soda |
| ½ cup shortening | 3 teaspoons cinnamon |
| 3 cups water | 1 teaspoon cloves |
| ½ teaspoon salt | 1 teaspoon allspice |

Cook raisins, sugar, shortening, water, and salt together for about 5 minutes, stirring. Cool, add sifted flour, soda, and spices. Stir well together. Bake in 2 small or 1 large greased and floured loaf cake pan in 350° oven for 45-60 minutes.

*Mrs. John Hillegas*

## SPICE CAKE II

1 cup sugar
1½ cups butter and shortening
2½ cups flour
2 heaping teaspoons baking powder

¼ teaspoon salt
¾ cup milk
1 teaspoon cloves
1 teaspoon cinnamon

Cream butter and sugar. Sift flour, baking powder, and salt. Sift into butter and sugar mixture, alternating with milk. Take out 1 cup batter and spice it with cloves and cinnamon. Return to batter, fold it carefully to give marbleized appearance. Bake in small loaf pan at 350° for about 35-40 minutes. Makes 1 cake.

*Mrs. Susan Laudenslager*

## CLOVE CAKE I

½ cup butter
2 cups sugar
1 teaspoon soda dissolved in a
    little hot water

1 cup sour milk
2 eggs
3 cups flour
1½ teaspoons cloves

Cream butter and sugar, dissolve soda in hot water and add to sour milk. Beat eggs lightly, add to butter and sugar. Sift in flour, add cloves, and milk. Bake in loaf tin in 350° oven for about 40 minutes. Makes 1 cake.

*Mrs. Victor Boyer*

## CLOVE CAKE II

¾ cup butter
2 cups sugar
3 eggs
4 cups flour

1 teaspoon soda
1 teaspoon cream tartar
1 teaspoon cloves
1 teaspoon cinnamon

1 cup milk

Cream butter and sugar. Beat eggs lightly and add. Sift flour, soda, cream tartar, and spices and add alternately with milk. Beat well. Bake in large loaf pan in 350° oven for about 45 minutes. Makes 1 large cake.

*Mrs. Susan Laudenslager*

## PUDDING DISH CAKE

1 pound powdered sugar
1 tablespoon butter
3 eggs
3 cups flour

3 teaspoons baking powder
¼ teaspoon salt
1 cup milk
1 teaspoon vanilla

Cream sugar and butter, add well-beaten egg yolks. Sift flour, baking powder, and salt, add alternately with milk. Fold in stiffly beaten egg whites. Add vanilla. Bake in deep pudding dish in 350° oven for about 45-50 minutes. May be served with custard sauce.

### Sauce

⅔ cup sugar
⅓ cup flour
Pinch of salt

2 cups milk, scalded
2 eggs
1 teaspoon flavoring

Sift together sugar, flour, salt. Place in bowl. Scald milk, stir into flour and sugar, and add slightly beaten eggs. Cook in double boiler over boiling water until sauce thickens. Cool and flavor. 6 portions.

*Mrs. Victor Boyer*

## MOCHA CAKE

4 eggs, beaten separately
1 cup confectioners' sugar
1 cup flour, scant

¼ teaspoon salt
1 teaspoon baking powder
¼ cup strong coffee

### Filling

2 teaspoons strong coffee
1 tablespoon confectioners' sugar

1 cup whipped cream
½ cup chopped nuts

Beat egg yolks and blend with sifted sugar, flour, and baking powder. Beat egg whites stiffly with salt. Fold in. Bake in 2 layers in 8-inch pans at 350° for about 35 minutes. For filling, mix coffee, sugar, and whipped cream lightly together. Add nuts. Spread between layers and over cake and serve at once, cutting in squares.

*Mrs. Arthur J. McShane*

## COFFEE CAKE

4 eggs
2 cups sugar
1 cup molasses
1 cup butter
1 cup strong, hot coffee
4½ cups sifted flour

1 teaspoon soda
1 teaspoon cream tartar
1 teaspoon cloves
1 teaspoon cinnamon
1 teaspoon nutmeg
½ cup chopped raisins

Beat eggs, cream with sugar, stir in molasses, mix well. Melt butter with hot coffee and add. Sift flour, soda, cream tartar, and spices over the bowl and mix into batter. Stir well until smooth. Dredge raisins lightly with flour and fold in. Bake in large loaf tin at 350° for about 1 hour. When cool spread with mocha icing if desired.

*Mrs. Arthur J. McShane*

## MOLASSES CAKE

1 cup brown sugar, closely packed
2 tablespoons shortening
1 cup water
2 cups molasses
1 level tablespoon soda
1 tablespoon vinegar
2¾ cups flour

Cream brown sugar and shortening. Stir in water, molasses, and soda dissolved in vinegar. Sift flour over the bowl. Mix, adding more flour if batter seems too soft. Bake in loaf pan at 350° for about 45 minutes.

*Mrs. Victor Boyer*

## OUR OWN GINGER CAKE

2 eggs
1 cup soft butter
1 cup sugar
1 cup molasses
1 level tablespoon soda
2½ cups flour
1 teaspoon ginger

Beat eggs lightly, cream butter and sugar, mix with eggs. Add molasses. Sift soda, flour, and ginger into the bowl. Mix well. Bake in 350° oven for about 40 minutes. Makes 1 cake.

*Mrs. Susan Laudenslager*

## GERMAN NUT CAKE

5 eggs
1½ cups sugar
1 cup flour
1½ teaspoons baking powder
1 teaspoon allspice
1 teaspoon cloves
1 teaspoon nutmeg
1 teaspoon cinnamon
1 cup blanched almonds, chopped
1 teaspoon vanilla
½ teaspoon almond extract

Beat eggs lightly, add sugar and stir together. Add flour, sifted with a pinch of salt, the baking powder, and the spices. Dredge almonds in a little flour and fold in. Add flavoring. Bake in a large, shallow pan in 350° oven, raising heat gradually to 375°. Bake from 45 minutes to 1 hour. Cool cake in the pan. Cut in squares. Makes 1 large cake.

*Mrs. Abram Samuels III*

## WALNUT CAKE

| | |
|---|---|
| ½ cup butter | 1 teaspoon vanilla |
| 1½ cups granulated sugar | 1¾ cups sifted flour |
| 4 eggs | 1 heaping teaspoon baking powder |
| ½ cup milk | ¼ teaspoon salt |

### Frosting

| | |
|---|---|
| 2 cups brown sugar | Butter, size of walnut |
| ⅔ cup milk | Chopped walnuts |

Cream butter and sugar, add well-beaten eggs. Mix. Add milk and vanilla and beat well. Sift in flour, baking powder, and salt. When well blended add stiffly beaten egg whites. Bake in greased, floured 8-inch layer cake pans at 350° for about ½ hour. Cool. Cook sugar, milk, and butter together over low heat until creamy. Remove from stove and beat until cool and thick. Add nuts. Spread on cake. If you prefer, substitute pecans for walnuts.

*Mrs. Elda Keck*


## BLACK WALNUT CAKE

| | |
|---|---|
| 1 cup sugar | 2 tablespoons baking powder |
| ½ cup butter | Pinch of salt |
| 2 eggs | ½ cup milk |
| 1½ cups flour | 1 cup black walnut meats |

Cream sugar and butter, add egg yolks and mix. Sift flour, baking powder, and salt over the bowl, alternately adding milk. Beat well together. Fold in stiffly beaten egg whites and nuts. Spread in 1 9-inch cake pan. Bake 40 minutes at 375°. Makes 1 cake.

*Alyse Kistler*


## SHAKER NUT CAKE

| | |
|---|---|
| ½ cup butter | 1½ cups sifted flour |
| 1 cup brown sugar | 1 heaping teaspoon baking powder |
| 2 beaten eggs | ¼ teaspoon salt |
| ½ cup water | 1 cup chopped hickory nuts |

Cream butter and sugar. Beat egg yolks and add. Sift flour and baking powder and add alternately with water. Beat egg whites stiffly with salt and fold in batter with chopped nuts, which have been lightly dredged with flour. Bake in 8-inch loaf pan at 350° for about 40 minutes. Cover with hickory nut icing when cool.

*Mrs. Elda Keck*

## HICKORY NUT CAKE

1 cup butter

1 pound powdered sugar

4 eggs

3 cups flour

¼ teaspoon salt

2½ teaspoons baking powder

1 cup milk

1 cup hickory nutmeats

1 teaspoon almond or vanilla flavoring

Cream butter and sugar, stir in beaten eggs. Sift flour with salt and baking powder and add alternately with milk. Flour the nutmeats lightly and fold into batter with 1 teaspoon almond or vanilla flavoring. Bake in loaf tin in 325° oven for 10 minutes, raise heat to 350°, bake about 40 minutes longer. Frost with hickory nut icing.

*Mrs. Victor Boyer*

## FIG CAKE

2 tablespoons butter

3 eggs

1½ cups sugar

2 cups sifted flour

2 teaspoons baking powder

1 cup cream, scant

1 teaspoon vanilla or lemon extract

Pinch of salt

*Filling*

½ pound chopped figs          ¼ cup water          ½ cup sugar

Cream butter, egg yolks, and sugar. Sift in flour and baking powder, alternately adding cream. Add vanilla, fold in stiffly beaten egg whites and salt. Bake in floured 8-inch layer cake pans in 350° oven for ½ hour. Cool. Steam figs in a little water until soft. If you used lemon flavoring in the cake, add a little lemon juice to the figs as they cook. When the water is cooked away the figs should be soft enough to chop or mash. Smooth to a paste with the sugar and spread between layers of cake. Dust top with confectioners' sugar.

*Mrs. Arthur J. McShane*

## COCONUT CAKE

½ cup soft butter

1½ cups sugar

3 eggs, beaten separately

2 cups flour

2 teaspoons baking powder

½ cup milk

Pinch of salt

1 teaspoon vanilla and almond
    extract

¾ cup grated coconut

*Icing*

2 cups sugar

1 cup water

Pinch of salt

2 egg whites

Pinch of cream tartar

1 teaspoon vanilla and
    almond extract

¾ cup grated coconut

Cream butter and sugar. Beat egg yolks lightly and add. Sift flour with baking powder and add to batter alternately with milk. Beat well to blend. Beat egg whites stiffly with salt and fold in. Fold in flavoring and coconut. Spread batter on 2 greased and floured layer cake pans and bake at 350° for about 25 minutes. Put together with icing when cool. Stir sugar and water over low heat until sugar is dissolved, then simmer until syrup threads from spoon (do not stir). Remove from stove and beat egg whites with salt on a cold platter. Add syrup gradually to egg whites. When all is whipped in, add cream tartar and flavoring. Spread between layers and thickly over top and sides of cake. Sprinkle coconut lightly over icing. Makes 1 9-inch cake.

*Mrs. Victor Boyer*

## MARBLE CAKE

*White Part*

½ cup butter
1½ cups granulated sugar
2 cups sifted flour
1 teaspoon baking powder
¼ teaspoon salt
½ cup milk
1 teaspoon vanilla
4 egg whites

*Dark Part*

½ cup soft butter
1 cup brown sugar, closely packed
4 egg yolks
½ cup molasses
2 cups flour
1 teaspoon cream tartar
½ teaspoon soda
3 teaspoons cinnamon
1 teaspoon cloves
½ cup sour milk

Mix white part by creaming butter and sugar, sifting flour, baking powder, and salt into mixture alternately with milk. Add vanilla. Beat egg whites stiffly and add. Mix dark part by creaming butter and brown sugar, mixing with egg yolks, adding molasses. Sift flour with cream tartar, soda, and spices, add to batter. Stir in sour milk. If desired a square of chocolate may be melted and added. Mix well. Pour into large loaf cake pan, alternating spoonfuls of light and dark mixtures, swirling in the spoonfuls lightly, to make marbleized effect. Bake in 350° oven for about 1 hour.

*Mrs. Victor Boyer*

## MORAVIAN CREAM CAKE

4 eggs, beaten separately
1 cup granulated sugar
½ cup cream

1 heaping cup flour
2 teaspoons baking powder
¼ teaspoon salt

1 teaspoon vanilla

Combine beaten egg yolks with sugar, add cream, and blend. Sift flour 4 times, resift with baking powder and salt into the bowl, and mix. Beat egg whites stiffly with salt, fold into batter with vanilla. Bake in a loaf tin at 350° for about ½ hour.

*Mrs. Arthur J. McShane*

## PEARL CAKE

½ cup soft butter
2 cups sugar
¼ cup cornstarch
2½ cups sifted flour

2 teaspoons baking powder
1 cup milk
1 teaspoon vanilla
5 egg whites

Pinch of salt

Cream butter and sugar. Sift cornstarch with flour 4 times. Resift with baking powder and add little by little to butter and sugar, stirring and blending. Add milk and vanilla and beat well. Fold in egg whites, stiffly beaten with salt. Bake in medium-sized loaf cake pan at 325° for about 40 minutes. When cool, cut in squares.

*Mrs. Elda Keck*

## POUND CAKE

1 pound butter
1 pound sugar
1 dozen eggs
1 teaspoon vanilla
½ teaspoon mace

1 pound cake flour
½ teaspoon cream tartar
½ teaspoon salt
2 tablespoons brandy or 10 drops
   rosewater

Cream butter and sugar until very light and smooth. Add eggs, beating them in vigorously, one at a time. Add vanilla and mace. Sift flour 4 times, then resift with cream tartar and salt. Sift into batter, a little at a time. Mix thoroughly. Add brandy or rosewater. Bake in 2 oiled loaf pans in 325° oven for about 1 hour.

*Mrs. Edward S. Shepherd*

## GOLD CAKE

2 cups sifted cake flour
½ teaspoon salt
2 teaspoons baking powder
8 egg yolks

1½ cups sugar
1 teaspoon lemon juice
2 teaspoons orange juice
1 tablespoon grated orange rind

1 cup milk

Sift flour 4 times. Resift with salt and baking powder. Beat egg yolks lightly until thick. Add sugar, lemon juice, orange juice, and milk. Stir well together. Sift in flour and baking powder. Fold in grated orange rind. Bake in floured loaf cake pan at 325° for about 50 minutes.

*Mrs. Victor Boyer*

## SILVER CAKE
### (To be made at same time as Gold Cake)

| | |
|---|---|
| 1 cup butter | ½ teaspoon salt |
| 2 cups sugar | 1 cup milk |
| 3 cups sifted flour | ½ teaspoon vanilla |
| 3 teaspoons baking powder | ½ teaspoon almond extract |

8 egg whites

Cream butter and sugar. Sift flour 4 times and resift with baking powder and salt. Sift into the bowl, stirring into batter little by little, alternating with milk and flavoring. Mix well. Beat whites of eggs stiffly and fold in. Bake in large tube pan in 325° oven for about 50 minutes.

*Mrs. Victor Boyer*

## MRS. KECK'S GLORY CAKE

| | |
|---|---|
| 1¼ cups granulated sugar | 7 eggs, beaten separately |
| 1 cup cake flour | ½ teaspoon almond extract |
| 1 level teaspoon cream tartar | ½ teaspoon vanilla |

½ teaspoon orange extract

### Icing

| | |
|---|---|
| 2 cups 4X sugar | ½ teaspoon almond extract |
| 2 heaping tablespoons butter | 1 tablespoon orange juice |
| Cream | 1 orange, grated rind |

Sift sugar 4 times. Sift flour 5 times. Beat egg whites on a platter with wire whisk. When stiff add sugar slowly, beating constantly. Beat egg yolks lightly in a bowl, sift in flour and cream tartar and stir together. Fold in white of egg and sugar mixture. Add flavoring. Bake in 9-inch tube pan in 325° oven for about 1 hour. When the cake is cool cream butter and sugar and add enough cream to make a free-spreading mixture. Stir in grated orange peel and add almond extract and orange juice. Spread thickly on cake.

*Edna Bachman*

## MY GRANDMOTHER'S SPONGE CAKE

6 eggs
2 half eggshells water

2 cups sugar
2 cups flour

Separate eggs and stir yolks just enough to break skins. Add water, stir in sifted sugar. Beat until thick and lemon-colored. Sift flour several times; add. Fold in stiffly beaten egg whites. Bake in ungreased loaf pan at 325° for about 1 hour.

*Mrs. Harry Hess Reichard*

## WATER SPONGE CAKE

2 cups sifted flour
2 heaping teaspoons baking powder
3 eggs
½ cup water

2 cups sifted sugar
¼ teaspoon salt
2 tablespoons orange juice
1 teaspoon grated orange rind

Sift flour and baking powder several times. Stir egg yolks with water until light and thick. Add half the sugar gradually and continue beating. Fold in flour and baking powder. Beat egg whites stiffly with salt and beat balance of sugar with them. Add flavoring. Fold this mixture into batter. Spread in ungreased loaf pan and bake at 350° for about 1 hour. Cool in pan. Makes 1 cake.

*Mrs. Susan Laudenslager*

## CREAM SPONGE CAKE

2 cups sugar
1½ cups flour
2 teaspoons baking powder
¼ teaspoon salt

2 eggs, broken into a cup
Cream to fill cup
½ teaspoon almond extract
½ teaspoon vanilla

Sift sugar 3 times. Sift flour 3 times. Resift flour with baking powder and salt. Mix sugar with eggs and cream. Add flour and blend thoroughly. Add flavoring. Beat well. Bake in small loaf pan in 375° oven for about ½ hour. Makes 1 cake.

*Mrs. Victor Boyer*

## GRANDMOTHER'S JELLY ROLL

3 eggs
1 cup confectioners' sugar
2 tablespoons ice water

1 heaping cup sifted flour
1 rounded teaspoon baking powder
½ teaspoon salt

Stir egg yolks lightly, add sugar. Stir until creamy. Add ice water and blend. Sift flour and baking powder several times, sift into bowl, stirring. Fold in stiffly beaten egg whites with salt. Bake in long, shallow pan at 400° for 15 minutes. Turn out on damp cloth and spread with grape jelly. Roll up while warm. When cool, dust with powdered sugar.

*Mrs. Edward S. Shepherd*

## ANGEL CAKE

1 cup sifted flour
1 cup sifted sugar
¼ teaspoon salt

9 egg whites (1 cup)
½ teaspoon cream tartar
1 teaspoon vanilla

2 teaspoons orange juice

Sift flour 5 times, sugar 5 times. Resift flour with salt and half the sugar. Whip egg whites on a platter with wire whisk until foamy. Add cream tartar and whip until stiff. Whip in balance of sugar, a little at a time. Fold in flavoring, then sifted flour and sugar, a little at a time. Pour into an ungreased 9-inch tube pan and bake in 325° oven for about 1 hour. When cool spread with orange icing.

*Mrs. Victor Boyer*

## MRS. FEGLEY'S ANGEL FOOD

1 heaping cup flour
1½ cups sugar
½ teaspoon salt

11 egg whites
1½ teaspoons cream tartar
½ teaspoon vanilla

½ teaspoon almond extract

Sift flour 5 times, sugar 5 times. Resift flour with half the sugar and the salt. Whip egg whites on a platter with wire whisk until they are foamy. Add cream tartar, whip until stiff. Whip in balance of sugar a little at a time. Fold in vanilla and almond extract. Fold in sifted flour and sugar, a little at a time. Pour batter into an ungreased 9-inch tube pan. Bake in 325° oven for about 70 minutes. Take from oven and turn upside down in pan. When cake is cool remove from pan. Makes 1 large cake.

*Mrs. Victor Boyer*

## BLACK JOE CAKE

2 cups brown sugar
¾ cup butter and lard
2 egg yolks
2 squares chocolate
½ cup lukewarm water

1 teaspoon soda
½ cup sour milk
2 cups flour
1 teaspoon baking powder
¼ teaspoon salt

1 teaspoon vanilla

Cream sugar and shortening, add egg yolks. Melt chocolate, add with warm water. Mix. Dissolve soda in sour milk and add, alternating with sifted flour and baking powder. Beat well. Add salt and 1 teaspoon vanilla. Bake in square loaf pan at 350° for about 35 minutes. Cool and ice.

*Mrs. Susan Laudenslager*

## CHOCOLATE CAKE

1 egg  
1½ cups sifted flour  
1 cup sugar  
½ teaspoon salt  

1 cup sour milk  
1 teaspoon soda  
1 teaspoon vanilla  
2 squares chocolate (2 ounces)  

1 tablespoon butter

### Icing

2 squares chocolate  
1 teaspoon butter  

2 cups 4X sugar  
Cream  

Mix beaten egg, sifted flour, sugar, and salt. Mix together sour milk and soda. Add to first mixture. Melt the chocolate and butter in separate pan and add to the mixture. Beat all together for 5 minutes, add vanilla. Bake 45 minutes in loaf cake pan at 350°. Cool. Melt chocolate, mix with butter. Add enough cream with the sugar to spread easily. Spread thickly on cake.

*Miss A. H. Fellenbaum*

## MRS. LEIBENSPERGER'S DEVIL'S FOOD

*Part 1*

1 cup brown sugar, closely packed  
½ cup butter  
3 egg yolks  
½ cup sour milk  
1 teaspoon soda  
2 cups sifted flour  
1 egg white  

*Part 2*

1 cup brown sugar, closely packed  
1 cup cocoa  
½ cup sweet milk  
Vanilla  

Mix ingredients for Part 2 in a saucepan and slowly bring to a boil. Cool. Mix ingredients for Part 1 by creaming sugar and butter, adding unbeaten egg yolks, soda dissolved in sour milk, sifted flour, and stiffly beaten egg white. Mix well and stir in Part 2. Bake in loaf cake pan in 350° oven for about 35-40 minutes.

*Mrs. John Joseph Stoudt*

## MRS. SCHILL'S DEVIL'S FOOD

1 teaspoon soda dissolved in
½ cup sour milk
2 ounces chocolate, melted in
hot water, to make ½ cup
½ cup shortening

2 cups brown sugar, loosely packed
3 egg yolks
1 teaspoon vanilla
½ cup hot coffee
2 cups flour

Mix soda and sour milk. Melt chocolate in cup by filling cup with hot water. Cream shortening with half the sugar. Beat egg yolks with balance of sugar and add this to butter and sugar. Beat well. Stir in chocolate and hot water, vanilla and hot coffee. Beat again. Stir in sifted flour, alternately with sour milk. Beat for 3 minutes. Bake in loaf cake pan for about 35 minutes at 350°.

*Mrs. Donald L. Helfferich*

## DEVIL'S FOOD III

2 squares chocolate (2 ounces)
½ cup boiling water
½ cup butter
1½ cups granulated sugar
2 eggs, beaten

½ cup sour milk
1 teaspoon soda, scant
2 cups sifted flour
1 teaspoon baking powder
½ teaspoon vanilla

Melt chocolate in boiling water and cool. Cream butter and sugar. Add well-beaten egg and chocolate. Dissolve soda in sour milk and add. Sift flour with baking powder into batter. Add vanilla. Beat hard. Bake in loaf cake pan in 400° oven for 15 minutes. Reduce heat to 350° and finish baking, about 15 minutes longer.

*Mrs. Karl L. Lubrecht*

## WHITE FRUIT CAKE

1½ cups sugar
1 cup butter
3 cups sifted flour
3 teaspoons baking powder
1 teaspoon mace
2 tablespoons orange juice
1 4-ounce glass white wine

1 cup white raisins
½ cup candied cherries
1½ pounds chopped citron
½ pound blanched almonds, chopped
6 egg whites
¼ teaspoon salt
1 cup grated coconut

Sift sugar 3 times. Cream butter with sugar. Sift flour 5 times and resift with baking powder and mace, adding gradually to batter with orange juice and wine. Dredge fruit and nuts lightly with flour. Fold into batter. Beat egg whites stiffly with salt, fold in. Add coconut last. Bake in 325° oven for about 1¼ hours.

*Mrs. Arthur J. McShane*

## FRUIT CAKE I

1 pound soft butter (2 cups)
1 pound brown sugar (about 3 cups)
12 egg yolks
1 pound browned flour (about
  3¾ cups)
1 teaspoon cinnamon
1 teaspoon cloves
1 teaspoon allspice
1 teaspoon ginger
1 teaspoon mace
1 level tablespoon nutmeg

1 cup molasses
1 glass sherry
2 ounces whisky
1 glass preserved strawberries
2 pounds currants
2 pounds seedless raisins
2 pounds prunes
1 pound figs
½ pound citron
1 pound almonds, blanched
12 egg whites

Cream butter, sift brown sugar, add gradually to butter. When thoroughly creamed, beat egg yolks lightly and stir into butter and sugar. Sift flour and set aside 1 cup to dredge fruit. Place balance of flour in spider and brown quickly, taking care not to let it stick or burn. Cool and resift with spices. Add to butter and egg mixture. Stir in molasses, sherry, whisky, and strawberries. Chop fruit, blanch and chop almonds. Dredge in flour that was saved. Beat egg whites stiffly, fold into batter, add floured fruit. Line loaf cake pans with heavy waxed paper and pour in batter. Bake in 300° oven for 2-3 hours, taking extreme care not to let cake burn. A large flat pan, filled with boiling water to height of 1 inch, will help prevent burning. Set cake pans in this while baking, adding boiling water as needed. Toward the end of baking, remove cakes from pan of water, move to upper shelf, and finish baking. Cool cakes in pans, remove, and peel off waxed paper. Wrap and store in tightly covered tin containers. Cakes may be wrapped in cloths saturated with brandy. This recipe makes about 11 pounds.

*Mrs. John Dodson*

## FRUIT CAKE II

1 cup figs
1 cup raisins
1 cup currants
4 ounces sherry wine
2 ounces brandy
1 cup butter
2 cups light brown sugar
4 eggs
2 teaspoons soda

1 cup sour milk
4 cups sifted flour
¼ cup citron
1 cup candied cherries
1 cup candied pineapple
1 cup English walnuts
1 teaspoon cinnamon
1 teaspoon cloves
1 teaspoon nutmeg

1 teaspoon mace

Chop figs, raisins, and currants and let stand overnight in wine and brandy. Cream butter and sugar, stir in egg yolks, mix well together. Dissolve soda in sour milk. Sift some of the flour over the bowl of fruit and turn over lightly until all fruit is coated. Sift balance of flour into batter gradually, alternating with sour milk. Beat hard. Add fruit, nuts, and spices and stir well. Fold in stiffly beaten egg whites. Fill a paper-lined loaf pan three-quarters with batter. Bake in 350° oven for 1-1¼ hours. Cool, remove from pan, peel off paper, and store in tin container. Cake may be wrapped in cloth dipped in brandy and a quartered apple tucked in with it will keep the cake fresh. Makes 1 4-5-pound cake.

*Mrs. Abram Samuels III*

# ICINGS AND FILLINGS

## PLAIN ICING

2 egg whites
½ pound powdered sugar

1 teaspoon vanilla, or
lemon or orange juice

Beat eggs to a froth and work in enough powdered sugar to stiffen. Add flavoring, increasing proportion if fruit juice is used.

*Mrs. Elda Keck*

## BOILED ICING

2 cups granulated sugar
½ cup cold water

1 egg white
1 teaspoon vanilla

Boil sugar and water together until syrup threads. Beat white of egg on a platter with wire whisk and add syrup little by little, beating all the time. When mixture thickens and cools, add flavoring and spread on cake at once.

*Mrs. Elda Keck*

## CONFECTIONERS' ICING

Confectioners' sugar
2 tablespoons cream

2 teaspoons melted butter
½ teaspoon vanilla

Pistachio nuts or blanched almonds

Add sugar to cream until mixture is very thick. Work in melted butter and flavoring, when it should be of proper consistency to spread on cake. Sprinkle with finely chopped pistachio nuts or blanched almonds.

## CARAMEL FROSTING

2 cups brown sugar                    3 tablespoons butter
                    6 tablespoons cream

Boil ingredients together until mixture threads from a spoon, or forms a soft
ball when dropped in cold water. Cool, add flavoring. Beat until of fudgelike
consistency. Spread quickly on cake. Splendid for nut or ginger cake.

*Mrs. W. H. Anewalt*

## ELLIE REIDER'S MOCHA ICING

4 teaspoons strong coffee            1 heaping cup confectioners' sugar
½ cup soft butter                    2 teaspoons cocoa
                    1 teaspoon vanilla

Pour hot coffee over butter, to melt. Add sugar and cocoa. Cream together. Stir
until smooth, add vanilla and spread on cake.

*Mrs. Susan Laudenslager*

## STRAWBERRY ICING

½ cup mashed strawberries            1 cup confectioners' sugar
                    3 tablespoons cream

Mash strawberries with a silver fork and combine with sugar, using only enough
cream to make a smooth paste. Stir until smooth and spread on cake.

## HICKORY NUT ICING

1 cup brown sugar                    Butter size of a walnut
1 cup sour cream                     1 cup chopped hickory nutmeats

Heat sugar and cream together over low flame for a few minutes until it thickens.
Add butter. Simmer until mixture forms a soft ball when dropped into cold
water from a spoon. Remove from stove, cool. Beat until of a fudgelike consistency.
Mix with nutmeats and spread quickly on the cake.

*Mrs. Susan Laudenslager*

## ORANGE FILLING

1 egg                                1 teaspoon butter
½ cup sugar                          1 orange, juice and grated rind
1 heaping tablespoon flour           1 teaspoon lemon juice

Mix egg, sugar, flour, and butter and simmer over low flame, stirring constantly, until it comes to a boil. Place in top of double boiler over boiling water, add orange juice and rind and lemon juice. Simmer for 10 minutes. Spread on cake.

*Mrs. Elda Keck*

## ALMOND FILLING

1 cup confectioners' sugar  
1 cup sour, whipped cream  
½ teaspoon almond flavoring  
½ teaspoon vanilla  
1 cup blanched almonds, chopped

Combine sugar and cream to a smooth consistency. Add flavoring and nuts. Spread on cake.

*Mrs. Abram Samuels III*

## MORAVIAN CREAM NUT FILLING

1 cup nutmeats  
1 egg  
⅔ cup sour cream  
⅓ cup sifted powdered sugar  
1 teaspoon vanilla

Chop nuts. Beat egg yolk, mix with sour cream and beat well. Add sugar, vanilla, beat until thick. Fold in chopped nuts and stiffly beaten egg white. Chill. Spread thickly on cake just before serving. Good on sponge or butter cake.

*Mrs. Elda Keck*

## COCONUT FILLING

1 cup grated coconut  
1 cup sugar  
1 cup milk  
1 egg yolk  
2 egg whites

Heat sugar and milk together, beat egg yolk, and add with freshly grated coconut. Simmer until mixture thickens. Remove from stove and quickly fold in stiffly beaten egg whites. Spread on cake at once and sprinkle thickly with more coconut.

*Mrs. C. D. Miller*

# Cookies

*Early view of Sun Inn, Bethlehem, Pennsylvania*

EVERY year, in December, the kitchens of Bethlehem, Pennsylvania, produce their wonderful Christmas cookies made from traditional Moravian recipes. Christmas in Bethlehem means not only the birth of the Christ-child but it is also Bethlehem's birthday. On a snowy Christmas Eve over two hundred years ago Count Zinzendorf, the leader of the Moravians, took shelter in the little town's one log dwelling. Noting that humans and beasts shared the same roof, as they had on that first Christmas in Bethlehem in Judea, the count snatched up his candle and led the way to the stable, singing

> Not Jerusalem
> Only Bethlehem. . . .

As the strains of the Moravian hymn died away he turned to his followers and said, "The name of this place is Bethlehem." And so it has been ever since.

Moravians have always been devout, and through many years and troubled times their faith has expressed itself in kindly hospitality in the name of Christ as well as in worship of Him. From their earliest days in the wilderness the Moravians have offered food and shelter to all comers, whether they were Indians, Revolutionary soldiers, or the Marquis de Lafayette. And because Christmas is the climax of their year, generations of Bethlehem housewives have toiled long and lovingly to make the Christmas holidays memorable. There is much visiting around at Christmas time in Bethlehem, and Bethlehem still is hospitable. Thus cakes and wine are frequently brought forth and the Moravians have developed Christmas cookies to superlative perfection.

Recipes for the famous Moravian cakes and cookies are passed from mother to daughter, just as the same cookie cutters have been preserved from early days and are still in use. The shape of a Moravian cookie is a reasonable indication of its content, since probably it has been made in the same shape and with the same ingredients for a century or two. It is true that some modern innovations may have made their way into the Christmas cookie field, but it would be considered a shabby household in Bethlehem that must resort to brownies or hermits for Christmas, when there are so many traditional recipes that are intricate and delicious. There used to be a saying in Bethlehem that you could estimate not only the housewife's culinary skill but the family's financial status from the quantity and variety of its Christmas cookies!

Bethlehem is also the home of the *Putz*. Every family has a crèche, as elaborate and detailed as can be contrived, to place under the Christmas tree. This Nativity scene, deriving from the German word *putzen*, to decorate, has been shortened in Pennsylvania Dutch to *Putz* and has come to mean whatever-decorates-the-space-under-the-Christmas-tree. It is particularly a crèche, but the term may include a toy village or an electric train, if the family wishes to elaborate. *Putzing*—visiting around to see the *Putzes*—is a Bethlehem holiday custom. It is also the occasion for the appearance of the holiday cookies and for general good will.

Bethlehem's loveliest Christmas custom by far is its candle-lighting service. This is beautiful and deeply religious. Anyone who has ever seen how myriads of twinkling candles can light a darkened church, who has whiffed the mingled odors of beeswax and balsam, who has followed antiphonally a small girl's singing of "Morning Star, O cheering sight . . ." has experienced one of the most moving Christmas services in the world. Then, when he has passed through the shining, candlelit gantlet of his singing neighbors and gone forth into the snowy evening, he has been truly in Bethlehem at Christmas.

## MORAVIAN WHITE CHRISTMAS COOKIES

| | |
|---|---|
| 1½ cups soft butter | 3 cups sifted flour |
| 3 cups powdered sugar | ½ teaspoon salt |
| 4 eggs | 3 tablespoons sherry |
| ½ tablespoon nutmeg | |

Cream butter and sugar, add well-beaten eggs. Beat together. Sift flour and salt together several times, add to other ingredients with wine and nutmeg. Stir well but do not beat. Place in refrigerator overnight. Next morning, roll out on floured board, very thin. Cut in shapes (hearts, stars, and diamonds) and bake in 350° oven. Makes about 80 cookies.

*Mrs. Philip B. Woodroofe*

## MORAVIAN BROWN COOKIES

| | |
|---|---|
| 1 cup light brown sugar, firmly packed | 1 teaspoon ginger |
| 1 cup butter and shortening | 1 cup sifted flour |
| 1 teaspoon salt | 1 egg |
| ¼ teaspoon nutmeg | 1 cup molasses |
| 1 tablespoon cinnamon | 1 teaspoon soda, dissolved in |
| ½ teaspoon cloves | ¼ cup hot water |
| | 4 cups sifted flour |

Cream sugar and shortening. Sift together salt, spices, and 1 cup of flour. Sift into mixing bowl, work sugar and shortening into flour, add egg well beaten and slightly warmed molasses. Add hot water and soda, stirring into mixture. Stir in 4 cups sifted flour, a little at a time. Chill in refrigerator overnight. Next morning roll out, very thin, on floured board. Shape with Christmas cookie cutters— men, deer, men on horseback, etc. Bake in 325° oven for about 15 minutes. Pierce with a darning needle when they come from the oven, so that they may be threaded to hang on Christmas tree. Cookies may be iced with colored frosting and decorated with pieces of fruit and nuts. This makes 6-8 dozen cookies.

*Mrs. Philip B. Woodroofe*

## MORAVIAN SCOTCH COOKIES

| | |
|---|---|
| ½ cup butter | Pinch of salt |
| ½ cup sugar | 1 egg |
| 3 cups sifted flour | 1 teaspoon caraway seed |

### Frosting

| | |
|---|---|
| 1 cup sugar | 1 egg white |
| 4 tablespoons water | Pink sugar |

Cream butter and sugar, sift flour several times with salt. Stir egg into mixture, sift in flour, add caraway seed. Stir well. Roll out on floured board, very thin. Cut in diamonds with a jagging iron, and bake on greased cookie sheet at 325° for about 15 minutes. Cool, cover with frosting: Boil water and sugar until syrup threads. Beat white of egg on cold platter with wire whisk. Beat syrup gradually into egg. When thick and smooth, spread quickly on cookies and sprinkle with pink sugar.

*Mrs. Philip B. Woodroofe*

## ANISE COOKIES

½ cup soft butter
½ cup powdered sugar
3 cups sifted flour
1 teaspoon hartshorn

1 egg
¼ teaspoon salt
1 lemon, juice and grated rind
1 tablespoon anise seed

Cream butter and sugar, stir in egg. Sift flour with salt and hartshorn, sift into mixture. Beat well. Add anise seed. Form into long, thin rolls and wrap in waxed paper. Chill in refrigerator overnight. Next morning slice very thin. Bake on greased cookie sheet in 325° oven about 15 minutes, being careful not to burn. Makes about 60 cookies.

*Mrs. Edward S. Shepherd*

## SPRINGERLE

6 eggs
3 cups powdered sugar
3 cups sifted flour

1 teaspoon hartshorn
1 lemon, juice and grated rind
1 tablespoon anise seed

### Pinch of salt

*Springerle* could mean a small, jumping horse, probably with a thought to old-time German cookies in shapes of horses and riders. It is also reminiscent of the German word for the knight in chess. So, whether it derives from a horse-shaped cookie or from the resemblance to a chessboard that a springerle board has, we can't tell. However, a springerle board is divided into squares with indentations of fancy patterns—animals, flowers, birds, and people. This board is pressed down upon the cookie dough and the design impressed, or you can buy springerle rollers with the designs hollowed out on the rolling pin, but they are difficult to use. Nowadays, many people content themselves with pressing the bottom of a star-patterned cut-glass tumbler upon each cookie. To be really beautiful, *Springerle* have to be made pretty much professionally. They are never given away with profusion because they are too much trouble to make! But there are sure to be one or two on every cookie plate at Christmas.

The old recipes required that sugar and eggs be beaten together for at least an hour. Then the flour was sifted several times, resifted with the hartshorn, added to the eggs and sugar, and the whole stirred again. Then lemon, anise seed, and grated rind were added and the dough rolled out. The pictures were separated along the dividing lines to form square cookies.

Bake on a greased cookie sheet in 300° oven for about 20 minutes, watching carefully to prevent burning and coloring. When baked they should be pale. Makes about 40.

## TORTELLEN
### (Tartlets)

½ lemon, grated rind
1 cup sugar
1 cup butter
2 egg yolks
1½ cups bread flour

1 egg white
1 tablespoon water
1 cup shredded almonds
½ cup sugar
2 tablespoons cinnamon

¼ teaspoon salt

Grate lemon rind and mix with sugar. Cream with butter and beat in egg yolks one at a time. Add flour gradually, sifting into batter to make rich dough. Form into balls the size of walnuts and flatten with the bottom of a glass. Beat egg white with water and brush over cookies. Blanch and shred the almonds, mix with sugar, cinnamon, and salt and sprinkle thickly over tops of cookies. Bake in 350° oven until golden brown. Makes 40.

*Julie Weder*


## MANDELRINGE
### (Almond Ring)

1 cup blanched almonds
6 egg whites
Pinch of salt

2 cups powdered sugar
¼ teaspoon nutmeg
1 teaspoon vanilla

Blanch and shred almonds, then toast lightly. Beat egg whites with salt on a platter and, when stiff, whip in sugar gradually. Stir mixture for ½ hour. Fold in almonds, nutmeg and vanilla. Grease a cookie sheet and shape batter on it in rings, with a spoon. Bake in 325° oven until golden brown. Take from oven and sprinkle with sugar. Makes 50.

*Mabel E. Mulock*


## MANDELPLAETTCHEN
### (Almond Wafers)

1 cup soft butter
1 cup sugar
2 eggs
1 teaspoon grated lemon rind
⅛ teaspoon salt

½ cup blanched, shredded almonds
¼ teaspoon nutmeg
2 ounces sherry wine
3 cups sifted flour
2 tablespoons cream

1 egg yolk

Cream butter and sifted sugar, beat in eggs one at a time. Add lemon rind, salt, almonds, nutmeg, and sherry. Sift flour and add with cream. Stir but do not beat for 15 minutes. Chill overnight. Next day roll out very thin on floured board and cut in shapes. Mix egg yolk with a little milk to thin, and brush tops of cookies. Bake on greased sheet in 350° oven until golden. Makes 75.

*Mabel E. Mulock*

## ALMOND COOKIES

| | |
|---|---|
| 1 cup butter, scant | 4 egg yolks |
| 1 cup confectioners' sugar | 3 tablespoons cream |

3 cups sifted flour

### Icing

| | |
|---|---|
| 2 egg yolks | Confectioners' sugar, to thicken |
| 2 tablespoons water | 2 cups finely chopped blanched almonds |

Cream butter and sugar, add eggs and cream. Stir. Sift in flour and mix. Scatter confectioners' sugar and flour on board and roll dough very thin to almost ¼-inch thickness. Cut in diamond shapes with jagging iron. Bake on greased sheet at 350° for about 15 minutes. Cool. Beat egg yolks lightly and stir in water. Work in enough sugar to make thick paste. Ice cookies generously and "strew thickly with almonds." Return to oven for about 3 minutes "to dry."

*Mrs. Elda Keck*

## LEBKUCHEN I
### (Ginger Cakes)

| | |
|---|---|
| ½ cup shortening | 1 teaspoon cinnamon |
| 1 cup brown sugar | 1 teaspoon cloves |
| 2 eggs | 1 teaspoon allspice |
| 1 cup molasses | ¾ teaspoon salt |
| 1 cup warm coffee | ¼ pound finely chopped citron |
| 1 teaspoon soda | ¼ pound shredded orange peel |
| 4½ cups flour | ¼ pound shredded lemon peel |
| 2 tablespoons cocoa | 1½ cups chopped nutmeats |

Cream shortening and sugar, add eggs separately, stirring. Add molasses, dissolve soda in hot coffee, and add. Sift flour and cocoa with spices and a pinch of salt. Add to mixture, alternating with mixed fruit and nuts. Grease large cookie sheets, spread batter on them to ½-inch thickness, allowing for spreading. Bake in 350° oven for 25 minutes. Cut in squares.

*Mrs. F. C. Wunder*

## LEBKUCHEN II

| | |
|---|---|
| 1 cup honey | 1 teaspoon cloves |
| 1 cup light brown sugar | 1 tablespoon cinnamon |
| ¼ pound blanched almonds | ½ teaspoon salt |
| ¼ pound chopped citron | 1 glass brandy |
| Grated rind of 1 lemon | 4½ cups sifted flour |
| 1 teaspoon nutmeg | 1 teaspoon hartshorn |

Boil the honey and sugar for a few minutes. Add shredded almonds, citron, lemon rind, and spices. Stir well into mixture. Add brandy, sift in flour and hartshorn. Stir for 10 minutes vigorously. Cover dough and chill overnight, not in too cool a place. Next day roll out floured board to ¼-inch thickness, cut in shapes (hearts or diamonds), and bake in 375° oven for about 15 minutes. Turn off heat, let stand in oven 5 minutes. Cool. Combine:

| | |
|---|---|
| 1 cup confectioners' sugar | 1 lemon, juice and grated rind |

Make a smooth, creamy paste, thinning with a little cream if necessary. Spread lightly on cookies. These are traditional Bethlehem Christmas cookies.

*From an old cook book*

## BASEL LECKERLEIN
### (Sweetmeats)

| | |
|---|---|
| 1 cup honey | 2 cups sifted flour |
| 1 cup sifted sugar | ½ lemon, juice and grated rind |
| 1 cup almonds, not blanched | 1 teaspoon nutmeg |
| | 2 ounces arrack or brandy |
| | 2 teaspoons mace |
| 1 teaspoon cloves | |

These cookies are thought to have come from Basel, Switzerland, and are a "lickerish" delicacy. The mace and cloves were not in the old recipe but can be added. The original instructions are as follows: "Melt the honey, add sugar and almonds, blend well, cover and set aside for 8 days (perhaps to ferment?). Then roll out, after adding other ingredients, to a paste half a finger thick, place on large pan lined with oiled paper and bake quickly in a hot oven. While still warm, cut in strips about 2 fingers broad and 1 finger long."

*From an old cook book*

## PEFFERNISS
### (Pepper Nuts)

| | |
|---|---|
| ¼ cup butter | 1 teaspoon baking powder |
| 3 cups brown sugar | 2 tablespoons cinnamon |
| 4 eggs | ¼ tablespoon cloves |
| 3 cups sifted flour | 1 tablespoon ground cardamom seed |

Cream butter and sugar, add beaten eggs. Sift flour with baking powder and spices. The dough should be extremely stiff and either rolled out thinly and cut in tiny rounds the size of a coin or, with addition of ½ cup cream, thinned and shaped into small balls and placed on greased cookie sheet. Bake until light brown in 350° oven about 10 minutes.

*Mabel E. Mulock*

## MANDELSPITZEN
### (Almond Peaks)

| | |
|---|---|
| 1 cup butter | 1 teaspoon lemon juice |
| 1 cup sugar | 1 cup sifted flour |
| 3 egg yolks | ½ teaspoon baking powder |
| 1 tablespoon orange juice | ½ cup blanched, shredded almonds |
| 1 tablespoon grated orange rind | |

Cream butter and sugar, add egg yolks one by one, orange and lemon juice. Sift in flour and baking powder, mix thoroughly and stir well. Dredge about ⅔ of almonds in little flour, fold into batter with grated orange rind. Stir some more. Pour the batter into a greased pan, spread over its surface but leave space for spreading. Bake in 350° oven for about 20 minutes. Cool and cut in squares.

### *Frosting*

| | |
|---|---|
| 1 cup sugar | 2 egg whites |
| 4 tablespoons cold water | ¼ teaspoon salt |

Boil water and sugar until syrup threads. Whip egg whites with wire whisk until stiff. Beat in syrup. When smooth and creamy, spread quickly on cookies, sprinkle with remaining almonds.

*Mary Ann Ochs*

## MRS. SCHAEFFER'S HICKORY NUT DROPS

| | |
|---|---|
| ½ cup butter | 2 teaspoons baking powder |
| 2 cups sugar | ½ cup milk or cream |
| 3 beaten eggs | 2 cups hickory nutmeats |
| 2½ cups sifted flour | ½ teaspoon flavoring |

Cream butter and sugar, add eggs, and blend. Sift flour and baking powder together, adding to batter alternately with milk. Dredge nuts with a little flour and add with flavoring. If batter seems too thin, add a little more flour at this point. Drop from spoon on buttered cookie sheet. Bake at 350° for about 10 minutes. Makes about 100.

*Mrs. Susan Laudenslager*

## "DUTCH" SHORTBREAD

| | |
|---|---|
| 1 lemon, grated rind | 3 cups sifted flour |
| ⅔ cup sugar | 1 egg white |
| 1 cup butter | Milk |
| 1 egg | ½ cup sugar |
| Pinch of salt | 2 tablespoons cinnamon |
| 6 hard-boiled egg yolks | ⅓ cup chopped nuts |

Grate the lemon rind and mix with sugar. Cream butter and add. Beat in egg and mix together. Add salt. Put hard-boiled egg yolks through a sieve and add. Stir in sifted flour. Roll balls from dough, the size of walnuts (using 1 scant teaspoon of dough for each will keep them uniform in size). Place on greased cookie sheet and flatten with a fork. Mix slightly beaten egg white with a little milk, dip balls in this, then in mixed sugar, cinnamon, and nuts. Return to cookie sheet and bake at 325° until lightly browned. Makes 80.

*Ellie Kofler*

## SLAPJACKS

| | |
|---|---|
| ¾ cup butter | 3 cups sifted flour |
| 3 cups brown sugar, loosely packed | 1 cup molasses |
| ½ tablespoon soda, dissolved in | ½ coconut, grated |
| 1 tablespoon warm water | ½ cup chopped nuts |

Cream butter and sugar. Add soda and water to molasses. Sift flour into bowl. Sir. Add molasses and stir vigorously. Fold in coconut and nuts. Let stand overnight in refrigerator. Next day, drop by teaspoonfuls on buttered sheet. Bake at 350° for 10-15 minutes.

*Mrs. W. H. Anewalt*

## BLACK WALNUT SQUARES

| | |
|---|---|
| 2 eggs | ¾ cup sifted flour |
| 1 cup sugar | ¾ teaspoon baking powder |
| ½ cup butter | 1 teaspoon vanilla |
| 2 squares unsweetened chocolate | 1 cup chopped, black walnuts |

Break eggs into bowl. Beat and add sugar gradually. Melt chocolate with butter, add and stir together. Sift flour and baking powder into bowl. Dredge nutmeats with a little flour and add with vanilla. Bake in thin sheets in a shallow pan at 350° for 15 minutes. Spread with frosting:

1 egg white, unbeaten        ¾ cup confectioners' sugar
3 tablespoons melted chocolate

Stir together until soft and creamy. As soon as baked sheets come out of the oven, spread with frosting. Cool, cut in squares with sharp knife. Makes 50.

*Mrs. Elda Keck*

### SCOTCH TAFFY CAKES

2 cups sifted flour        ¾ cup New Orleans molasses
2 cups brown sugar        ½ teaspoon soda dissolved in water
⅓ cup melted lard        ½ coconut, grated

Sift flour several times, then sift with sugar. Mix with melted lard. Slightly warm molasses and add. Dissolve soda in a little hot water and add. Mix well, chill in refrigerator overnight. Next day add coconut, drop from teaspoon on greased cookie sheet about size of hickory nut and 3 inches apart. Bake at 350° for about 15 minutes.

*Mrs. Thomas B. Keck*

### ALINE DILLINGER'S JUMBLES

1 cup butter        2 cups sifted flour
2 cups white sugar        1 lemon, grated rind and juice
2 eggs, lightly beaten        1 grated coconut

Cream butter and sugar, stir in eggs, mix. Sift flour into bowl, mix into batter, add lemon juice. Fold in lemon rind and coconut. Roll out lightly on board sprinkled with powdered sugar, very thin, cut in shapes. Bake at 350° for about 10 minutes.

*Mrs. Thomas B. Keck*

### WALNUT DROPS

2 cups powdered sugar        ¼ teaspoon salt
3 eggs        1 level tablespoon baking powder
6 tablespoons sifted flour        2 cups English walnut meats

Mix sugar and eggs, sift flour, salt, and baking powder into bowl, mix well with sugar and eggs. Fold in walnut meats. Add whatever flavoring you prefer. Drop from a teaspoon on a buttered cookie sheet and bake in 350° oven about 10 minutes. Makes about 90.

*Mrs. Victor Boyer*

## CURRANT DROPS

½ cup butter
1 cup sugar
2 eggs

½ cup sour cream
½ teaspoon soda
1 cup sifted cake flour

1 cup currants

Cream butter and sugar and stir in lightly beaten eggs. Dissolve soda in sour cream, mix with egg and butter mixture, sift in flour. Dredge currants in a very little flour and fold into batter, with whatever flavoring you prefer. Drop from teaspoon on greased cookie sheet. Bake at 350° for 10 minutes. Makes about 4 dozen.

*Mrs. Victor Boyer*

## TOUCH ME NOTS

1 cup hickory nutmeats
4 egg whites

Pinch of salt
1 cup granulated sugar

Chop hickory nuts finely. Beat egg whites on cold platter with salt. Add sugar a little at a time, beating. Fold in nutmeats. Drop from teaspoon on greased cookie sheet, well separated. Bake about 10 minutes at 350°.

*Mrs. Susan Laudenslager*

## FRUIT COOKIES

⅔ cup butter
1 cup granulated sugar
2 eggs
1 teaspoon soda, dissolved in
1 tablespoon hot water

2 cups sifted flour
1 cup chopped English walnuts
1 cup chopped raisins
1 scant teaspoon cloves
1 teaspoon cinnamon

½ teaspoon mace

### Icing

1 cup sugar
4 tablespoons water

1 egg white
½ teaspoon almond extract

Cream butter and sugar, stir in eggs, add soda dissolved in water and sifted flour. Mix. Dredge nuts and fruit in a little flour, fold into batter, sift in spices. Drop from a teaspoon on buttered cookie sheet, well separated, bake at 350° for about 20 minutes. Cool. Boil water and sugar together until syrup threads from spoon. Beat egg whites on cold platter with wire whisk. Add flavoring and beat in syrup gradually. Drop a little of this on each cookie.

*Mrs. Elda Keck*

## FRUITED COOKIES

3 eggs
1 cup granulated sugar
3 squares chocolate
½ cup melted butter, scant
1½ cups sifted flour

¾ teaspoon baking powder
¾ teaspoon salt
½ cup broken nutmeats, scant
½ cup candied cherries, scant
¾ teaspoon vanilla

Beat eggs lightly, add sugar, and cream together. Melt chocolate and add, with melted butter. Sift flour, measure, resift with baking powder and salt into the batter. Add vanilla. Mix well. Dredge nuts and cherries in a little flour and stir in. Drop by half-teaspoonfuls on buttered and floured baking sheet. Bake at 350° for 8-10 minutes. Makes about 90.

*Miriam Wertman*

## AUNT SUE'S FIG COOKIES

3 teaspoons baking powder
½ teaspoon salt
3 cups flour
½ teaspoon nutmeg

1 cup granulated sugar
1 cup butter and lard
¼ cup milk
1 cup chopped figs

Sift baking powder, salt, flour, and nutmeg. Cream sugar with butter and lard, add flour mixture and milk alternately. Dredge chopped figs in a little flour, fold into the batter. Roll out lightly on a floured board. Cut in squares. Bake in 350° oven about 25-30 minutes.

*Mrs. John Joseph Stoudt*

## DATE STRIPS

3 eggs, lightly beaten
1 cup sugar
¾ cup pastry flour

½ teaspoon salt
1 teaspoon baking powder
1 pound chopped dates

1 cup walnut meats

Add sugar gradually to beaten eggs. Sift in flour, salt, and baking powder and mix well. Dredge dates and nuts lightly with flour, fold into batter. Spread in a greased pan, leaving space around edges for spreading. Bake at 350° for about 40 minutes. Cool, cut in strips. Makes about 40.

*Mrs. John H. Adams*

## SPICED GINGER COOKIES

¾ cup brown sugar
½ cup shortening
¾ teaspoon baking soda, dissolved in
½ teaspoon vinegar

½ cup molasses
2-2½ cups sifted flour
¼ teaspoon ginger
¼ teaspoon cloves

1½ teaspoons cinnamon

The vinegar is to make the cookies snap. Cream sugar and shortening, add soda and vinegar. Place molasses in large mixing bowl, add mixture to the molasses, sift in flour and spices. If dough seems not stiff enough, add a little more flour. Roll out thin on floured board and cut in shapes. Bake in 350° oven from 10-15 minutes. Makes about 80 cookies.

*Mrs. W. H. Anewalt*

## ALINE DILLINGER'S SPICE COOKIES

½ cup melted butter
½ cup brown sugar
1 cup molasses
½ teaspoon soda dissolved in
1 tablespoon hot water

2½ cups sifted flour
½ teaspoon salt
1 teaspoon cinnamon
1 teaspoon ginger
1 egg

Mix melted butter, sugar, and molasses in a bowl. Add soda in water. Sift in flour, salt, and spices, mix well. Stir in egg and beat for 5 minutes. Chill in refrigerator overnight. Next day roll out very thin on floured board, cut in shapes, bake at 350° for 10-15 minutes. Makes about 7 dozen.

*Mrs. Thomas B. Keck*

## CINNAMON COOKIES

⅓ cup butter
1 cup sugar
1 egg
2 cups flour

2 teaspoons baking powder
1 tablespoon cinnamon
½ teaspoon salt
½ cup milk

Cream butter and sugar. Beat egg lightly and stir in. Add alternately sifted flour, baking powder, cinnamon and salt and milk. Mix well. Roll out on floured board, cut in shapes. Bake at 350° for about 15 minutes. Makes about 70.

*Mrs. Victor Boyer*

## MOLASSES COOKIES

| | |
|---|---|
| 1 cup molasses | ½ tablespoon lard |
| 1 teaspoon soda, dissolved in | 1 egg |
| 1 tablespoon hot water | 2-2½ cups sifted flour |
| | ⅛ teaspoon ginger |

Place molasses in bowl, add soda in water, melted lard. Mix. Add slightly beaten egg, sifted flour, and ginger. Beat well, and if the dough seems too soft, add enough more sifted flour to make a stiff batter. Chill. Roll out on a floured board, very thin, and cut in animal shapes. Bake on cookie sheets in 350° oven for 10-15 minutes. Makes about 5 dozen.

*Mrs. Donald L. Helfferich*

## MOLASSES CREAMS

| | |
|---|---|
| 1 cup baking molasses | ¼ cup sour cream |
| ½ cup lard or shortening | Flour to stiffen, starting with 2 cups |
| ½ cup sugar | 1½ teaspoons ginger |
| | 1½ teaspoons soda |

Place molasses in mixing bowl, adding melted lard, sugar, and sour cream. Mix. Sift flour, ginger, and soda and sift into bowl. Mix to consistency of biscuit dough, roll out, not too thin, on floured board and cut in squares. Bake in 350° oven for about 10 minutes. Then ice with:

| | |
|---|---|
| ½ cup granulated sugar | Small lump butter |
| 1½ tablespoons water | Vanilla |

Boil together until firm, soft ball can be formed when tested in water. Beat a little until cool and creamy, add a little vanilla, and spread on cookies.

*Mrs. Elda Keck*

## SOFT MOLASSES COOKIES

| | |
|---|---|
| 1 cup lard | 2 teaspoons soda, dissolved in |
| ½ cup sugar | 1 tablespoon hot water |
| 1 cup molasses | 3 cups sifted flour |
| 1 cup sour milk | ½ teaspoon salt |

Soften lard, cream with sugar, mix with molasses. Add sour milk and soda and water. Mix well. Sift in flour and salt. Roll out quickly and lightly on floured board to ⅜-inch thickness. Cut with a teacup-sized cutter and bake in greased, cookie pans at 350° for about 12 minutes. This is the big soft molasses cookie that melts in your mouth, especially if eaten as it comes from the oven. It is my grandmother's recipe and I remember that she used to spread a hot cookie with butter for me, just as it came from the oven. Nothing has ever tasted so good since.

## SPICE TONGUES

1 cup molasses
½ cup lard
¼ cup brown sugar
2 teaspoons soda, dissolved in
¼ cup hot water

1 tablespoon vinegar
¾ teaspoon nutmeg
¾ teaspoon cinnamon
¾ teaspoon cloves
2½ cups sifted flour

Place molasses in mixing bowl, heat lard, and pour over molasses. Add brown sugar and soda with vinegar. Stir. Sift in spices with flour and beat well. Shape bits of dough in tongue shapes, roll them in granulated sugar. Bake on cookie sheet in 350° oven for about 15 minutes.

*Mrs. Irene Herman*

## BUNNY'S COOKIES

1½ cups shortening
2 cups brown sugar
3 eggs
5 cups flour

1 teaspoon cinnamon
1 teaspoon soda
¼ teaspoon salt
1 cup chopped nuts

Cream butter and sugar, stir in eggs. Sift in flour, cinnamon, soda, and salt and beat well. Dredge nuts in a little flour and fold in. Shape into 4 rolls, wrap in waxed paper, and chill in refrigerator overnight. Next day slice rather thin and bake at 325° about 20 minutes. Makes 160.

*Mrs. John C. Weigand*

## MOTHER'S OATMEAL COOKIES

1 cup melted butter
3 cups dark brown sugar
1 egg

3 cups oatmeal (uncooked)
Pinch of salt
1 tablespoon vanilla

Melt butter, mix with sugar, add egg, and beat. Add oatmeal, salt, and vanilla. Beat well. Drop from teaspoon on buttered cookie sheet and bake at 325° until lightly browned.

*Miriam Wertman*

## DINAH'S SHAKER COOKIES

¾ teaspoon soda
1 cup shortening
1 cup brown sugar
2 eggs, well beaten

2 cups sifted flour
½ teaspoon salt
2 cups rolled oats
1 cup chopped raisins

⅞ cup milk

Dissolve soda in a little water. Cream shortening with sugar, beat in eggs, sift in flour and salt, add rolled oats and raisins. Stir in soda and water. This will seem to be a very stiff batter but can be dropped from teaspoon on greased baking sheet. Bake at 375° until cookies are lightly browned. Makes about 100.

*Mabel E. Mulock*

## FILLED COOKIES

1 cup chopped raisins
½ cup sugar

½ cup water
1 tablespoon flour

½ cup chopped walnuts

Place these ingredients in a saucepan and cook together until thick and syrupy. Set aside to cool.

½ cup shortening
1 cup sugar
½ teaspoon salt
1 egg

½ cup cream
1 teaspoon vanilla
3½ cups flour
1 teaspoon baking powder

1 teaspoon soda

Cream shortening, add sugar and salt, beaten egg, cream, and vanilla. Sift flour with baking powder and soda and add to mixture. Turn out and roll on floured board, very thin. Cut in shapes with round cookie cutter. On half the rounds spread filling that has cooled. Top these cookies with the rest of the rounds, pressing top and bottom firmly together at edges. Bake in 350° oven, in greased pans, for 15-20 minutes.

*Mrs. Ira F. Zartman*

## BUTTERTHINS

2 cups butter
3½ cups confectioners' sugar
5 eggs, lightly beaten
4 cups sifted flour

1 teaspoon soda, dissolved in
½ cup sour cream
1 teaspoon vanilla
¼ teaspoon salt

Cream butter and sugar, stir in eggs. Sift in flour, stir in sour cream and soda, add vanilla and salt. Mix well. Chill. Roll out very thin on floured board, cut in shapes. Bake on greased cookie sheet at 350° for about 10 minutes. Makes 100.

*Mrs. Victor Boyer*

## SCHOOLBOY COOKIES

| | |
|---|---|
| 2 eggs | ½ teaspoon salt |
| 1 cup sugar | ½ teaspoon soda |
| ¾ cup sour cream | 1 teaspoon baking powder |
| 2 cups sifted flour | 1 teaspoon vanilla |

Beat eggs lightly and mix with sugar. Add sour cream. Sift in salt, soda, baking powder with flour, mix well to form a soft batter. Add vanilla. Mix and drop in buttered gem pans, about half full. Not meant to be as large as cup cakes. Sprinkle a little granulated sugar and a few currants over the tops. Bake at 375°-400° for 10 minutes.

*Mrs. Elda Keck*

## SALLY HOFFMAN'S CHOCOLATE COOKIES

| | |
|---|---|
| 1 cup granulated sugar | 2 ounces chocolate |
| 1 cup brown sugar | 3 cups sifted flour |
| 1 cup butter | 1 teaspoon cinnamon |
| 4 eggs | 1 teaspoon cloves |

Cream sugar and butter, adding eggs and melted chocolate. Sift in spices with flour and blend to form a stiff dough. Roll out on a board spread with confectioners' sugar and flour, very thin. Bake at 350° for about 10 minutes. Makes 90-100 cookies.

*Mrs. Susan Laudenslager*

## CHOCOLATE COOKIES II

| | |
|---|---|
| 2 cups granulated sugar | 2 ounces chocolate, grated |
| 1½ cups soft butter | ½ teaspoon soda, dissolved in |
| 4 eggs | 1 tablespoon vinegar |
| 2½ cups sifted flour | |

Cream sugar and butter, add eggs and grated chocolate. Stir well. Add soda in vinegar and enough sifted flour to form a stiff dough, using more than 2½ cups if needed. Mix well, chill in refrigerator overnight, next day roll out on floured board, very thin. Bake at 350° on greased cookie sheets for about 10 minutes. Makes about 80.

*Mrs. W. H. Anewalt*

## BROWN SUGAR SAND TARTS

2 cups brown sugar
1 cup butter or shortening
2 egg yolks
3 cups sifted flour

¼ teaspoon salt
1 egg white (reserve the other)
Cinnamon and sugar
Raisins

Cream sugar and shortening, add egg yolks. Sift in flour and salt, a little at a time, blending well. Sprinkle board with powdered sugar, roll out dough, very thin. Cut in squares. Beat reserved egg white and, with a brush, spread a little on each cookie. Sprinkle with brown sugar and cinnamon, top with raisins. Bake on greased cookie sheet at 325° for 10-15 minutes, watching to prevent burning. Makes about 80.

*Mrs. John H. Adams*

## SAND TARTS

Blanched almonds
1 cup soft butter
2 cups granulated sugar

3 eggs
4 cups sifted flour
1 teaspoon vanilla

Sugar and cinnamon, mixed

Blanch and split almonds (because a whole almond presents no flat side to stick to a cookie). Cream butter and sugar, stir in eggs, blend well. Sift in flour to make a stiff batter, adding vanilla. Roll out on board sprinkled with powdered sugar, very thin. Cut in shapes—usually rounds, sometimes hearts, stars, and half moons. Brush tops with a little egg white, then shake a very little cinnamon and sugar on top. Press down half an almond at center of each cookie. Bake at 325°-350° for 8-10 minutes, watching to prevent burning. Cookies are done when they just begin to change color. Should not be allowed to brown. Better when chilled overnight before rolling and cutting. Makes about 100.

*Mrs. Edward S. Shepherd*

## APEES

These are cousins of the sand tart—simple cookies but with a complicated history. For the first edition of this book I collected at least twenty variants of the recipe and finally used five, chiefly because each one spelled the name differently. At about that time Frances Lichten dug up, in Watson's *Annals of Philadelphia*, a story to the effect that a young woman named Ann Page had made the first of these cookies, scratching her initial on each one, hence AP's. But if Ann did invent them one thing is sure, the Pennsylvania Dutch took to them with alacrity.

For any number of recipes can be found, labeled variously apees, apeas, apace, apice, epise, epees, and eepies, to name a few. Miss Lichten sent me some more notes:

"1817—'flat cakes that will keep long in the house good.'"

"In 1831 they played a game called *I Love My Love* and said, 'He took me to the Anchor and treated me to apees and almonds.'"

"Widdifield's recipe (1856):

| | |
|---|---|
| 1½ pounds flour | 1 pound butter |
| 1 pound sugar | 1 gill milk |

"Mrs. Rorer used the Widdifield recipe word for word. In 1853 she had used it, halved, adding a teaspoon of nutmeg and dropping the milk. In the 1902 edition of her book it was no longer included."

Here is Miss Lichten's own recipe:

## APEES

| | |
|---|---|
| ¾ pound butter | 3½ cups flour |
| 1 pound "A" sugar | ½ teaspoon cream tartar |
| 3 eggs, beaten separately | 1 cup sour cream |

Cream butter and sugar, add egg yolks, and blend. Sift flour with cream tartar into the bowl, little by little. Mix together. Add sour cream and fold in egg whites. Chill overnight in refrigerator. Next day roll out on floured board, shape with scalloped circular cutter, the traditional shape for apees. Bake on greased cookie sheets in 325° oven about 10 minutes, watching to prevent burning.

*Frances Lichten, who wrote* The Folk Art of Rural Pennsylvania

# Other Desserts

*Moravian Buildings, Bethlehem,*
*Pennsylvania*

EVERYONE knows that Pennsylvania's favorite desserts are, of course, pies and cakes. But that's not to say that there's nothing else to eat! Usually pie and cake appear at the same time—and more than one kind of each. But just in case someone might have a hankering for a dish of custard or an apple dumpling, well, there'd better be dessert. Anyhow, cake is an accompaniment, isn't it; meant to go with something else? A pudding, maybe? It would never do for anyone to go away from a Pennsylvania Dutch table hungry—as though he could! But it's just as bad if he goes away thinking of something he wished Mom had made and didn't. To be on the safe side, Mom decides to have fruit fritters for dinner, or perhaps a cherry pudding. Although quantity is the word, it is not to be supposed that there is any lack of quality. There is always plenty of country butter in the dessert, often it is made with cream and almost always with dozens of eggs. Probably the Pennsylvania Dutch make more use of eggs and flour in their cookery than any other cooks on earth! And the cream! There'd better be a pitcher of it handy; it's good poured over a pudding. Or perhaps there ought to be a sauce for the pudding. . . . And so, for a couple of centuries, hearty desserts have followed hard upon hearty meals. Not for the Pennsylvania Dutch is the slight confection, the dessert so ephemeral that all you remember about it afterward is the flavor. Oh no! Pennsylvania desserts are rich and substantial, aimed at providing satisfactory nourishment and the comfortable feeling, when you push back your chair (if you can) , that you sat down to eat and that's what you've been doing. But in the meantime pass the pie—and the cake—and I guess there ought to be a dish of pudding to go with the cake.

## CHEESE PUDDING

12 ounces cottage cheese
¾ cup cream

1 tablespoon sugar
1 lemon, juice and grated rind
Cinnamon

Press cheese through a sieve and mix with cream, sugar, and lemon juice. Fold in most of the grated rind, sprinkle the rest on top with a little cinnamon. Mold, chill, and serve—with a spoonful of strawberry or cherry preserves on top of each serving. Serves 4.

*Amy Kerr*

## FEINPUDDING
### (Delicate Pudding)

2 cups milk
3 level tablespoons cornstarch
½ cup sugar

½ teaspoon salt
2 egg whites
1 tablespoon vanilla

Place milk in top of double boiler over boiling water. Moisten cornstarch with a little extra milk, add it to the hot milk, stir until thick and smooth. Add sugar and salt. Beat egg whites stiff and pour the mixture, while hot, into the bowl with them. Stir, add vanilla, pour into a mold, and cool. Serves 4.

*Mrs. Elda Keck*

## RAHMPUDDING
### (Cream Pudding)

3 egg yolks
3 tablespoons sour cream
1 heaping teaspoon sugar
½ teaspoon cinnamon

1 cup soft white bread or
    cake crumbs
3 egg whites
Pinch of salt

Stir egg yolks with sour cream, add other ingredients, folding in egg whites last, stiffly beaten with the salt. Pour into buttered pudding dish, cover with waxed paper or foil, steam over boiling water for 45 minutes. Chill. Unmold and serve with wine- or vanilla-flavored custard sauce.

### Sauce

2 cups milk
½ cup sugar

3 eggs
¾ teaspoon vanilla

Scald the milk. Beat the egg yolks and mix with sugar until creamy. Add hot milk to egg yolks gradually and, when mixed together, return to double boiler.

Stir until sauce thickens. Remove from stove, stir in beaten egg whites, add vanilla. Cool. Serves 4.

*From an old cook book*

## LEMON PUDDING

| | |
|---|---|
| Butter, size of an egg | 2 tablespoons cornstarch |
| 1 lemon, juice and grated rind | 2 eggs |
| 1 cup boiling water | 2 cups sugar |

Place butter, lemon juice, and boiling water in a saucepan and bring to a boil. Moisten cornstarch with a little water, add, stir until mixture is smooth. Cool, beat in yolks, sugar, and lemon rind. Turn into buttered pudding dish and bake in 350° oven for about ½ hour. Remove from oven and spread with meringue (made by combining the stiffly beaten egg whites with 2 tablespoons confectioners' sugar and ¾ teaspoon flavoring). Return to oven, bake 10 minutes longer or until meringue is lightly browned. Serves 4.

*Mrs. Elda Keck*

## BAVARIAN CREAM

| | |
|---|---|
| 1 tablespoon gelatine | ½ cup sugar |
| ¼ cup ice water | 1½ teaspoons vanilla |
| 4 eggs | ¼ teaspoon salt |

2 cups cream

Soak gelatine in a cup with ice water. Place cup in shallow bowl of hot water until gelatine is dissolved. Cool. Beat egg yolks lightly with half the sugar. Add gelatine and vanilla. Beat egg whites until stiff with the salt. Beat in balance of sugar. Whip cream until stiff, combine with egg yolk mixture, fold in egg whites. Turn into a wet mold and chill. May be served with shredded, blanched, toasted almonds. Serves 6.

*Mrs. Abram Samuels III*

## CHOCOLATE PUDDING

| | |
|---|---|
| 1½ cups bread bits, tightly packed | ¼ teaspoon salt |
| 2 cups milk | 1 tablespoon sugar |
| 1 egg | 2 ounces chocolate |

½ teaspoon vanilla

Soak bread in milk for about an hour. Beat egg with salt and sugar. Grate chocolate, melt, add with vanilla. Stir all ingredients together. Bake in buttered pudding dish at 350° until pudding is set. Serve hot, with hard sauce:

1 cup confectioners' sugar
½ cup soft butter

⅛ teaspoon salt
1 teaspoon vanilla

1 egg

Sift sugar and cream it with the butter. Add salt and flavoring. Beat in the egg. When sauce is smooth chill until firm. Serves 4.

*Mrs. W. H. Anewalt*

## CHOCOLATE SPEISE
### (Chocolate Pudding)

The literal translation would be *food*, in the sense of angel food or devil's food, but in this case it is a pudding.

¼ cup grated chocolate
2 tablespoons flour
½ cup milk
2 rounded tablespoons butter

2 tablespoons sugar
3 eggs
Vanilla

Mix chocolate and flour with a little of the milk. Add balance gradually, blending. Place in saucepan over low heat. Add butter and stir to a smooth paste until mixture leaves side of the pan. Add sugar, beat in; cool. Add egg yolks one at a time, then vanilla. Fold in stiffly beaten egg whites. Pour into a buttered pudding dish and steam over boiling water for about an hour. Chill and unmold. Serve hot with custard sauce, or cold, or baked in the oven, as a cake! Serves 4.

*From an old cook book*

## COTTAGE PUDDING

½ cup butter
1 cup sugar
1 cup milk

2 cups sifted flour
1 heaping teaspoon baking powder
1 cup raisins or chopped figs

### Sauce

1 cup sugar
2 tablespoons butter
2 cups boiling water

1 tablespoon flour with
1 tablespoon cold water
1 teaspoon vanilla

Mix creamed butter and sugar with milk and flour, sifted with baking powder. Dredge fruit with a little flour and fold in. Bake in a breadpan in 350° oven for about ½ hour. For the sauce, cream sugar and butter, add mixed flour and water, and stir together. Stir mixture into the boiling water and simmer over low heat until sauce clears. Add vanilla. Serves 6-8.

*Mrs. Karl Lennert*

## FRUIT PUDDING

¾ cups sugar
2 tablespoons butter
⅓ cup milk

¾ cup flour
1 teaspoon baking powder
1 teaspoon vanilla

Fruit

Cream sugar and butter, add milk. Mix. Sift flour and baking powder into bowl with mixture. Stir in vanilla. Mix to a dough. Butter a pudding dish, place fruit (cherries, peaches, or apples) in it, and bake ½ hour at 375°. Serves 4.

*Elsie Singmaster, who has written many books about Pennsylvania*

## CHERRY PUDDING

1 tablespoon butter
½ cup sugar
1 egg

½ cup milk
1 cup flour
1 teaspoon baking powder

1 cup sweet cherries

Cream butter and sugar, stir in lightly beaten egg, add milk, sift in flour and baking powder. Fold in cherries. Butter gem pans, fill two-thirds with batter, bake at 350° for about 25 minutes. Serve with cream or custard sauce. Serves 4.

*Mrs. Abram Samuels III*

## PEACH PUDDING

3 tablespoons melted butter
½ cup sugar
1 beaten egg
1 cup milk

1½ teaspoons baking powder
2 cups sifted flour
Pinch of salt
2 cups sliced peaches

Cream butter and sugar, add beaten egg and milk. Sift in baking powder, flour, and salt and mix well. Butter a loaf pan, line with sliced peaches, pour batter over peaches. Bake at 350° for about ½ hour. Serves 6.

*Mrs. Arthur J. McShane*

## HUCKLEBERRY PUDDING WITH LEMON SAUCE

1 heaping tablespoon butter
1 cup sugar
3½ cups flour

1 teaspoon soda
2 cups sour milk
Pinch of salt

1½ cups huckleberries

Cream butter and sugar, sift flour and soda into the bowl, add sour milk and salt and mix. Dredge huckleberries in a little flour and fold into batter. Bake in a shallow, greased pan in 350° oven for about ½ hour. Serves 6.

### Lemon sauce

1 tablespoon cornstarch
1 egg
1 tablespoon butter

½ cup sugar
2 cups boiling water
1 lemon, juice and grated rind

Place cornstarch, egg, butter, and sugar in a bowl and beat well. Pour boiling water over them. Mix. Transfer to top of double boiler, over boiling water, and stir until mixture thickens. Remove, add lemon juice and grated rind or, if preferred, juice of 2 lemons and grated rind of 1 orange.

*Mrs. Elda Keck*

## FIG CUSTARD PUDDING

3 eggs
½ cup sugar
¼ teaspoon salt
½ teaspoon vanilla

2 cups milk
Dried figs, boiled and split
2 tablespoons bread crumbs
½ cup shredded, blanched almonds

Beat eggs lightly, add sugar, salt, and vanilla. Scald milk and stir in the mixture. Place in top of double boiler over boiling water, and stir until mixture coats the spoon. Cook figs in water until they are soft (with a slice or 2 of lemon), line a pudding mold with them. Stir bread crumbs and shredded almonds into the custard and pour it over the figs. Chill, remove from mold, and serve with whipped cream. Serves 6.

*Mrs. Abram Samuels III*

## APPLE PUDDING

3 or 4 apples
1 cup sugar
2 tablespoons butter
⅓ cup milk

1 egg
½ cup flour plus 2 tablespoons
¾ teaspoon baking powder
⅛ teaspoon salt

1 teaspoon cinnamon

Peel and slice the apples. Butter a baking dish and spread the apples across the bottom. Sprinkle with 6 tablespoons of the sugar and the cinnamon. Cream balance of sugar with butter, adding beaten egg and milk. Sift flour, baking powder, and salt into the bowl, and mix batter. Pour over apples. Sprinkle a little cinnamon on top and bake in 350° oven for 40-45 minutes. Serve with a pitcher of heavy cream. Serves 4.

## RED RASPBERRY PUDDING

3 cups raspberries

2 cups sugar plus 2 tablespoons

2 tablespoons butter

1 cup flour plus 2 tablespoons

1½ teaspoons baking powder

½ teaspoon salt

5 tablespoons butter

⅓ cup milk

1 egg

Whipped cream

Use a square, shallow cake pan, 9 x 9 x 2. Butter it and sprinkle with a little flour. Dredge the berries in the extra 2 tablespoons of flour and place in the pan. Spread the extra sugar over them. Dot with the 2 tablespoons butter. Cream butter and sugar, mix with egg. Sift in flour, baking powder, and salt. Stir in milk. Beat well. Drop batter from spoon onto the fruit—do not pour it in. Bake at 350° for about ½ hour. Serve warm with whipped cream and a few whole berries on top.

## LEMON CUSTARD

3 eggs

2 cups milk

2 tablespoons flour

1 lemon, juice and grated rind

1 cup sugar

Separate the eggs and beat the yolks lightly. Bring milk to a boil, turn down heat, simmer. Moisten flour with a little cold milk and add to hot milk in saucepan with lemon juice and sugar. Stir and mix well until custard thickens. Then stir in the egg yolks. Remove from stove, fold in stiffly beaten egg whites, pour into butter pudding dish, and bake in 350° oven for about 40 minutes. Serves 6.

*Mrs. Victor Boyer*

## PEACH CUSTARD

2 cups milk

½ cup sugar

¼ teaspoon salt

1 lemon, juice and grated rind

3 egg yolks

Ripe peaches, halved

Place milk, sugar, salt, lemon juice, and egg yolks together in top of double boiler and cook slowly, stirring, over boiling water. When thick and creamy, fold in grated lemon rind and set aside to cool. Line a mold with peeled peach halves, pour custard over the fruit when partly cooled, and place in refrigerator. To serve turn out of mold and top with whipped cream to which a very little almond extract has been added.

*Mrs. Elda Keck*

## CUP CUSTARD

4 eggs                                     4 cups milk
½ cup sugar                              1 teaspoon vanilla

Beat eggs until light. Add sugar, milk, and flavoring. Stir until sugar is dissolved. Pour into custard cups. Place in a pan of boiling water and put the pan in a 350° oven. Bake until custard is set. Cool and serve. 8 cups.

*Mrs. Elda Keck*

## KUGELHOPF
### (Turk's Cap)

2 cups milk                              4 cups sifted flour
1 cup butter                             ⅛ teaspoon salt
8 eggs                                    1 tablespoon confectioners' sugar
1 yeast cake                             ¾ cup raisins, citron or other
                                              candied fruit

Mix milk, butter, and eggs and warm slowly in a saucepan. When well warmed, turn into a bowl. Dissolve yeast in a little warm water. Add. Sift in flour, salt, and sugar. Knead and form into a ball. Turn out onto a floured board and knead; add fruit. Grease a round baking dish or a Turk's Cap mold, put in the dough, and set aside to rise. When doubled in size, place in oven and bake at 325° for 50-60 minutes.

*From* The Pennsylvania German, *1907*

## APPLE DUMPLINGS

1 egg                                     ¼ teaspoon salt
⅔ cup milk                              6 apples
2½ cups sifted flour                   Cinnamon and sugar
2½ teaspoons baking powder        6 tablespoons butter
                          ½ cup brown sugar
                          ½ cup butter

Mix egg and milk together in a bowl and sift in flour, baking powder, and salt. Stir to make a soft dough. Turn out on floured board and knead lightly. Roll and cut in 6 squares. Place in centers a peeled, cored apple that has been quartered. Sprinkle with sugar and cinnamon, dot with butter, and bring up corners of dough to enclose apple. Pinch and seal. Place dumplings in a large pan, not touching. Bake at 425° for 10 minutes, then at 350° for 45 minutes. Test by pricking with toothpick and, if apples are tender, they are done. Sprinkle with a little sugar and cinnamon. Cream brown sugar and butter, add flavoring if desired and spoon on hot dumplings when served. 6 servings.

*Irma Weber*

## MRS. FUNK'S APPLE DUMPLINGS

| | | |
|---|---|---|
| 4 cups sifted flour | | 4 cups sifted flour |
| 2 cups sour cream | | Butter, size of an egg |
| 1 teaspoon soda | OR | Pinch of salt |
| Pinch of salt | | 2 level teaspoons baking powder |
| | | Milk to make stiff batter |
| | | |
| 8 tart apples | | Cinnamon |
| Sugar | | Butter |

Peel and halve the apples, remove cores, fill with sugar, sprinkle with cinnamon, and dot with a good-sized piece of butter. Put halves together. Mix the dough as for biscuits, roll out lightly on a floured board, divide into 8 parts and wrap these squares around the apples. Seal edges with a little milk and pinch together. Drop into boiling water, cover tightly, serve in 15 minutes. If steamed, place in steamer over hot water for 30 minutes. If baked, remove from oven when nicely browned. Serve with cream and sugar. 8 dumplings.

*From* The Pennsylvania German, *1907*

## TOKEY

| | |
|---|---|
| 3 eggs, separated | 15 chopped dates |
| 1 cup granulated sugar | 2 tablespoons flour |
| 1 cup rolled English walnuts | 3½ teaspoons bread crumbs |

Beat egg yolks and sugar together, add other ingredients, beaten egg whites last. Bake in lightly greased sheet pan in 350° oven for about 30 minutes. Cool, cut in squares, cover with whipped cream. Serve with a cherry in center. Serves 6-8.

*Mrs. John H. Adams*

## COMFORTS

| | |
|---|---|
| 2 eggs | ¼ teaspoon salt |
| 1 cup sugar | 3 teaspoons baking powder |
| 2½ cups sifted flour | 1 cup milk |

Blend beaten eggs with sugar, add sifted flour, salt, and baking powder. Stir in milk. Drop from a spoon into hot lard and fry quickly. Drain on brown paper, sprinkle with powdered sugar, and serve hot.

*Mrs. Elda Keck*

## SNOWBALLS

2 eggs
1 cup sugar
3 cups sifted flour
3 tablespoons baking powder

¼ teaspoon salt
1 cup milk
Confectioners' sugar
Freshly grated coconut

Mix beaten eggs with sugar, add sifted flour, baking powder, and salt. Stir in milk. Drop from spoon into hot fat, fry quickly, drain on brown paper. Shake in bag with confectioners' sugar and coconut. Serve hot.

*Mrs. Elda Keck*

## FRUIT FRITTERS

2 eggs
½ cup milk
1 cup sifted flour
2 tablespoons sugar

2 tablespoons melted butter
½ teaspoon salt
1 lemon, juice and grated rind
½ teaspoon nutmeg

*Fruit:* sliced apples, bananas, peaches, oranges; elderberry blossoms.
Beat eggs until light, add milk. Sift flour into a bowl, pour into it egg and milk mixture. Beat until smooth. Add sugar and melted butter. Mix. Beat vigorously for 5 minutes. Beat egg whites stiffly with salt, and add to the batter. Stir in lemon juice, grated rind, and nutmeg. Dip fruit into batter, coating well. Drop from spoon into hot fat. Fry quickly about 3 minutes. Drain on brown paper. Sprinkle with confectioners' sugar and serve hot.

*Mrs. Elda Keck*

## ORANGE PUFFS

¼ cup butter
½ cup sugar
2 egg yolks

1¼ cups sifted flour
1 teaspoon baking powder
½ cup milk

### Sauce

3 egg whites
1 cup confectioners' sugar

2 oranges, juice and grated rind
Juice of 1 lemon

Cream butter and sugar, add beaten egg yolks. Sift baking powder with flour and add alternately with milk. Mix. Bake in buttered gem pans at 350° for about 25 minutes. Beat egg whites until stiff, fold in confectioners' sugar, orange and lemon juice and grated rind. Serve puffs hot and pour sauce over them. Makes 10.

*Mrs. W. H. Anewalt*

## CREAM PUFFS

½ cup butter                    ¼ teaspoon salt
1 cup sifted flour              1 cup water
                    3 eggs
                  *Filling*
2 cups milk                     ½ cup sugar
2 tablespoons cornstarch        4 eggs
½ teaspoon salt                 ½ teaspoon vanilla

Melt butter in saucepan, take from stove, blend with flour and salt. Return to stove, add water gradually, stirring to a smooth paste. Remove from stove, beat in eggs one by one. Drop from spoon to greased cookie sheet, about 2 inches apart. Place in preheated oven, 400°, bake for 30 minutes. (Reduce to 350° during last 5 minutes of baking.) Cool, slit sides, fill with custard or whipped cream. To make filling, scald the milk. Sift together cornstarch, salt and sugar, add and blend. Place in top of double boiler over hot water and cook until mixture thickens. Cool, add egg yolks lightly beaten and vanilla. If you prefer, beat egg whites stiff and fold in, but they can be omitted. Makes 10 or 12 large puffs.

*Mrs. Abram Samuels*

## GRISCHDAGRINGEL
### (Christmas Ring)

1 cup chopped dates             2 tablespoons flour
1 cup chopped nuts              3 eggs
½ cup brown sugar               1 teaspoon vanilla
1 teaspoon baking powder        1 wine glass sherry
                  ¼ teaspoon salt
                  *Garnish*
1 cup heavy cream               Maraschino cherries
2 tablespoons confectioners' sugar   Candied orange peel
1 teaspoon vanilla              Candied citron

Dredge dates and nuts with a little flour. Combine with sugar, baking powder, and flour, sifted together. Stir in egg yolk, vanilla, and sherry. Mix well. Fold in egg whites, stiffly beaten with salt. Bake in buttered ring mold at 350° for about 30 minutes. Cool in pan. Remove from ring, place on large plate. Whip cream very stiff, fold in sugar. Add vanilla. Spread thickly over top of ring. Garnish with cherries for berries and strips of citron and orange peel for leaves, making a wreath all around the top of pudding. For Christmas dinner. Serves 6-8.

*Anna Schaeffer*

## MORAVIAN PLUM PUDDING

1½ cups sifted flour
1 teaspoon baking powder
½ cup chopped suet
½ cup currants
½ cup raisins
¼ cup citron
½ cup molasses

½ teaspoon cinnamon
½ teaspoon cloves
½ teaspoon nutmeg
¼ teaspoon salt
1 cup brown sugar
½ cup cream
1 wineglass brandy

Sift flour several times and resift with baking powder. Prepare fruit and suet, dredge lightly with flour. Resift balance of flour with spices, salt, and brown sugar. Combine with fruit and suet and mix with molasses. Add cream and brandy. Pour batter into large, greased pudding mold and cover tightly. Steam for 3 hours over boiling water. Uncover, place in 300° oven for 15 minutes to dry a little. Serve with wine sauce or hard sauce. Serves 8.

*Mrs. Elda Keck*

## PLUM PUDDING II

1 pound bread crumbs
1 pound eggs (!)
1 pound sweet raisins
1 pound currants
1 pound sugar

¼ pound citron, chopped
2 gills brandy
2 nutmegs, grated
2 teaspoons cinnamon
¼ teaspoon mace

This one is just for the record. Who wants to grate nutmegs—and where can you find them these days? Anyhow, if you don't mind weighing the ingredients, especially those eggs, this how you make the pudding: Dredge fruit in a little flour. Combine ingredients, place in a bag, tie up, and steam or boil for 2½ hours. Dry out in 300° oven for 15 minutes. Serve hot with hard sauce or lemon sauce, but first pour brandy over it and bring it flaming to the table.

*From the* Willing Workers' Cookbook, *Allentown, 1902*

## WINE SAUCE

1 cup confectioners' sugar
½ cup butter

1 egg
1 cup wine
½ teaspoon nutmeg

Cream sugar and butter, add egg. Blend. Place bowl in a pan of boiling water and stir until mixture melts. Add wine and nutmeg.

*Mrs. Elda Keck*

## VANILLA SAUCE

| | |
|---|---|
| 4 tablespoons butter | 2 tablespoons sugar |
| 2 tablespoons flour | 1 cup boiling water |

1½ teaspoons vanilla

Melt butter. Stir in flour and sugar until well blended, add hot water. Simmer this mixture until it comes to a boil, stirring, then place in top of double boiler over boiling water and simmer for 15 minutes. Flavor and serve hot.

*Amy Kerr*

## LEMON SAUCE

| | |
|---|---|
| ⅔ cup confectioners' sugar | 3 egg yolks |
| 3 tablespoon butter | ⅓ cup boiling water |

1 lemon, juice and grated rind

Sift sugar, cream with butter, beat in egg yolks. Add boiling water. Place mixture in top of double boiler, over boiling water, and stir until it thickens. Add lemon juice, blend, stir in grated rind. Serve hot.

*Amy Kerr*

## HARD SAUCE

| | |
|---|---|
| 1 cup confectioners' sugar | ⅛ teaspoon salt |
| ½ cup soft butter | 1 teaspoon vanilla or other flavoring |

Sift sugar, cream with butter. Add salt and flavoring. If preferred, beat in 1 egg. When sauce is smooth, chill until firm.

*Mrs. W. H. Anewalt*

## CUSTARD SAUCE

| | |
|---|---|
| 2 cups milk | ½ cup sugar |
| 3 eggs | 1 teaspoon vanilla |

Scald milk in top of double boiler over boiling water. Beat eggs and sugar until light and creamy. Only yolks need be used, but if preferred use whole eggs. Gradually add hot milk to beaten eggs and sugar, and return whole mixture to double boiler, stirring carefully until sauce begins to thicken. Remove from stove, add vanilla. Pour from one container to another several times to make sauce foam. Cool. If cooked to proper consistency the sauce will coat a silver knife blade when dipped in it.

*Mrs. Elda Keck*

# Candies

*Washington's Headquarters, Valley Forge, Pennsylvania*

IN THE early, hard days in the Pennsylvania Dutch country, candy was an unheard-of luxury, of course. Sweetening was hard to come by, sugar was precious, molasses had many uses, and maple syrup was a godsend. Probably the first Pennsylvania candy was a little maple syrup stirred in a saucer with the last snow of winter—a special treat for good children. When at last the day came when there could be popcorn balls, apples dipped in taffy, even taffy pulls, that was luxury indeed.

As soon as sugar could be had there were lemon drops, butterscotch, and horehound candy. The Moravians began to make their famous mints. But the special holiday treat was marzipan, a carry-over of Old World confectionery that appeared on days of high feasting. These charming molded fruits were delicious but so beautiful that they were saved as treasures rather than eaten. They were brought here by way of Switzerland, probably on their way from a lot of other places, for marzipan seems to be universal.

It used to be considered a poor Christmas if, along with ornamented, dangling cookies, there were not strings of sugar candy, clear toys, and candy canes on every Pennsylvania Dutch Christmas tree. And at Easter, in addition to the traditional dyed eggs, there was something wrong if there were not also some of the chocolate-covered eggs filled with mashed potato and sugar in combination.

Times have changed, but many of us remember these candies and some of them are still with us. You will find recipes for some of them in the pages that follow. I have not tried to bring them up to date; they are described pretty much as they have been made hereabouts for a long time.

219

## MOLASSES TAFFY I

4 cups New Orleans molasses   ½ cup butter
2 tablespoons white sugar   ¼ teaspoon soda
2 tablespoons vinegar   1 teaspoon vanilla

Boil molasses, sugar, vinegar, and butter together. Simmer until it hardens when dropped in cold water. Remove from stove, stir in soda, and cool. When cool enough to handle, add vanilla, butter the fingers, and pull. When pulled break into 1-inch pieces.

*Mrs. Elda Keck*

## MOLASSES TAFFY II

2 cups sugar   1 tablespoon vinegar
1 cup molasses   1 tablespoon butter
½ cup water

Boil ingredients together until mixture forms a ball when tested in cold water. Cool. Butter the fingers, pull, and break into small pieces.

*Mrs. Herman Oswald*

## CHOCOLATE TAFFY

2 cups granulated sugar   1 scant tablespoon butter
3 ounces grated chocolate   2 teaspoons vanilla
½ cup boiling water   ⅛ teaspoon salt

Mix sugar, chocolate, and water. Boil until nearly done, then add butter. Simmer and when candy snaps remove from stove. Cool. Add 1 teaspoon vanilla and pull with buttered fingers. Break into small pieces.

*Mrs. Elda Keck*

## CREAM TAFFY

1 pound white sugar   1 teaspoon cream tartar
3 tablespoons vinegar   ½ cup water
1 teaspoon vanilla

Moisten the sugar with the water, simmer together with vinegar and cream tartar until candy hardens when tested in cold water. Add vanilla (or mint flavoring if preferred). Pour on buttered pan to cool. Pull with buttered fingers. Break into pieces.

*Mrs. Elda Keck*

## HAZELNUT TAFFY

1 teaspoon vinegar  
⅛ teaspoon salt  
¼ teaspoon cream tartar  
½ cup water  

2 tablespoons butter  
1 pound loaf sugar  
2 cups hazelnut meats  
1 teaspoon vanilla  

Mix vinegar, salt, cream tartar, and water in a bowl and blend thoroughly. Melt butter, add sugar and the mixture in the bowl. Stir over medium heat until candy boils. Add nuts, beat until thick, add vanilla. Pour into buttered tins. Cool. Mark in squares.

*Mrs. Arthur J. McShane*

## TAFFY CHIPS

1 cup molasses  
1 cup sugar  
2 tablespoons vinegar  

2 tablespoons butter  
1½ teaspoons vanilla  
4 ounces chocolate  

Boil molasses, sugar, vinegar, and butter slowly until mixture hardens when tested in cold water. Stir gently as syrup thickens. Add vanilla, pour on a buttered plate, and cool. Cut in 1-inch squares. When cool melt chocolate over warm water and dip the pieces in it. Cool on waxed paper.

*Amy Kerr*

## BUTTER TAFFY

1½ cups light brown sugar  
3 tablespoons molasses  
1½ tablespoons vinegar  

¼ teaspoon salt  
1½ tablespoons hot water  
3 tablespoons butter  

1 teaspoon vanilla

Mix sugar, molasses, vinegar, salt, and hot water, put on stove and bring slowly to a boil. Simmer until candy is brittle when tested in cold water. Add butter, cook one minute longer. Remove from stove, add vanilla. Pour into buttered pans. Cool and mark in squares.

*Mrs. Arthur J. McShane*

## BLACK WALNUT TAFFY

½ cup maple syrup  
¼ cup water  
1 cup sugar  

1 tablespoon vinegar  
1 heaping tablespoon butter  
1 cup black walnuts  

Combine maple syrup, water, sugar, vinegar and cook over low heat, stirring, until mixture hardens when tested in cold water. Add butter, cook 1 minute longer.

Remove from stove, add black walnut meats. Pour into buttered pan and cool. Break into pieces.

*Amy Kerr*

## BUTTERSCOTCH

2 cups brown sugar          ⅓ cup butter
                           ½ cup water

Simmer together without stirring. When mixture hardens when tested in cold water, pour into buttered tins. Cool. Mark in squares when almost cool.

*Mrs. Elda Keck*

## MOSCHIES

4 cups brown sugar          A little water
1 tablespoon butter          1 cup black walnut meats

Combine sugar, butter, and water and simmer over low heat. Try in cold water and when candy hardens add 1 cup black walnut meats. Simmer a little longer, until mixture begins to sugar. Pour into patty pans to depth of ½ inch and cool.

*Mrs. Elda Keck*

## HOREHOUND CANDY

2 cups granulated sugar          2 tablespoons horehound tea

Make a strong tea of fresh or dried horehound. Simmer to keep it hot. Place sugar in heavy iron spider and stir over brisk flame. At first it will be hard and lumpy but keep on stirring until it melts and boils. Add strained horehound tea. Keep stirring. "When it hardens so as to crack with the teeth" pour into buttered tins. Cool, cut in squares "and stand away to harden."

*From an old Bethlehem cook book*

## BURNT ALMOND CANDY

1 cup coarsely chopped almonds          1½ cups sugar
                          3 tablespoons boiling water

Place almonds, sugar, and boiling water in a saucepan and stir while cooking at low heat, until mixture becomes syrupy. When all the water has evaporated and the sugar has "balled up" and then changed back to syrup, it is time to pour candy into buttered pans. Crease into squares with a sharp knife. Cool and break.

*Mrs. Arthur J. McShane*

## PEANUT CANDY

2 cups granulated sugar          4 cups shelled peanuts

Shell and chop the peanuts and heat in a pan in the oven. Melt sugar over low heat to avoid burning. When it boils, stir in the hot peanuts, pour into buttered pans, and cool. Cut in squares.

*Mrs. Elda Keck*

## MRS. SOLELIAC'S CARAMELS

2 tablespoons butter
1 can table syrup
1 cup brown sugar

½ cup milk
3 ounces chocolate
1 teaspoon vanilla

Melt the butter, add syrup and then brown sugar, milk, and grated chocolate. Stir and watch carefully as candy simmers. When it threads from a spoon, remove from stove and add vanilla. Pour into greased pans, cool, and cut in squares.

*Mrs. W. H. Anewalt*

## LEMON CARAMELS

2 cups granulated sugar
⅔ cup boiling water

½ cup cream
1 heaping tablespoon butter

Boil sugar and water together until candy snaps when dropped in water. Add cream and butter. Simmer and stir and test again. When candy hardens in cold water, remove from stove, add ½ teaspoon lemon extract, and pour into buttered pans to cool. Mark in squares.

*Mrs. Arthur J. McShane*

## COCONUT CREAM CANDY

1 grated coconut and milk          1 cup granulated sugar
1 teaspoon vanilla

Grate coconut and reserve milk. Heat coconut milk with sugar until sugar melts. Simmer 5 minutes over medium flame, add grated coconut, simmer 20 minutes, stirring to prevent stocking, add vanilla. Pour on buttered plates and set aside overnight to harden. Cut in squares.

*Mrs. Elda Keck*

## COCONUT STEEPLES

3 eggs, beaten together
2 cups confectioners' sugar

1 tablespoon flour
2 cups coconut
Pinch of salt

Beat eggs and mix with sugar and flour. Add coconut with a pinch of salt. Drop on buttered paper, well apart. Bake in 300° oven for about 1 hour.

*Mrs. Elda Keck*

## SUGARED ALMONDS

1 cup blanched almonds                    1 cup granulated sugar
                  ¼ cup water

Blanch almonds. Let stand until they are dry. Boil sugar and water until syrup hairs when dropped from spoon. Toss in almonds. Cook them in syrup, stirring occasionally until they are delicately browned. When syrup begins to change color remove from stove. Stir rapidly until syrup turns back to sugar and coats the nuts. Cool on buttered plate.

*Mrs. Elda Keck*

## PEANUT CREAM CANDY

2 cups granulated sugar                   2 beaten egg whites
¾ cup table syrup                         Pinch of salt
¼ cup water                               1 teaspoon vanilla
                  1 cup peanuts

Cook sugar, syrup, and water together until mixture threads from the spoon. Beat egg whites with a pinch of salt on a cold platter. When they are stiff, beat in syrup gradually. Add vanilla and peanuts. Pour in buttered tins and cool. Mark in squares.

*Mrs. Arthur J. McShane*

## NUT KISSES

6 egg whites                              2 cups confectioners' sugar
Pinch of salt                             2 teaspoons vanilla
2 tablespoons flour                       2 cups chopped nutmeats

Beat egg whites stiff with salt. Add sifted sugar and flour. Stir together lightly, then add vanilla and nutmeats. Drop on buttered cookie sheet and bake in 300° oven for about ½ hour until golden brown.

*Mrs. Elda Keck*

## GUMMY CHOCOLATE CANDY

2 cups brown sugar                        1 lump butter
1½ cups baking molasses                   3 ounces chocolate
                  1 teaspoon vanilla

Boil sugar, molasses, butter, and chocolate together until syrup threads when dropped in cold water. If boiled too long, candy will be brittle. Try it after cooking slowly 15 minutes. If it is ready, add vanilla. Pour on buttered plates, cool, mark in squares.

*Mrs. Mae Sieger*

## POTATO CANDY

1 baked potato                    Vanilla
Confectioners' sugar              Melted chocolate

As soon as the potato is baked, warm a mixing bowl and scoop the potato from
its skin. Mash and add confectioners' sugar, stirring and adding until mixture
can be kneaded with the hands. Knead well, keeping warm, add vanilla and
form into small balls. Dip quickly in melted chocolate kept warm over hot
water and drop on waxed paper. Or shape like Easter eggs and dip. Potato balls
can be flattened and topped with English walnut halves, the mixture can be used
to stuff dates, which are then rolled in sugar, or it can be rolled out like dough,
spread with peanut butter, rolled up and sliced, then dipped in coconut.

*Mrs. Elwood Shaub*

## HUGUENOT NOUGAT

*First Mixture*                    *Second Mixture*

1 cup granulated sugar             2 cups granulated sugar
½ cup boiling water                1 cup table syrup
                                   1 cup boiling water

Boil together until syrup
    threads from spoon. Beat       Boil this until thick.
    into it:                       Stir into first mixture.

3 egg whites

Beat all together, add 1 tablespoon vanilla or preferred flavoring, add 1 cup
nuts. When mixture begins to harden as it is beaten, pour into buttered tins.
Cool and mark in squares.

*Mrs. Elda Keck*

## MORAVIAN MINTS

2 cups granulated sugar            ¼ teaspoon cream tartar
1 teaspoon confectioners' sugar    12 drops peppermint extract
¾ cup water                        or 3 drops oil of peppermint

Simmer granulated sugar and water together until syrup threads from the spoon.
Take from stove, add confectioners' sugar, cream tartar, and peppermint. (An
old recipe says that the sugar and water should be first brought to a boil, then
"boil hard, long enough to count twelve slowly.") Beat until creamy and drop
from spoon on waxed paper. For wintergreen flavor, use wintergreen extract

and add pink vegetable coloring. Use mint flavoring and green coloring, lemon flavoring and yellow coloring.

*Mrs. Philip B. Woodroofe*

## POPCORN BALLS

1 cup popcorn
1 teaspoon salt
2 cups peanuts (optional)

1 tablespoon butter
1 cup molasses
½ cup sugar

Pop the corn to make about 12 cups. Place in large bowl, remove imperfect kernels, and sprinkle with salt. Place butter, molasses, and sugar in a saucepan and stir over low heat only long enough for sugar to dissolve. Simmer until syrup cracks against side of glass when tested in cold water. Pour over corn, add peanuts if desired, and form into balls with buttered fingers.

*Mrs. Philip B. Woodroofe*

## CANDIED APPLES

### Syrup

2⅔ cups sugar
1⅓ cups water
1 cup corn syrup

¼ teaspoon cloves
Red vegetable coloring
Lemon juice or vinegar

Select perfect apples of medium size. Cook sugar, water, and syrup together without stirring until syrup colors. When it turns pale yellow and threads from the spoon, add cloves and coloring. Remove from stove, add a few drops of lemon juice or a very little vinegar. Set the pan in another pan filled with ice water, then in a pan of hot water to keep syrup from hardening. Dip apples in syrup quickly and cool on greased cookie sheet until coating hardens.

*Amy Kerr*

## CANDIED ORANGE PEEL

Orange peel
½ cup water

1 cup sugar
Sugar

Cut orange peel into strips and drop it into a saucepan filled with cold water. Bring slowly to a boil. Remove from stove and drain orange peel. Repeat 4 times. Combine water and sugar and simmer together. Drop in the peel and simmer until orange peel has taken up all the syrup. Remove and cool. Roll pieces in sugar and spread on waxed paper until thoroughly dried. May be dipped in melted chocolate.

*Mary Rose McWilliams*

## CHOCOLATE CREAMS

2 cups sugar
½ cup cold water

¼ teaspoon cream tartar
1 teaspoon vanilla

4 ounces melted chocolate

Boil together sugar, water, and cream tartar. Do not stir. When syrup threads from end of spoon, take from stove and let stand for 5 minutes. Beat until white and creamy. Form into balls and set aside to harden. Melt the chocolate over warm (not hot) water, dip well-hardened creams, place on waxed paper to cool.

*Mrs. Elda Keck*

## CREAMED DATES

1 package dates
½ cup cold water

¼ teaspoon cream tartar
1 teaspoon vanilla

2 cups sugar

Remove stones from dates. Boil sugar, water, and cream tartar, but do not stir. When mixture threads from spoon, remove from stove. Let stand 5 minutes. Add vanilla and beat until thick and creamy. Stuff the dates and roll in granulated sugar.

*Mrs. Elda Keck*

## MARZIPAN I

1 pound blanched, grated almonds
1 pound fine, sifted flour

1 pound "flour sugar"
12 drops rosewater

4 drops bitter almond extract

Marzipan requires infinite care in preparation. Nowadays it can be bought in the shops at holiday time and few care to try to make it. Grandmother always gave each of us a few marzipan fruits at Christmas time, and I remember that I treasured my marzipan strawberries, apples, and peaches for months. If there was a potato in the lot, I ate that immediately because I didn't consider potatoes beautiful. Besides, I knew it would be solid with almond. There was less coloring used on the potato, and it had no little wire with artificial leaves stuck into it to mar the flavor. The potato was perfect for eating purposes. The fruits, however, were carefully placed behind the glass door of the bookcase, there to glow enticingly all through the winter months. As spring housecleaning time approached I would decide to eat my marzipan fruits, but alas by that time they were hard as rocks and were flavored with leather and varnish. . . .

The recipe above is from Frau Henriette Davidis' *Praktische Kochbuch,* much used by Pennsylvania Dutch housewives back in the eighties. Frau Davidis gives detailed (and more or less explicit) directions: First, the almonds must be blanched and spread out to dry for twelve hours; then mixed with sugar, flour, and rosewater, to form a solid dough, having been grated "fine as flour." Now sprinkle the board with sifted sugar, divide the dough into three round balls, and roll out carefully, "not too brittle, not too soft." Roll "to the thickness of the back of a knife." Or if you prefer mold the dough into fruit shapes. From the rolled-out dough Frau Davidis tells you also how to cut out and make marzipan baskets. You are told to sprinkle the board with rosewater, cut small rounds of dough for bases, and then build up the baskets by applying small rolls at the edge. "With the top strip, notch or prick with a fork on one side, to make the top of the basket. Now your marzipan is insofar finished." I hope so! There are more instructions, however, if you want to make the fruits. They must be molded and colored: "So you heat a pan on live coals to a red glow, place your cakes on a paper-lined tin, and set the tin on the pan to bake. After baking, place on a flat vessel to cool. Blend one pound of sifted sugar with rosewater, stir for three-quarters of an hour, fill the paté to the edge. When the filling has stiffened, top with preserves." I'm confused—how about you? No, I do not think I could make marzipan from this recipe. Here is a modern method:

## MARZIPAN II

2 cups blanched and grated almonds  
2 cups sugar  
1 cup water  
Juice of 1 orange  

12 drops rosewater  
2 egg whites  
Salt  
2 cups confectioners' sugar  

Lemon juice

Blanch and grate the almonds, dry them thoroughly. When well dried, pound them in a bag. Boil sugar and water together and when the syrup threads from a spoon, add powdered almonds, orange juice, and rosewater. Simmer 2 minutes longer, then stir until mixture is thick and creamy. Dust a marble slab with confectioners' sugar, toss out the dough, and knead until it cools. Fill a pint jar with the paste and store in a cool place for a week to season. Beat egg whites with a very little salt, until fluffy, and work into the almond paste. Add enough confectioners' sugar to make paste easy to handle. If too stiff, add lemon juice, drop by drop. Knead paste on sugared board. Mold into shapes and either roll in confectioners' sugar or brush with vegetable coloring, to make lifelike fruits. Wrap them in waxed paper and store in a cool place.

Sometime when we have a long, cold winter and time lies heavy on the hands, I'm going to stir up the live coals, hunt out a marble slab, and make marzipan. As an occupation it should engross me until the snowplow breaks through.

# Index

Almond Balls for Soup, 13
  Cookies, 192
  Filling, 186
  Peaks, 194
  Rings, 191
  Wafers, 191
Almonds, Sugared, 224
Amish Half-Moon Pies, 161
  Preaching Pies, 161
  Preaching Soup, 8
Angel Cake, 180
Angel Food, Mrs. Fegley's, 180
Anise Cookies, 190
Apees, 204, 205
  Widdifield's, 205
Apple Butter, 134
Apple Cake, 27
Apple Custard Pie, 159
Apple Dumplings, 213, 214
Apple Fritters, 54
Apple Pudding, 211
Apple Rings, 110
Apple Sauce, 134
Apple Sauce Cake, 170
Apple Stuffing, 87
Apple Tarts, 160
Apples and Dumplings, 71, 72
Apples, Baked, 134
  Candied, 226
Apricot Jam, 137
Artichokes, Pickled, 148

Ball Cheese, 96
*Basel Leckerlëin*, 193
Bavarian Cream, 208
Bean Soup, Amish Preaching, 8
  Dried, 6

Beans, Baked, Holland House, 119
  Baked Lima, 118
  Mustard, 148
  Pork and, 118
  Sour, 119
  String, 119
Beef and Potato Pie, 62
Beef Heart, Stuffed, 65
Beef Kidney Stew, 66
Beef Liver and Onions, 65
Beef Pie, No-Crust, 63
Beef, Roast, with Onion Sauce, 58
  Rolled Pot Roast, 59
  Short Ribs, 64
  Sour Roast, 57
  Stew, Brown, 58
  Stew II, with Potato Dumplings, 59
    with Onions, 61
Beef Tongue, Baked, 65
  Boiled, 64
Beets, Pickled, 147
Beets, Sour-Sweet, 125
Birdseye Sauce, 144
Biscuits, 46
  Raised, 34
Blackberry Pie, 167
Blackberry Shrub, 112
Black Joe Cake, 180
Black Walnut Cake, 174
Black Walnut Squares, 195
Black Walnut Taffy, 221
*Blitzkuchen*, 41
*Boovashenkel*, 60, 71
Bran Muffins, 48
Bread, 19, 20
Bread, Brown, 42
  Cinnamon, 23

Bread—*Continued*
  Coffee, 24
  Corn, 42
  Date and Nut, 45
  Egg, 94
  Federal, 20
  *Grumbera* Twist, 21
  Mennonite Egg, 94
  Mush, 23
  Nut, 44, 45
  Poppy Seed Twist, 21
  Potato Twist, 21
  Raised Corn Meal, 22
  Raised Nut, 28
  Raisin, 27
  Rich, 22
  Rye, 23
  Whole Wheat, 24
Bread and Butter Pickles, 146
Bread Filling, 86
Breakfast Cake, *Der Benner,* 40
  Molasses, 43
Breakfast Cakes, 39
Breakfast Mackerel, 105
Brown Beef Stew, 58
Brown Bread, 42
Brown Cookies, Moravian, 189
Brown Flour Potato Soup, 2
Brown Sugar Crumb Cake, 41
Brown Sugar Sand Tarts, 204
Buckwheat Cakes, 51, 52
  Raised, 52
Bunny's Cookies, 201
Buns, Cinnamon, 31, 32
Buns, Sticky, 33
Burnt Almond Candy, 222
Butter, Apple, 134
  Gooseberry, 135
  Grape, 135
  Tomato, 141
Butter Balls for Soup, 11, 12
Butter Taffy, 221
Buttermilk-Pop, 5
Butterscotch, 222
Butterscotch Pie, 157
*Buttersemmeln,* 30
Butterthins, 202

Cabbage, Coleslaw, 129, 130
  Creamed, 122
  Filled, 123

Cabbage—*Continued*
  Red, 123
  Roll-Ups, 60
  Sauerkraut, 76
  Sauerkraut, Baked, 76
  Stuffed, 123
  with Caraway Seeds, 123
Cake, Angel, 180
  Angel Food, 180
  Apple, 27
  Applesauce, 170
  Aunt Sue's Feather, 169
  Black Joe, 180
  Black Walnut, 174
  *Blitzkuchen,* 41
  Breakfast, 39, 40, 43
  Brown Sugar Crumb, 41
  Cheese, 98, 99
  Children's, 169
  Chocolate, 181
  Clove, 171
  Coconut, 175
  Coffee, 25, 40, 172
  Cream, 176
  Cream Sponge, 179
  Crumb, 40, 41
  Crumb, Brown Sugar, 41
  Crumb, Lancaster County, 41
  *Der Benner* Breakfast, 40, 181, 182
  Dutch, 40
  Easter 155
  Feather, 169
  Fig, 175
  Fruit, 182, 183
  Funny, Mrs. Reinert's, 155
  German Nut, 173
  Ginger, 43, 44, 173
  Glory, Mrs. Keck's, 178
  Gold, 177
  Grandmother's Jelly Roll, 179
  Have-Some-More, Abe's, 154
  Hickory Nut, 175
  Hurry Up, 169
  Jelly Roll, 179
  Journey (Johnny), 42
  Lancaster County Crumb, 41
  Light, with Dollars, 26
  Lightning, 41
  Marble, 176
  Mocha, 172
  Molasses, 173

Cake—*Continued*
  Molasses Breakfast, 43
  Moravian Cream, 176
  Mrs. Leibensperger's, 181
  Mrs. Reinert's, 155
  Mrs. Schill's, 182
  *Nochkuche,* 154
  *Osterfladen,* 155
  Our Own Ginger, 173
  Pearl, 177
  Poor Man's, 168
  Pound, 177
  Pudding Dish, 171
  Schwenkfelder, 25
  Shaker Nut, 174
  Short, 46, 47
  Silver, 178
  Sour Milk, 170
  Spice, 170, 171
  Sponge, 179
  *Streusel*-Filled Coffee, 40
  Walnut, 174
  Water Sponge, 179
  White Fruit, 182
Cakes, Breakfast, 39
  Buckwheat, 51, 52
  Coffee, 25, 40, 172
  Crumb Griddle, 50
  Flannel, 51
  Fried, 38
  Funnel, 53
  Ginger, 192
  Hot, Cornmeal, 51
  Moravian Sugar, 29
  Raised, 28
  Raised Buckwheat, 52
  Scotch Taffy, 196
Candied Apples, 226
Candied Orange Peel, 226
Candies:
  Almonds, Sugared, 224
  Black Walnut Taffy, 221
  Burnt Almond, 222
  Butter Taffy, 221
  Butterscotch, 222
  Candied Apples, 226
  Candied Orange Peel, 226
  Caramels, Lemon, 223
  Caramels, Mrs. Soleliac's, 223
  Chips, Taffy, 221
  Chocolate Creams, 227

Candies—*Continued*
  Chocolate Taffy, 220
  Coconut Cream, 223
  Coconut Steeples, 223
  Cream Taffy, 220
  Creamed Dates, 227
  Gummy Chocolate, 224
  Hazelnut Taffy, 221
  Horehound, 222
  Kisses, Nut, 224
  Lemon Caramels, 223
  Marzipan, 227, 228
  Mints, Moravian, 225
  Molasses Taffy, 220
  *Moschies,* 222
  Nougat, Huguenot, 225
  Nut Kisses, 224
  Peanut, 222
  Peanut Cream, 224
  Popcorn Balls, 226
  Potato, 225
  Sugared Almonds, 224
  Taffy Chips, 221
Caramel Frosting, 185
Catsup, Mother's, 142
Catsup, Walnut, 104
Celery Sauce, 93
Centre County Dandelion Salad, 126
Cheese, Ball, 96
  Cake, 98, 99
  Cottage, 96
  Cup, 96
  Custard Pie, Mrs. Hollenbach's, 98
  Pie, 97
  Pudding, 207
Cherries, Pickled, 136
  Spiced, 137
Cherry Crumb Pie, 162
  Hash, 136
  Pie, Sour, 161
  Pudding, 210
  Tart, 161
Chestnut Soup, 9, 10
Chestnut Stuffing, 87
Chicken, with Almond Balls, 13
  Baked, 80
  and Corn Pie, 82
  Corn Soup, 12
  with Dumplings, 82
  Fried, 79
  Noodle Soup, 11

Chicken—*Continued*
  Potpie, 80, 81
  Roast, 83
  Stewed, 80
Children's Cake, 169
Chili Sauce, 142
Chips, Taffy, 221
Chocolate Cake, 181
  Candy, Gummy, 224
  Cookies II, 203
  Creams, 227
  Pie, 159
  Pudding, 208
  *Speise,* 209
  Taffy, 220
Chowchow, Green, 143
Christmas Cookies, Moravian, 188, 189
Christmas Ring, 216
Cinnamon Bread, 23
Cinnamon Buns, 31, 32
Cinnamon Cookies, 199
*Citronenkuchen,* 158
Clam Soup, 7
Clams, Deviled, 103
Clove Cake, 103, 171
Cocktail, Hot Tomato, 110
Coconut Cake, 175
Coconut Cream Candy, 223
  Filling, 186
  Pie, 159
  Steeples, 223
Coffee Bread, 24
  Cake, 25, 40, 172
  Cakes, 38, 39, 40, 41
Coleslaw, 129, 130
Comforts, 214
Confectioners' Icing, 184
Conserve, Grape, 135
  Plum, 135
Cookies, Almond, 191
  Almond Peaks, 194
  Almond Ring, 191
  Almond Wafers, 191
  Anise, 190
  Apees, 204, 205
  *Basel Leckerlein,* 193
  Black Walnut Squares, 195
  Brown Moravian, 189
  Brown Sugar Sand Tarts, 204
  Bunny's, 201

Cookies—*Continued*
  Butterthins, 202
  Chocolate, Sally Hoffman's, 203
  Chocolate, II, 203
  Christmas, 188, 189
  Cinnamon, 199
  Currant Drops, 197
  Date Strips, 198
  Dinah's Shaker, 202
  "Dutch" Shortbread, 195
  Fig, 198
  Filled, 202
  Fruit, 197
  Fruited, 198
  Ginger Cakes, 192
  Hickory Nut Drops, 194
  Jumbles, Aline Dillinger's, 196
  *Lebkuchen,* 192, 193
  *Leckerlein, Basel,* 193
  *Mandelplaettchen,* 191
  *Mandelringe,* 191
  *Mandelspitzen,* 194
  Molasses, 200
  Molasses Creams, 200
  Molasses, Soft, 200
  Moravian Brown, 188, 189
  Mother's Oatmeal, 201
  Mrs. Schaeffer's, 194
  *Pefferniss,* 194
  Peppernuts, 194
  Sally Hoffman's, 203
  Sand Tarts, 204
  Sand Tarts, Brown Sugar, 204
  Schoolboy, 203
  Scotch, Moravian, 189
  Scotch Taffy, 196
  Shaker, 202
  Shortbread, 195
  Slapjacks, 195
  Soft Molasses, 200
  Spice, 199
  Spice Tongues, 201
  Spiced Ginger, 199
  *Springerle,* 190
  Sweetmeats, 193
  Taffy Cakes, Scotch, 196
  Tartlets, 191
  *Tortellen,* 191
  Touch-Me-Nots, 197
  Walnut Drops, 196
  White Moravian, 188

Corn:
  Bread, 42
  and Chicken Pie, 82
  and Chicken Soup, 12
  Dried, 120
  Fritters, 54
    Oyster, 122
  Pie, 121
  Pudding, 122
  Salad, 144
  Soup, 6
Corn Meal Bread, Raised, 22
  Hot Cakes, 51
  Muffins, 48
Cottage Cheese, 96
  Pudding, 209
Crab Apples, Spiced, 137
Crab Meat, Deviled, 102
Crab Patties, 102
Cream, Bavarian, 208
Cream Cake, Moravian, 176
Cream Nut Filling, Moravian, 186
Cream Pudding, 207
Cream Puffs, 216
Cream Sponge Cake, 179
Cream Taffy, 220
Cream Waffles, 54
Creams, Chocolate, 227
Creams, Molasses, 200
Crown Roast of Lamb, 69
Crullers, 38, 39
Crumb Cake, 40, 41
Crumb Griddle Cakes, 50
Crumb Omelet, 91
Crumb Pie, 155
  Cherry, 162
Cucumber Pickles, 145
Cucumbers in Sour Cream, 130
Cup Cheese, 96
Cup Custard, 213
Currant Drops, 197
Currant Jelly, 140
Custard, Cup, 213
  Fig, 211
  Lemon, 212
  Peach, 212
Custard Pie, 158
  Apple, 159
  Cheese, 98
Custard Pudding, Fig, 211
Custard Sauce, 218

Dandelion Greens, 126
Dandelion Salad, Centre County, 126
Dandelion Wine, 111, 112
Date and Nut Bread, 45
Date Strips, 198
Dates, Creamed, 227
Delicate Pudding, 207
*Der Benner* Breakfast Cake, 40
Deviled Clams, 103
Deviled Crabmeat, 102
Devil's Food, Mrs. Leibensperger's, 181
  182
Dinah's Shaker Cookies, 202
Dough, Sweet, 151
Doughnuts, Raised, 36
*Drechterkuche*, 53
Dressing, for Spinach, 128
Dressing, Mustard, for Greens, 127
Dried Bean Soup, 6
Dried Corn, 120
Duck, Roast, 84
Dumplings, Apple, 213
  for *Levverknepp Supp*, 14, 15
  for Pepperpot, 8
  for Poor Man's Dinner, 15, 61, 62
  for Sauerkraut, 76
  Potato, 57
  with Chicken, 82
  with *Schnitz*, 71, 72
  with Soup, 16
Dutch Cake, 40
Dutch Hash, 107
Dutch Pepperpot, 8
Dutch Potato "Salad," 117
Dutch Roll-Ups, 31
Dutch Salad, 127
"Dutch" Shortbread, 195

Easter Cake, 155
Easy Piecrust, 151
*Ebbelkuche* (cake), 27
  (tart), 160
Egg Balls for Soup, 15
Egg Bread, 94
Egg *Hexel*, Mrs. Weaver's, 108
Eggplant, Fried, 120
Eggs, Baked, 90
  Baked Omelet, 92
  Creamed, 92
  Crumb Omelet, 91
  Pickled, 93

Eggs—*Continued*
  Poached, 90
  Poached in Milk, 90
  Poached with Vinegar, 90
  Scrambled, 91
  Scrambled with Celery, 91
  Scrambled with Ham, 91
  Square, 90
  Stuffed, 93
  Stuffed, with Celery Sauce, 93
  Tomato Omelet, 92
Elderberry Jelly, 140
Endive and Potato Salad, 128

*Fastnachtkuche*, 35
*Feinpudding*, 207
Fig Cake, 175
Fig Cookies, Aunt Sue's, 198
Fig Custard Pudding, 211
Filled Cabbage, 123
Filled Cookies, 202
Filling, Almond, 186
  Bread, 86
  Coconut, 186
  Moravian Cream Nut, 186
  Mushroom, 87
  Orange, 185
  Oyster, 87
Fish, Baked, 103
  Boiled, with Parsley Sauce, 103
Flank Steak with Dressing, 63
Flannel Cakes, 51
*Flitche*, Milk, 153
  Molasses, 153
Fourteen-Day Pickles, 145
Fritters, Apple, 54
  Corn, 54
  Corn, Oyster, 122
  Fruit, 215
  Hominy, 111
  Oyster Corn, 122
Frosting, Caramel, 185
Fruit Cake, 182, 183
  Cookies, 197
  Fritters, 215
  Pudding, 210
Fruited Cookies, 198
Funeral Pie, 156
Funnel Cakes, 53
Funny Cake, Mrs. Reinert's, 155

German Nut Cake, 173
Ginger Cake, Our Own, 173
Ginger Cakes, 192
Ginger Cookies, Spiced, 199
Ginger Pears, 138
Ginger Pickles, 147
Gingerbread, Soft, 44
Glory Cake, Mrs. Keck's, 178
Gold Cake, 177
Goose, Roast, 85
Gooseberry Butter, 135
Gooseberry Tart, 163
Graham Muffins, 48
Grape Butter, 135
Grape Conserve, 136
Grape Juice, 112
Grape Pie, 164
Greens with Hot Sauce, 127
Greens with Mustard Dressing, 127
Griddle Cakes, Crumb, 50
Griddle Muffins, 50
*Grischdagringel*, 216
*Grumbera Knepp*, I (with Sauerbraten), 57
  II (with Beef Stew), 59
*Grumbera Supp*, 3
*Grumbera* Twist, 21
Gummy Chocolate Candy, 224

Half-Moon Pies, Amish, 161
Ham, Baked, 70
  Milk, 72
  Holland House, in Blanket, 70
  with Scalloped Potatoes, 116
  with Scrambled Eggs, 91
Hard Sauce, 218
Hash, Cherry, 136
  Dutch, 107
  Pepper, 144
*Hassenpeffer*, 77
Have-Some-More Cake, Abe's, 154
Hazelnut Taffy, 221
*Hexel*, 107
*Hexel*, Mrs. Weaver's Egg, 108
  Mush and Creamed Beef, 108
Hickory Nut Cake, 175
Hickory Nut Drops, 194
Hickory Nut Icing, 185
Hominy Fritters, 111
Honey, Quince, 136
Horehound Candy, 222

Huckleberry Meringue Pie, 166
  Muffins, 49
  Pancakes, 50
  Pie, 164
  Pudding, 211
Hurry Up Cake, 169

Icing, Boiled, 184
  Confectioners', 184
  Hickory Nut, 185
  Mocha, Ellie Reider's, 185
  Plain, 184
  Strawberry, 185

Jam, Apricot, 137
  Red Raspberry, 136
  Strawberry, 137
Jelly, Currant, 140
  Elderberry, 140
Jelly Roll, Grandmother's, 179
Journey Cake (Johnny), 42
Jumbles, Aline Dillinger's, 196

*Kaffeekuche,* 25
*Karschekuche,* 161
Kidney Stew, Wagner's, 66
*Knepp, Grumbera,* 57, 59
  *Schnitz un,* 71, 72
*Kuche, Blitz,* 41
  *Drechter,* 53
  *Ebbel,* 27, 160
  *Kaffee,* 25
  *Karsche,* 161
  *Noch,* 154
*Kuchen, Citronen,* 158
  *Rosina,* 156
*Kugelhopf,* 213

Lamb, Crown Roast, 69
  Roast with Mint Sauce, 68
  Stew, 69, 70
*Lattwerk,* 134
*Lebkuchen,* 192, 193
*Leckerlein, Basel,* 193
Lemon, Caramels, 223
  Custard Pudding, 212
  Pie, 157
  Pudding, 208
  Sauce, 211, 218
  Sponge Pie, 157
  Strip Pie, 154
  Tarts, 158

Lentil Soup, 9
Lettuce, Wilted, 131
*Levverknepp Supp,* 14
Lickin' Good Pie, 153
Light Cake with Dollars, 26
Lightning Cake, 41
Lima Beans, Baked, 118
Liver, Beef and Onions, 65
Liver Dumpling Soup, 14

Mackerel, Breakfast, 105
*Mandelplaettchen,* 191
*Mandelringe,* 191
*Mandelspitzen,* 194
Marble Cake, 176
Marmalade, Peach, 139
  Pear, 138
  Tomato, 141
Marrow Ball Soup, 14
*Marzipan,* 227, 228
Maw, Stuffed Pig's, 74
Meat Loaf, 60
Milk *Flitche,* 153
Mince Pies, 166
Mint Sauce, 68
Mints, Moravian, 225
Mocha Cake, 172
Mocha Icing, Ellie Reider's, 185
Molasses Breakfast Cakes, 43
  Cake, 173
  Cookies, 200
  Cookies, Soft, 200
  Creams, 200
  *Flitche,* 153
  Taffy, 220
Moravian Brown Cookies, 189
  Cream Cake, 176
  Cream Nut Filling, 186
  Mints, 225
  Plum Pudding, 217
  Scotch Cookies, 189
  Sugar Cakes, 29
  White Cookies, 188
*Moschies,* 222
Muffins, Bran, 48
  Corn Meal, 48
  Feather, 48
  Graham, 48
  Griddle, 50
  Huckleberry, 49
  Raised. 49

*Mummix,* 107
  Mrs. Granseleiter's Hot, 107
  Noodle and Prune, 108
  Tomato, 108
Mush and Creamed Beef *Hexel,* 108
Mush Bread, 23
Mush, Fried, 109
Mushroom Filling, 87
Mushrooms, Pickled, 148
Mustard Beans, 148
Mustard Dressing, with Greens, 127
Mustard Pickles, 147

*Nochkuche,* 154
No-Crust Beef Pie, 63
Noodle and Prune *Mummix,* 108
Nougat, Huguenot, 225
Nut Bread, 44, 45
Nut Cake, German, 173
  Shaker, 174
Nut Kisses, 224

Oatmeal Cookies, Mother's, 201
Omelet, Baked, 92
  Crumb, 91
  Tomato, 92
Onion Pie, 124
Onion Sauce, with Roast Beef, 58
Onion Soup, 3, 4
Onions, Baked, 124
  with Beef, 61
  with Beef Liver, 65
Orange Filling, 185
  Peel, Candied, 226
  Puffs, 215
*Osterfladen,* 155
Oven Pork Chops, 75
Oyster Corn Fritters, 122
  Filling, 87
  Patties, 101
  Pie, 101
  Stew, 6
  Stew, Small, 7
Oysters, Grandfather Shepherd's Fried, 101
  Panned, 102

Pancakes, Huckleberry, 50
  Raised Buckwheat, 52
  Sour Cream, 50
*Pannhaas,* 76

Parsley Sauce, with Boiled Fish, 103
Paste, Puff, 101
Pastry, 151
  Rich, 151
Patties, Crab, 102
  Oyster, 101
Pea (Split) Soup, 9
Peach Custard, 212
  Marmalade, 139
  Pudding, 210
Peaches, Pickled, 139
  Spiced, 139
Peanut Candy, 222
  (Peanut) Cream Candy, 224
Pear Marmalade, 138
Pearl Cake, 177
Pears, Ginger, 138
  Spiced, 138
Peas, Sugar, 125
*Pefferniss,* 194
Pepper Hash, 144
Pepper Nuts, 194
Pepperpot, Dutch, 8
  Philadelphia, 7
Picalilli, Grandma Bertels', 143
Pickle, Watermelon, 140, 141
Pickles, Adams County 14-Day, 145
  Bread and Butter, 146
  Cucumber, Quakertown, 145
  Ginger, 147
  Mixed, 146
  Mustard, 147
  Sweet, 145
Pie, Amish Half-Moon, 161
  Apple Custard, 159
  Beef and Potato, 62
  Beef, No-Crust, 63
  Blackberry, 167
  Butterscotch, 157
  Cheese, 97
  Cheese Custard, 98
  Cherry Crumb, 162
  Chicken and Corn, 82
  Chocolate, 159
  *Citronenkuchen,* 158
  Coconut, 159
  Corn, 121
  Crumb, 155
  Crumb Cherry, 162
  Custard, 158
  Custard, Apple, 159

Pie—*Continued*
  *Ebbelkuche,* 160
  Funeral, 156
  Funny, 155
  Grape, 164
  Huckleberry, 164
  Huckleberry Meringe, 166
  *Karschekuche,* 161
  Lemon, 157
  Lemon Sponge, 157
  Lemon Strip, 154
  Lickin' Good, 153
  Milk *Flitche,* 153
  Mince, 166
  Molasses *Flitche,* 153
  Montgomery, 153
  *Nochkuche,* 154
  No-Crust Beef, 63
  Onion, 24
  *Osterfladen,* 155
  Oyster, 101
  Poor Man's, 152
  Potato, 117
  Preaching, 161
  Pumpkin, 165
  Raisin, 156
  Raspberry, 164
  Rhubarb, 165
  *Rosina Boi,* 156
  *Rosina Kuchen,* 156
  *Schleck Boi,* 153
  Shoofly, 43, 44
  Sour Cherry, 161
  Strawberry, 162
  Taffy, 152
  Vinegar, 152
  Walnut, 163
  Wineberry, 165
  *See also* Tart, Tarts
Piecrust, Easy, 151
Pig, Roast Young, 73
Pig's Maw, Stuffed, 74
Pig's Stomach, with Sausage, 74
Plum Conserve, 135
Plum Pudding, Moravian, 217
Pocketbook Rolls, 34
Poor Man's Cake, 168
Poor Man's Dinner, 15, 61, 62
Poor Man's Pie, 152
Poor Man's Turkey, 61
Popcorn Balls, 226

Popcorn Soup, 5
Poppy Seed Twists, 21
Pork and Beans, 118
Pork, Roast, 73
Pork, Spareribs, 74
Pork Chops, Baked, 75
  Oven, 75
  Stuffed, 75
Pot Roast, Rolled, 59
Potato and Endive Salad, 128
Potato Balls, Sweet, 118
  Cakes, 116
  Candy, 225
  Dumplings, 57, 59
  Pie, 117
  Pie, Beef and, 62
  Salad, 129
    "Dutch," 117
    "Hot," 117
  Soup, 3
  Soup, Brown Flour, 2
  Stuffing, 86
  Twists, 21
Potatoes, Creamed, 116
  Fried, 115
  Raw Fried, 115
  Scalloped, with Ham, 116
Potpie, Chicken, 80, 81
  Veal, 67
Poultry Stuffing, 86
Pound Cake, 177
Preaching Pie, 161
Pressed Veal, 67
Pretzel Soup, 5
Pretzels, 109
Prune Stuffing, 88
Pudding, Apple, 211
  Cheese, 207
  Cherry, 210
  Chocolate, 208, 209
  Corn, 122
  Cottage, 209
  Cream, 207
  Cup Custard, 213
  Delicate, 207
  *Fein,* 207
  Fig Custard, 211
  Fruit, 210
  Huckleberry, 211
  Lemon, 208
  Lemon Custard, 212

Pudding—*Continued*
  Peach, 210
  Peach, Custard, 212
  Plum, Moravian, 217
  *Rahm,* 207
  Red Raspberry, 212
  *Speise,* Chocolate, 209
Pudding Dish Cake, 171
Puff Paste, 101
Puffs, Cream, 216
  Orange, 215
Pumpkin Pie, 165

Quince Honey, 136

Rabbit, Fried, 77
*Rahmpudding,* 207
Raisin Bread, 27
  Pie, 156
  Tarts, 156
Raspberry Jam, 136
  Pie, 164
  Pudding, 212
  Vinegar, Aunt Sue's, 111
Raw Fried Potatoes, 115
Red Cabbage, 123
Relish, Mother's, 143
Rhubarb Pie, 165
*Rivvel Supp,* 2
Rolled Pot Roast, 59
Rolls, Pocketbook, 34
Roll-Ups, Cabbage, 60
  Dutch, 31
*Rosina Boi,* 156
*Rosina Kuchen,* 156
Rusks, 49
Rye Bread, 23

Salad:
  Coleslaw, 129, 130
  Corn, 144
  Dandelion, Centre County, 126
  Dandelion Greens, 126
  Dutch, 127
  Dutch Potato, 117
  Greens, with Hot Sauce, 127
    with Mustard Dressing, 127
  Hot Potato, 117
  Lettuce, Wilted, 131
  Potato and Endive, 128

Salads—*Continued*
  Potato, 129
    "Dutch," 117
    "Hot," 117
  Spinach, with Dressing, 128
  Tomato, Bald Eagle Valley, 131
  Wilted Lettuce, 131
Sand Tarts, 204
Sauce, Apple, 134
  Birdseye, 144
  Celery, 93
  Chili, 142
  Custard, 218
  Hard, 218
  Hot, for Greens, 127
  Lemon, 211, 218
  Mint, 68
  Onion, 58
  Parsley, 103
  Pudding, 207, 209
  Sour, with Veal, 68
  Vanilla, 218
  Wine, 217
Sauerbraten, 57
Sauerkraut, Baked, 76
  with Dumplings, 76
Scalloped Potatoes, with Ham, 116
*Schleck Boi,* 153
*Schmierkase,* 96
*Schnecke,* 29
*Schnitz un Knepp,* 71, 72
Schoolboy Cookies, 203
*Schwenkfelder* Cake, 25
Scotch Cookies, Moravian, 189
Scotch Taffy Cakes, 196
Scrambled Eggs, 91
  with Celery, 91
  with Ham, 91
*Scrapple,* 76, 77
*Semmeln,* Butter, 30
Shad, Baked, 104
Shaker Cookies, Dinah's, 202
Shaker Nut Cake, 174
Shoofly Pie, Lancaster County, 43
  Lehigh County, 44
Shortbread, "Dutch," 195
Shortcake, 46, 47
Short Ribs of Beef, Baked, 64
Shrub, Blackberry, 112
Silver Cake, 178
Slapjacks, 195

Small Oyster Stew, **7**
Snails, 29
Snowballs, 215
Soap, 112
Soup, Amish Preaching, 8
  Bean, 8
  Brown Flour Potato, **2**
  Buttermilk Pop, **5**
  Chestnut, 9, 10
  Chicken Corn, 12
  Chicken Noodle, 11
  Chicken with Almond Balls, **13**
  Clam, **7**
  Corn, **6**
  Dried Bean, 6
  *Grumbera*, 3
  Lentil, 9
  *Levverknepp*, 14
  Liver Dumpling, 14
  Marrow Ball, **14**
  Onion, **3**, 4
  Oyster, 6, 7
  Pea, Split, 9
  Pepperpot, 7, **8**
  Poor Man's Dinner, 15, 61, 62
  Popcorn, 5
  Potato, **3**
  Pretzel, 5
  *Rivvel*, **2**
  Split Pea, 9
  Tomato, 4
  Turkey Bone, 13
  *Tzvivvelle*, 3, 4
  Vegetable, 10, 11
  with Dumplings, 16
  with Egg Balls, 15
Sour Beans, 119
Sour Cherry Pie, 161
Sour Cream Pancakes, 50
Sour Milk Cakes, 170
Sour Roast, 57
Sour Sauce with Veal, 68
Sour-Sweet Beets, 125
Souse, 68
Spareribs, Roast, 74, 75
*Speise*, Chocolate, 209
Spinach with Dressing, 128
Split Pea Soup, 9
*Springerle*, 190
Squabs, Roast, 85

Steak, Flank, with Dressing, 63
  Swiss, 64
Stew, Brown Beef, 58
  Great-Great-Grandmother Wagner's, 66
  Huguenot, 70
  Lamb, 69, 70
  Liver Dumpling, 14
  Oyster, 6, 7
Strawberry Icing, 185
  Jam, 137
  Pie, 162
  Tart, 162
*Strickle* Sheets, 30
String Beans, 119
Stuffing, Apple, 87
  Chestnut, 87
  Potato, 86
  Poultry, 86
  Prune, 88
Sugar Cakes, Moravian, 29
Sugar Peas, 125
Sugared Almonds, 224
Swiss Steak, 64

Taffy, Black Walnut, 221
  Butter, 221
  Cakes, Scotch, 196
  Chips, 221
  Chocolate, 220
  Cream, 220
  Hazelnut, 221
  Molasses, 220
  Pie, 152
Tart, Apple, 160
  Berks County Apple, 160
  Cherry, 161
  Gooseberry, 163
  Strawberry, 162
Tartlets, 191
  Brown Sugar Sand, 204
Tarts, Lemon, 158
  Raisin, 156
  Sand, 204
*Tokey*, 214
Tomato Butter, 141
  Cocktail, Hot, 110
  Marmalade, 141
  *Mummix*, 108
  Omelet, 92
  Preserve, Yellow, 142

Tomato Butter—*Continued*
  Salad, 131
  Soup, 4
Tomatoes, Fried, 120
Tongue, Baked, 65
  Boiled, 64
Tongues, Spice, 201
*Tortellen*, 191
Touch-Me-Nots, 197
Trifles, 110
Turkey, Bone Soup, 13
  Poor Man's, 61
  Roast, 83
Turk's Cap, 213
*Tzitterle*, 68
*Tzivvelle Supp*, 3, 4

Vanilla Sauce, 218
Veal Potpie, 67
  Pressed, 67
  with Sour Sauce, 68

Vegetable Soup, 10, 11
Vinegar Pie, 152
  Raspberry, 111

Waffles, 53
  Cream, 54
  Sally Hoffman's, 54
Walnut Cake, 174
  Catsup, 104
  Drops, 196
  Pie, 163
  Pickled, 149
Water Sponge Cake, 179
Watermelon Pickle, 140, 141
*Wiener Schnitzel*, 66, 67
Wilted Lettuce, 131
Wine, Dandelion, Aunt Sue's, 111, 112
Wine Sauce, 217
Wineberry Pie, 165

Zwieback, 109